THE KINGDOM OF SAUDI ARABIA

The Royal Pavilion at King Khaled International Airport combines the arches and enclosed masses of traditional Arab architecture with an innovative design, based on a triangular floor-plan, providing facilities for both the efficient movement of passengers and for the reception of heads of state and other important visitors to the Kingdom.

THE KINGDOM OF SAUDI ARABIA

STACEY INTERNATIONAL
LONDON AND NEW JERSEY

Editor-in-Chief
William Facey

Senior Editors
Anthony Guise
Jill Waters

Design
Keith Savage
Anthony Nelthorpe
John Fitzmaurice

Arabic Usages
E. F. Haddad   Greg Shapland
Ahmed Mostafa   Samir Shishkali

Indexers
Michèle Clarke
Gertrude Mittelmann

Editorial Research
Anthony Lejeune   Charlotte Breese
Angela Milburn   Jane Rawlinson

Stacey International
128 Kensington Church Street, London W8 4BH
Telex: 298768 STACEY G
Fax: 071-792 9288

British Library Cataloguing in Publication Data

The Kingdom of Saudi Arabia
—9th fully rev. ed.
    Arabic 1. Saudi Arabia – History
    I. Anderson, Norman
    953'.8   DS244.52

Library of Congress Cataloguing in Publication
Information

The Kingdom of Saudi Arabia

    Bibliography: P.
    Includes Index.
    1. Saudi Arabia. I. Anderson, J. N. D. (James
Norman Dalrymple), Sir, 1908-
DS204.K56   1986   953'.8   86-14471
ISBN 0-905743-67-9

Set in Linotronic Century by
SX Composing Limited, Essex, England
Colour originations by
Dai Nippon Printing Company Limited, Tokyo
Printed and bound in Singapore by
Tien Wah Press (Pte) Ltd.

4

Principal contributors

Contributors were attached to the organizations listed at the time of writing.

Professor Sir Norman Anderson
Institure of Advanced Legal Studies,
University of London
H. St. John Armitage, O.B.E.
Dr. Randall Baker
University of East Anglia
Jeremy Barnett and John Ewart
British Council, Riyadh
Dr. Richard A. Chapman
University of Durham
Hajj D. Cowan
School of Oriental and African Studies,
University of London
Peter Duncan
Stanford Research Institute, Riyadh
Dr. Abdullah S. El-Banyan
Ministry of Labour and Social Affairs, Riyadh
Professor William Fisher
University of Durham
Dr. Hassan H. Hajrah
King Abdul Aziz University, Jiddah
G. R. Hawting
School of Oriental and African Studies,
University of London
Professor T. M. Johnstone
School of Oriental and African Studies,

University of London
Dr. Fadil K. Kabbani
Deputy Minister for Mineral Resources,
Saudi Arabia
Dr. Geoffrey King
School of Oriental and African Studies,
University of London
James P. Mandaville
Saudi Arabian American Oil Company,
Dhahran
Elizabeth Monroe, C.M.G.
St. Anthony's College, University of Oxford
Dr. Theodore Prochazka
University of Riyadh
Dr. Fazlur Rahman
University of Chicago
Dr. George Rentz
Hoover Institution, Stanford, California
Cecile Rouchdy
Dar el-Hanan School, Jiddah
Dr. Mahmoud Esma'il Sieny
The Arabic Language Institute,
University of Riyadh
Dr. Ibrahim Zaid
General Organization for Social Insurance,
Saudi Arabia

Principal Photographer: Peter Carmichael

Abbey Hanson Rowe 162; G. Adams (Frank Spooner
Pictures) 33 234(2); Aga Khan Award 33; S. Al-
Ghamdi, Saudi Aramco 20(2), 28, 156; Al-Khalifa,
Saudi Aramco 36, 89, 99(3), 102, 105, 106(4), 159,
176-7, 182, 210-1, 221(2), 222-3, 233; Al-Majalla 127;
Al-Rushaid 155; Mohammed S. Al-Shabeeb 240; Al-
Yousif, Saudi Aramco 85; S.M. Amin, Saudi
Aramco 13, 86, 87, 100, 107(2), 147(2), 158, 175, 177,
180; Saudi Aramco 12-13, 28, 34, 71, 80, 85, 105,
147(3), 174, 198; British Aerospace 126; J. Caldow
(FSP) 123, 213, 245; Central Press 28, 101, 130-1(3),
135, 137, 140, 152, 153(2), 163; G. Charpy (Scorpio
Films Prod.) 43, 188, 194-5, 209; M. Clarke
(MEPhA) 157; A. Y. Dobais 31; G. Duncan 157, 163;
Wayne Eastep 54; M. Evans 140, 147, 163, 164;
H.M.S. Farsi 29; Clifton Foster 154-5(2), 161(2);
Frank Spooner Pictures 52, 91; Bernard Gerard
(Hutchison Picture Library) 164, 191, 199, 204, 221,
224(2), 234, 237; Christopher Gent 26, 214(2); A.
Greenway (John Topham Picture Library) 163,
164-5; Francois Guenet (FSP) 206, 206-7, 233, 235;
D. Hadley 24(2), 40; Dr. D. Harrison 20, 21(2), 22;
Hutchison Picture Library 76, 213; Islamic Press
Agency 31, 153, 212, 224; S. Kay (JTPL)35;
Keystone Press Agency Ltd. 87; T. Kilsgaard 24(2);

Dr. G. King 36(4); King Khalid International
Airport 2-3; C. Kutschera 56, 63, 65, 85, 114-5; Jane
Lewis (IPA) 30; J. Mandaville 20(4), 21, 22; K.
Constable-Maxwell 215; MEPhA 108, 109, 148, 187,
225, 245; Ministry of Information, Riyadh 10, 11, 33,
90, 147(2); Tchekof Minosa (Scorpio Films Prod.) 42,
45, 57, 58, 61, 144, 153, 190, 203, 208, 231, 235; B.H.
Moody, Aramco 84(2), 132-3, 143, 174-5, 176, 201,
203; S. Naamani 103, 105, 106, 107(2), 109; NAAS
94-5; NASA 247(2); Oger International 192(2); M.
Oppersdorg 13, 36-7, 49, 58(3), 59, 63; S. Orakzai
(FSP) 234; S. Pendleton 53, 54, 83, 233; Dr. A.
Pesce (Ministry of Information, Riyadh) 50-1: W.
Pridgeon 22(2); Robert Harding 127; R. Roberts 24;
H. Ross 118(2); Royal Commission for Jubayl &
Yanbu 35, 154, 155(3), 159(2), 200, 201, 218, 221(2),
222-3(5), 241, 244, 245(2), 246(2), 247(2); Royal
Geographical Society 78(6); P. Ryan (FSP) 70, 71(2),
96, 136, 160(2), 162; Samarec 123; Saudi British
Bank 140; Saudia 13, 20(5), 145: D. Shirreff
(MEPhA) 138, 153, 157; Skidmore Owings & Merrill
96, 97; Mike Sparrow (FSP) 33, 123, 143, 154, 234;
S. Tart 32; Tony Stone Associates 106; John
Topham 117(3), 119(6); Zuhair Fayez Associates
123(2), 162.

The publishers gratefully acknowledge help from the following organizations and individuals:

Fuad al-Angawi; Abdul Rahman al-Ansari;
Mohammed El Aqeel, Ministry of
Communications, Riyadh; Mohammed Al-
Awwam, Royal Commission for Jubayl and
Yanbu; Aramco World Magazine; Majid Elass;
Salem Azzam, C.V.O.; British Council, Riyadh;
British Embassy, Riyadh; British Library,
London; British Museum (Natural History);
Ministry of Planning, Riyadh; Riccardo Cesati,
Milan; Cusdin, Burden and Howitt, London;
H.E. Dr. Fouad Al-Farsy; H.E. Mohammed Said
Farsi; Fauna Preservation Society, London; Dr.
David Harrison; Osman Himmat; David
Howard; Hassan Husseini, K.F.U.P.M.,

Dhahran; Mohammed Khayyat; Colonel Brian
Lees, OBE; Ministry of Information, Riyadh;
National Geographical Society, Washington
D.C.; Ismail 1. Nawwab; Reda Nazer; Bob
Nordberg, Saudi Aramco; Central Statistics
Office, Riyadh; Dr. Angelo Pesce; Fuad al-Rayis;
Royal Geographical Society, London; Royal
Institute of International Affairs, London; Saudi
Arabian Embassy, London; Saudi Arabian
Monetary Agency; Saudia; H.E. Sheikh Fahd K.
Al-Sedayri; Said Sieny; Habib A. Shaheen,
Royal Embassy of Saudi Arabia, Washington.
H.E.Dr. Abdul Aziz al-Sowayegh; Dr. Abdullah
al-Wohaibi; World Wildlife Fund.

Maps   Diagrams

Charts, diagrams and maps are based on the latest facts available at the time of their preparation, but subsequent developments may have superseded information contained therein.

Contents

NOTE: The Publishers and Contributors crave the indulgence of the reader who finds that the latest developments
have overtaken the facts and figures recorded in this work. Saudi Arabia is a Kingdom on the move, and fine books
are not made in a day. But the mere difficulty of leaping astride a galloping horse is no reason for allowing Saudi
Arabia's achievements to go unrecorded in durable print.

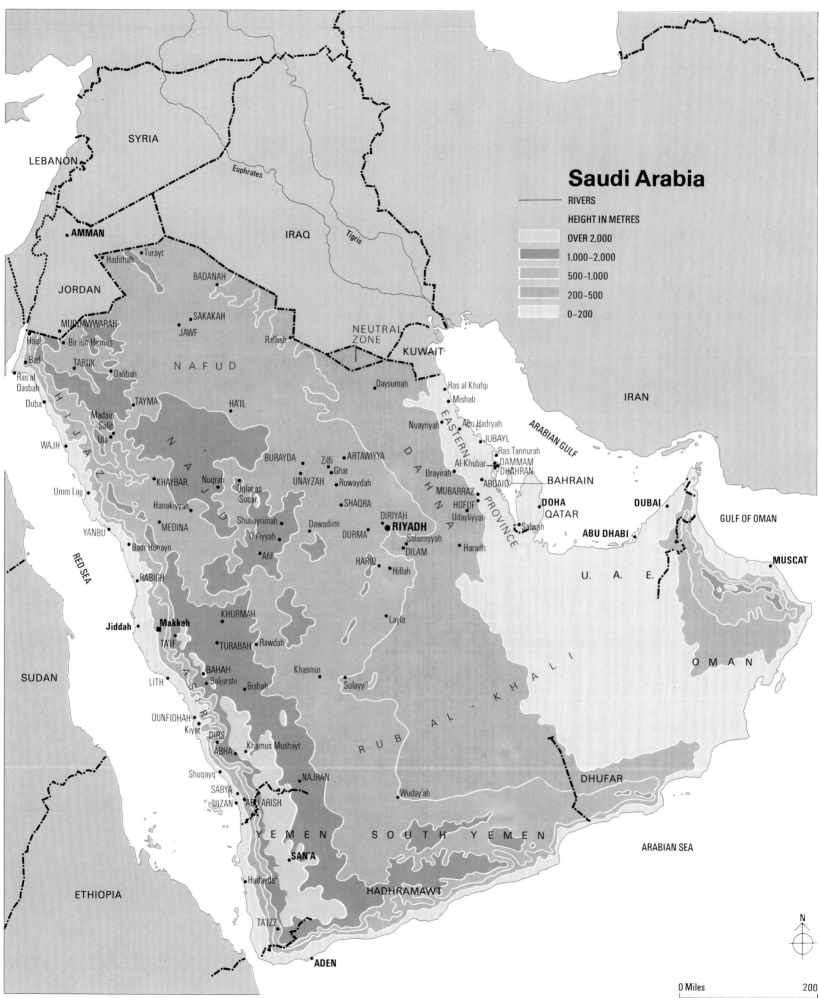

Saudi Arabia

RIVERS

HEIGHT IN METRES

OVER 2,000
1,000–2,000
500–1,000
200–500
0–200

LEBANON

SYRIA

Euphrates

Tigris

IRAQ

AMMAN

Hadithah • Turayt

JORDAN

MUDAWWARAH

Haql
Bir ibn Hirmas

BADANAH

SAKAKAH

• JAWF

Rafhah

NEUTRAL
ZONE

KUWAIT

Ras al
Qasbah

Bad

TABUK

Qalibah

N A F U D

Qaysumah

Ras al Khafqi

Mishab

IRAN

Duba

TAYMA

HA'IL

Nuayriyah

Abu Hadryah

ARABIAN GULF

E
A
S
T
E
R
N

Madain
Salih

N

JUBAYL

Ula

A

Ras Tannurah

HIJAZ

WAJH

F

BURAYDA

Zilfi

ARTAWIYYA

Al-Khubar

DAMMAM

DHAHRAN

D

J

Ghat

UNAYZAH

Ruwaydah

Urayirah

ABQAIQ

BAHRAIN

Umm Lajj

KHAYBAR

Nuqrah

D

Oqlat as
-Suqar

SHAQRA

MUBARRAZ

HOFUF

DOHA

QATAR

DUBAI

Hanakiyyah

A

Shubayrimah

Dawadimi

DIRIYAH

Udayliyyah

H

N

A

GULF OF OMAN

MEDINA

N

Qa'iyyah

DURMA

RIYADH

Salwah

ABU DHABI

YANBU

J

Afif

Salamiyyah

Haradh

U. A. E.

MUSCAT

Badr Hunayn

DILAM

RABIGH

RED SEA

HABIO

Hillah

Layla

Jiddah

Makkah

KHURMAH

O M A N

TA'IF

TURABAH

Rawdah

A

BAHAH

Khasmin

R

LITH

Baljurshi

Bishah

Sulayyil

R U B   A L   K H A L I

QUNFIDHAH

Kiyat

DIRS

ABHA

Khamus Mushayt

Shuqayq

NAJRAN

Wuday'ah

DHUFAR

SABYA

JIZAN

ABU ARISH

YEMEN

S O U T H   Y E M E N

ARABIAN SEA

SUDAN

ETHIOPIA

Hudaydah

SAN'A

HADHRAMAWT

TA'IZZ

ADEN

N

0 Miles   200

8

The Islamic calendar

Comparative Tables of AH and CE Dates

The Islamic era is based on the Hijrah, the migration of the Prophet Muhammad from Makkah to al-Madinah, which took place on 16 July 622 CE. The Islamic year is lunar, and has 354 days. There are approximately 103 Hijri years to a Gregorian century; AH stands for Anno Hegirae (hegira being the Latinized form of Hirjah), and CE for Christian Era. The Hijri year begins on the day of the month indicated.

THE HIJRAH MONTHS	AH	CE		AH	CE		AH	CE		AH	CE	
Muharram	1	622	16 July	600	1203	10 September	1160	1747	13 January	1362	1943	8 January
Safar	10	631	9 April	610	1213	23 May	1170	1756	26 September	1363	1943	28 December
Rabi al Awwal	20	640	21 December	620	1223	4 February	1180	1766	9 June	1364	1944	17 December
Rabi al Thani	30	650	4 September	630	1232	18 October	1190	1776	21 February	1365	1945	6 December
Jumada'l Awwal	40	660	17 May	640	1242	1 July	1200	1785	4 November	1366	1946	25 November
Jumada'l Thani	50	670	29 January	650	1252	14 March	1210	1795	18 July	1367	1947	15 November
Rajab	60	679	13 October	660	1261	26 November	1220	1805	1 April	1368	1948	3 November
Shaban	70	689	25 June	670	1271	9 August	1230	1814	14 December	1369	1949	24 October
Ramada	80	699	9 March	680	1281	22 April	1240	1824	26 August	1370	1950	13 October
Shawwal	90	708	20 November	690	1291	4 January	1250	1834	10 May	1371	1951	2 October
Dhu'l-Qadah	100	718	3 August	700	1300	16 September	1260	1844	22 January	1372	1952	21 September
Dhu'l-Hijjah	110	728	16 April	710	1310	31 May	1270	1853	4 October	1372	1953	10 September
	120	737	29 December	720	1320	12 February	1280	1863	18 June	1374	1954	30 August
	130	747	11 September	730	1329	25 October	1290	1873	1 March	1375	1955	20 August
	140	757	25 May	740	1339	9 July	1300	1882	12 November	1376	1956	8 August
	150	767	6 February	750	1349	22 March	1310	1892	26 July	1377	1957	29 July
	160	776	19 October	760	1358	3 December	1318	1900	1 May	1378	1958	18 July
	170	786	3 July	770	1368	16 August	1319	1901	20 April	1379	1959	7 July
	180	796	16 March	780	1378	30 April	1320	1902	10 April	1380	1960	26 June
	190	805	27 November	790	1388	11 January	1321	1903	30 March	1381	1961	15 June
	200	815	11 August	800	1397	24 September	1322	1904	18 March	1382	1962	4 June
	210	825	24 April	810	1407	8 June	1323	1905	8 March	1383	1963	25 May
	220	835	5 January	820	1417	18 February	1324	1906	25 February	1384	1964	13 May
	230	844	18 September	830	1426	2 November	1325	1907	14 February	1385	1965	2 May
	240	854	2 June	840	1436	16 July	1326	1908	4 February	1386	1966	22 April
	250	864	13 February	850	1446	29 March	1327	1909	23 January	1387	1967	11 April
	260	873	27 October	860	1455	11 December	1328	1910	13 January	1388	1968	31 March
	270	883	11 July	870	1465	24 August	1329	1911	2 January	1389	1969	20 March
	280	893	23 March	880	1475	7 May	1330	1911	22 December	1390	1970	9 March
	290	902	5 December	890	1485	18 January	1331	1912	11 December	1391	1971	27 February
	300	912	18 August	900	1494	2 October	1332	1913	30 November	1392	1972	16 February
	310	922	1 May	910	1504	14 June	1333	1914	19 November	1393	1973	4 February
	320	932	13 January	920	1514	26 February	1334	1915	9 November	1394	1974	25 January
	330	941	26 September	930	1523	10 November	1335	1916	28 October	1395	1975	14 January
	340	951	9 June	940	1533	23 July	1336	1917	17 October	1396	1976	3 January
	350	961	20 February	950	1543	6 April	1337	1918	7 October	1397	1976	23 December
	360	970	4 November	960	1552	18 December	1338	1919	26 September	1398	1977	12 December
	370	980	17 July	970	1562	31 August	1339	1920	15 September	1399	1978	2 December
	380	990	31 March	980	1572	14 May	1340	1921	4 September	1400	1979	21 November
	390	999	13 December	990	1582	26 January	1341	1922	24 August	1401	1980	9 November
	400	1009	25 August				1342	1923	14 August	1402	1981	30 October
	410	1019	9 May		*Transfer from Julian to*			1343	1924	2 August	1403	1982	19 October
	420	1029	20 January		*Gregorian calendar*			1344	1925	22 July	1404	1983	8 October
	430	1038	3 October				1345	1926	12 July	1405	1984	27 September
	440	1048	16 June	1000	1591	19 October	1346	1927	1 July	1406	1985	16 September
	450	1058	28 February	1010	1601	2 July	1347	1928	20 June	1407	1986	6 September
	460	1067	11 November	1020	1611	16 March	1348	1929	9 June	1408	1987	26 August
	470	1077	25 July	1030	1620	26 November	1349	1930	29 May	1409	1988	14 August
	480	1087	8 April	1040	1630	10 August	1350	1931	19 May	1410	1989	4 August
	490	1096	19 December	1050	1640	23 April	1351	1932	7 May	1411	1990	24 July
	500	1106	2 September	1060	1650	4 January	1352	1933	26 April	1412	1991	13 July
	510	1116	16 May	1070	1659	18 September	1353	1934	16 April	1413	1992	2 July
	520	1126	27 January	1080	1669	1 June	1354	1935	5 April	1414	1993	21 June
	530	1135	11 October	1090	1679	12 February	1355	1936	24 March	1415	1994	10 June
	540	1145	24 June	1100	1688	26 October	1356	1937	14 March	1416	1995	31 May
	550	1155	7 March	1110	1698	10 July	1357	1938	3 March	1417	1996	19 May
	560	1164	18 November	1120	1708	23 March	1358	1939	21 February	1418	1997	9 May
	570	1174	2 August	1130	1717	5 December	1359	1940	10 February	1419	1998	28 April
	580	1184	14 April	1140	1727	19 August	1360	1941	29 January	1420	1999	17 April
	590	1193	27 December	1150	1737	1 May	1361	1942	19 January	1421	2000	6 April

Introduction

Custodian of the Two Holy Mosques, HM King Fahd of Saudi Arabia.

This comprehensive work records a seminal period in the history of Saudi Arabia, as one of the most exceptional countries in the world emerges into modern statehood.

As the extent of the bounty of its natural resources became apparent, the ancient land of Arabia, under Saudi leadership, had various options. That it chose firmly to seize its opportunities and accept its full responsibilities both to itself, now and in the future, and in the Islamic, Arab and world communities, is a measure of the quality of the Saudi Arabian people and the leadership they have enjoyed.

King Faisal (1964-1975 CE) was responsible for establishing the direction of the country's domestic and foreign policy. His wisdom and devotion to the brotherhood of Muslims dictated the development of social policy and investment in infrastructure at home, and guided relations with Islamic countries and the industrialised world. His policies were pursued by King Khalid (1975-1982CE), under whom the nation experienced a period of unprecedented prosperity.

Since 1982, King Fahd has assumed the full direction of policy in domestic and foreign affairs, which have continued to be rooted in the country's commitment to Islam from which, as King Fahd has said, "emanate all our ideals." In the context of Islam the Five Year Plans have further evolved, bringing radical improvements in the standard of living of Saudi Arabians, their welfare and social security, their education and personal expectations. In industry and agriculture maximum self-sufficiency have become the goal, securing the future with sound husbandry of today's finite resources.

A similar continuity prevails in foreign policy, rooted in the reign of the late King Abdul Aziz ibn Saud. Put simply, it is one of peace and Islamic solidarity – a policy which proved its value when Saudi Arabia and the GCC, together with forces from around the world, acted decisively in coming to the aid of Kuwait. The Kingdom remains a force for stability on a global scale.

On becoming King, Fahd bin Abdul Aziz spoke of seeking the glory of Arabs and Muslims. He reaffirmed his determination in the "march of progress and development". All members of Government, he declared, were committed to helping in the realisation of the hopes and ambitions of the people, while adhering to divine teaching and the Prophet's tradition.

HRH Prince Abdullah ibn Abdul Aziz, Crown Prince of Saudi Arabia

HRH Prince Sultan ibn Abdul Aziz, Second Deputy Prime Minister

1 The Country

The heat is often forbidding, the face of the landscape often cruelly dry. And yet temperatures and seasons vary greatly, and parts of Saudi Arabia's vast area enjoy dependable rains. Underground water from past geological eras can be tapped to bring the powdery soils into rich bloom. Even the great sand deserts blossom after winter rains. Though they always defy cultivation, they provide spring pastures for the nomads, and can be made to yield their mineral wealth.

In contrast to Saudi Arabia's familiar image, the green uplands of Asir, in the south-west (far left), are well watered and have sustained a settled population from ancient times. Condemned by lack of rain to barrenness, much of the dun landscape of sand and gravel scrub desert (top picture) would bring forth plentifully. The second picture (above) shows the typical low-lying terrain of the Gulf coast and islets. The great sand deserts of the Nafud in the north, and the Rub al-Khali or Empty Quarter (bottom picture) in the south, resist settlement but support nomads in winter and spring.

Geography & Climate

THE Arabian peninsula, of which the Saudi Arabian state forms by far the largest part, covers well over three million square kilometres (Saudi Arabia itself comprises 2,300,000 square kilometres – nearly 900,000 square miles). The whole area is thought to be a detached fragment of an even larger continental mass which included Africa (*see also* page 20). Large rifts developed because of thermal currents in the lower mantle of the earth, forcing apart surface masses or "plates". The Arabian plate is held to have drifted northwards, impelled by the opening of the Red Sea and Gulf of Aden, and by subsequent spreading of the sea floors – a gradual movement that continues today.

As it moved, the Arabian plate tilted, with the western side upraised and the eastern side lowered. Shallow ancient seas covered the east, laying down layers of younger sedimentary rocks, and leading to the formation of oil deposits. In the west, volcanic disturbances associated with the opening of the Red Sea led to much upwelling of magma, which has produced the extensive lava fields *(harrah)* that occur all along the west side of the country, mostly in the Makkah-Jiddah-al-Madinah area. With ancient resistant rocks in the west, capped here and there with more recent lava, and progressively younger rocks towards the east, Saudi Arabia exhibits in its geography, very broadly speaking, a north-south running "grain".

In the extreme west, along the Red Sea, there is a coastal plain (Tihamah), flat and usually very narrow, except in the Jiddah area where it offers a small but useful lowland gap giving access to Makkah and the interior. Then immediately to the east is a formidable succession of high plateaux with steep scarp edges dominating the Tihamah below. Here occur the highest peaks in Saudi Arabia; particularly south of Makkah, where heights of 2,500 metres are reached. East again of this high land zone is an extensive region of

The mountains of the south-west plunge from plateaux of 2,400 metres and peaks of 3,000 metres to lowland valleys, where regular crops are grown.

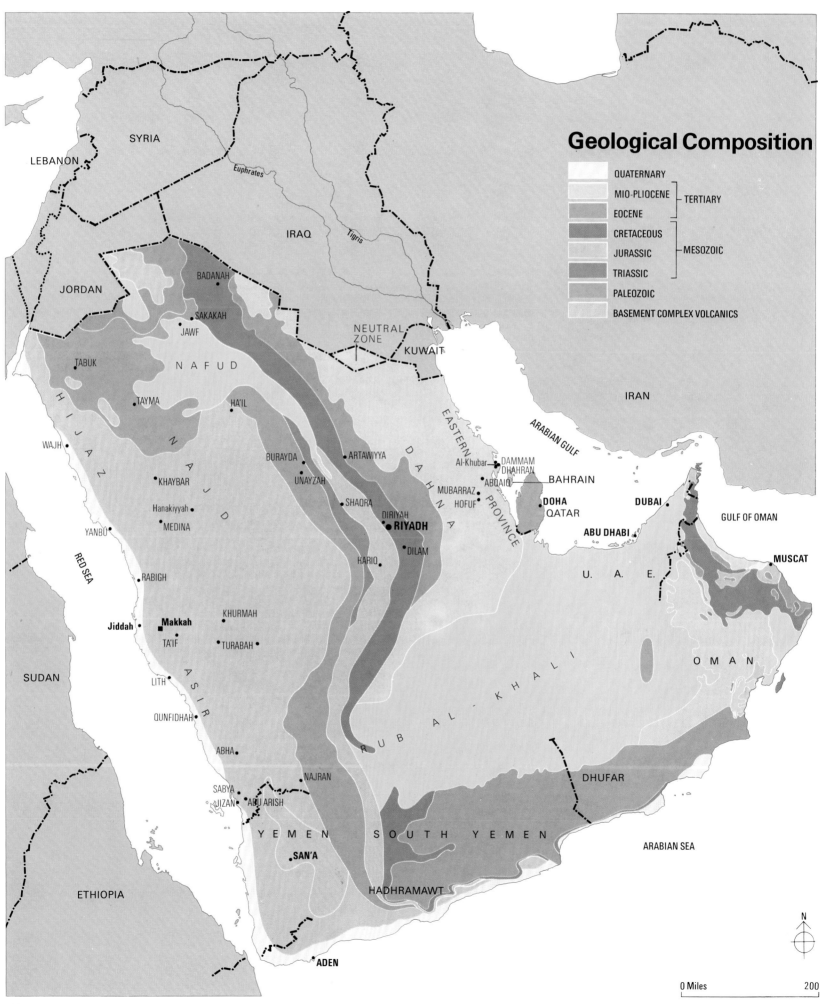

Geological Composition

- QUATERNARY
- MIO-PLIOCENE ⎱ TERTIARY
- EOCENE
- CRETACEOUS
- JURASSIC ⎱ MESOZOIC
- TRIASSIC
- PALEOZOIC
- BASEMENT COMPLEX VOLCANICS

LEBANON

SYRIA

Euphrates

JORDAN

IRAQ

Tigris

BADANAH

SAKAKAH

JAWF

NEUTRAL ZONE

KUWAIT

TABUK

N A F U D

TAYMA

HA'IL

IRAN

H I J A Z

WAJH

ARTAWIYYA

BURAYDA

EASTERN

ARABIAN GULF

Al-Khubar   DAMMAM
DHAHRAN

KHAYBAR

UNAYZAH

MUBARRAZ   ABQAIQ

BAHRAIN

N A J D

Hanakıyyah

SHAQRA

HOFUF

D A H N A

DOHA
QATAR

DUBAI

YANBÚ

MEDINA

DIRIYAH

RIYADH

P R O V I N C E

ABU DHABI

GULF OF OMAN

RED SEA

RABIGH

HARIQ

DILAM

U. A. E.

MUSCAT

KHURMAH

Jiddah   Makkah

TA'IF   TURABAH

O M A N

SUDAN

A S I R

LITH

R U B   A L - K H A L I

QUNFIDHAH

ABHA

NAJRAN

DHUFAR

SABYA

JIZAN   ABU ARISH

Y E M E N   S O U T H   Y E M E N

ARABIAN SEA

ETHIOPIA

SAN'A

HADHRAMAWT

ADEN

N

0 Miles   200

16

irregular plateaux and upland basins, where collection of sub-surface water allows human settlement on a larger scale, as at al-Madinah.

Further east, altitude gradually declines, but then occurs a whole succession of younger, sedimentary rocks – sandstones, limestones and marls. The harder series stand out as scarps or isolated ridges, with lower, flatter valleys formed in the less resistant strata between. The most imposing of these scarps is the Jabal Tuwayq, a limestone ridge that attains 3,200 feet and extends in a sinuous curve north-west and south-west of Riyadh. Gradually, altitude diminishes eastwards, until one of the last of these scarps occurs near Hofuf, after which the surface drops to form the low-lying coastal plain of Hasa.

Although some lowland areas or basins consist of bare rock pavement, most tend to be covered in loose rock deposits eroded by wind, by shattering due to temperature contrasts and, in the recent geological past, by water action. Near hill or plateau bases are stony areas of larger rock fragments; further away are outwash gravels, while in areas of low relief sand predominates, with silts in valley bottoms. Sand covers large areas. In the north, the Great Nafud is an expanse of sand dunes (*uruq*), often reddish in colour, interspersed with areas of bare rock pavement. A narrower zone of sand, the Dahna, links the Nafud to an even larger expanse of sand, indeed the largest sand desert in the world – the Rub al-Khali or Empty Quarter, which occupies much of the south of Saudi Arabia. In the extreme west the Rub al-Khali is a "sand sea" surrounded by gravel plains: in the east, there are massive dunes with salt flats (*sabkhah*). The whole area was for long an extreme barrier to human movement, but oil prospecting and the discovery of artesian water have reduced its difficulty.

Of all the sizeable countries on earth, Saudi Arabia is probably the driest. It derives its weather mainly from the north and west: climatically it is linked to the eastern Mediterranean and adjacent lands, in that it has a long, hot and almost totally dry summer, with a short cool winter season during which a little rain occurs. This is because air masses reaching Arabia have been largely exhausted of their moisture. Although Arabia is surrounded on three sides by sea, aridity is the dominant feature. With the sole exception of Asir in the extreme

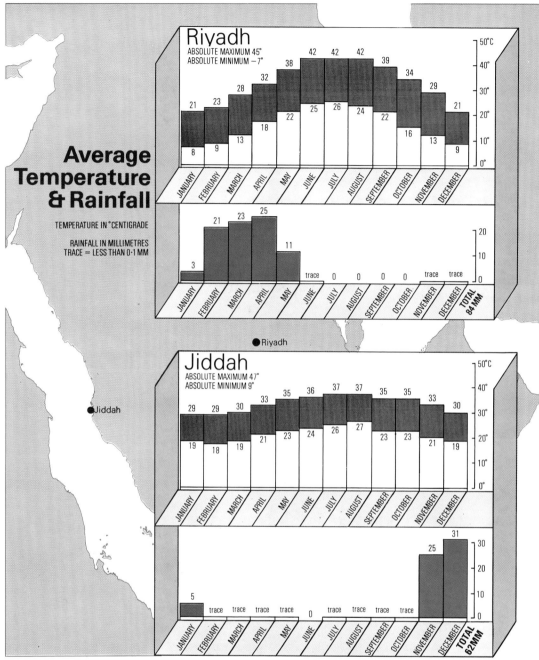

Average Temperature & Rainfall

TEMPERATURE IN °CENTIGRADE

RAINFALL IN MILLIMETRES
TRACE = LESS THAN 0·1 MM

The surface of the Arabian peninsula is slightly on the tilt – higher in the west, and dropping gently from the geologically very ancient Western Plateau towards the Gulf.

The sea keeps temperatures fairly constant in the coastal regions; in the interior day/night and summer/winter temperatures vary sharply. Rain, though scarce, can cause flooding.

south-west, any influences from the southern tropical zones are excluded by the highland rim that runs from Oman through the Hadhramawt to the Yemens.

Because of the dryness of the air reaching Saudi Arabia, and the consequent lack of cloud, insolation is considerable, prodlucing very high summer temperatures – up to 45 or 50°C, and sometimes even more in the southern deserts. But the cloudlessness also allows heat to escape from the surface at night, especially in winter; so temperatures drop quite markedly between day and night,

and between summer and winter. The night coolness, with a 10 to 22°C drop at both seasons, is a boon in summer but leads to sporadic frost in the interior of the centre and north during winter; temperatures as low as -7°C have been recorded at Riyadh.

Rainfall is irregular and unreliable, occurring mostly during the months from October to April. Except along the southern Red Sea coast, and inland over the mountains of Asir, summers are practically rainless, and in the interior several years may elapse without rain. The extreme south of Saudi Arabia, the

While Saudi Arabia has no permanent rivers reaching the sea, a dependable flow of water nourishes the deep wadis of the south-west in winter months.

virtually uninhabited Rub al-Khali, is almost entirely without rain – one of the driest areas on earth; but over the rest of the country (Asir excepted) annual totals amount to about 100 mm, though 150 mm have been known to fall locally within twenty-four hours. Because of temperature contrasts, winds can be strong, even violent, raising dust storms from time to time. On the coasts relative humidity is high, due to sea breezes that bring in moisture; this effect is, however, local, and most of the interior is extremely dry. The mean figures given on page 17 for Jiddah and Riyadh illustrate the principal features of the Saudi Arabian climate, as well as the contrasts between coast and interior. The hills of Asir, however, do participate in the marked summer rainfall which benefits the Yemen plateau.

Until recently the difficulty of the terrain, its aridity and the consequent scarcity of good soil sharply controlled the ways of life within Saudi Arabia. Apart from a few fishermen and traders, Saudi Arabia was able to support only a small population, estimated at 1.5 to 2 million in the 1930s. Possibly half of this could be regarded as "rural settled" – cultivators, village craftsmen and shepherds moving locally over short distances with their animals. At least a quarter of the population was wholly nomadic, following a regular pattern of rough grazing of sheep, goats and camels, which involved considerable annual movement. Both ways of life depended upon the use of wells which tapped water-tables at moderate or shallow depth; for there is no perennial river.

In some cases, catchment of water is local, from rapid percolation of rainfall, but over many parts of Saudi Arabia there is a much larger series of water-tables that allow "creep" of water underground from the better watered south-west through to the east coast. Some of the wells which tap this kind of water-table are large; Makkah and al-Madinah have a number, and others occur, for example, at Mudawwara, Tabuk and Ula. Some of this underground water is from wetter climatic phases of an earlier geological time, and is not replaced by present-day rainfall when drawn off.

Today, with the advent of irrigation and exploitation of deeper underground water resources, four or five times the former population is supported, and major cities have rapidly evolved at Riyadh, Jiddah and Makkah.

*The giant groundsels and bearded
lichen on evergreen trees (seen on the
right) characterize the sub-tropical
Alpine vegetation of highland Asir.*

The remarkable variety of Saudi Arabia's flora is due to the country's range of climate and soils. In some areas a sudden rain-fall will make an apparent desert bloom in a matter of hours. Many other "garden" species only sur-vive if regularly watered.

The yellow cassia

A young pomegranate

The spiny echinops

A flowering hibiscus

Centaurea sinaica (thistle)

Acacia ehrenbergiana

Anthemis deserti

Rumex vesicarius

Cistanche Tubulosa

Echinops

Opuntia

The Tamarisk survives the fierest droughts.

Calatropis Procera

Flora and Fauna

MAPS and geography books make Ara-bia a part of Asia, but plant and animal life clearly bear out the theory that it is really an extension of Africa. The desert steppes which now link the peninsula with Asia are the bottom of an ancient sea which once divided the continents. The Red Sea is a rift through a single mass of igneous rock, the Arabian-African Shield.

Saudi Arabia's wildlife is thus a com-plex of evolving and mingling species: the tropical African, the oriental from the Asian mainland, the Palaearctic from Europe, North Africa and northern Asia, and a few species endemic to the peninsula.

The animals and plants of northern and north-eastern Saudi Arabia are generally closely related to or identical with Saharan species. To the south and the west, wildlife assumes its older, tropical African character. Only in the Oman mountains, known to be geolog-ically related to the highlands across the Gulf, do we find strong Asiatic elements.

Plant Life

Except in parts of the Asir highlands, where the juniper, the wild olive, and some other larger trees grow together over large areas, there are no forests in Saudi Arabia. In some parts, scattered small acacia trees are common. Further east and north the vegetation is typical of arid steppes – hundreds of square kilo-metres of small, drought-adapted shrubs, a metre or less high. Often one species, such as the *rimth* saltbush or the yellow-flowered *arfaj* shrublet, domi-nates the landscape. The ground be-tween these shrublets is green for only two to three months of the year, when winter rains bring forth a host of herbs. Among these annuals, known collec-tively as *usht* by the Beduin, are the desert *Anthemis* or camomile, many species of the mustard family, and a striking iris.

Only the salt-impregnated bottoms of *sabkhahs*, small areas of rock-floored desert, and a few fields of actively mov-ing dunes do not support any plants. Even most parts of the Rub al-Khali have scattered shrublets of the prickly *hadh* saltbush, a *Tribulus*, or the scarlet-fruited *abal*.

Mammals

The largest wild mammal of Saudi Arabia is the Arabian oryx. This 100-kilogramme antelope with long, straight horns, which was known in this area in Biblical times became extinct in the wild in the early 1960s, but a herd has been successfully bred in Arizona from captured specimens, and the oryx has now been re-introduced into its natural habitat in Oman. With the effective new hunting laws and game parks the oryx is expected to re-establish itself successfully in Saudi Arabia.

Graceful gazelles were once common throughout most of Arabia, but their numbers are now much diminished, due to overhunting in the 1930s and 40s. The lovely *rheem* is known to survive on the edge of the Rub al-Khali; the *idhmi* still inhabits the mountains and foothills of the south and west; the *afri* is extant but rarely encountered, while its endemic sub-species, the dorcas, which used to range the south-east of the country, is alas probably extinct. Like the oryx, the gazelles of Arabia have adapted to desert life, obtaining much of their water needs from the scanty vegetation.

The ibex was also once widespread, but it is now rarely to be encountered except in the mountains of the north-west, and possibly the Hijaz and south-west.

The cheetah was not unknown on the broad plains of the far north and south, but is now considered extinct. The caracal lynx probably still exists in the north, while the leopard has been reported from the highlands of Asir and the rare sand cat, amazingly like a domestic cat in appearance, in barren sand country.

The Arabian wolf, *canis lupus arabicus*, jackals, foxes, and the striped hyena are found in Arabia, as are the hedgehog, the porcupine and the ratel, or honey badger. More common rodents are the small Arabian hare and the jerboa, or kangaroo rat. The rat-like jerd and mouse-sized gerbil burrow beneath desert shrubs, while the shy, brown hyrax lives amongst rocks. Baboons are not unusual in the central Hijaz and Asir highlands, where they raid the terraced croplands.

Birds

Several million birds, including flamingoes, storks, swallows, wagtails, warblers and many more, pass through Arabia on their spring and autumn migrations. Many end their journeys in Saudi Arabia to winter there. The birdlife of the country is consequently rich and varied and includes African, oriental and northern species.

Among the true desert residents are six species of sandgrouse and several larks, including the sweet-voiced hoopoe lark, known to the desert Arab as *Umm Salim*, "Salim's mother".

Game birds in Saudi Arabia include the *hubara* bustard, the quail, partridges, doves, the stone curlew, and the courser. Among the birds of prey are harriers, buzzards, several species of eagle, and falcons which are often trained to catch hares and *hubara*. Water birds, such as ibises, herons, egrets, gulls and pelicans inhabit the rich tropical coastal areas. The ostrich, which has figured in Arabic poetry and rock art since pre-Islamic times, is now extinct. One of the last sightings was in 1938.

Reptiles

The water-conserving body structure of reptiles makes them well adapted for life in arid lands, but many cannot endure extremes of heat and must lead nocturnal or subterranean lives. Thus, although some fourteen species of snake have been reported from Saudi Arabia, few are seen. One of these might be the small, thick-bodied sand viper, a venomous but seldom lethal creature that moves like the sidewinder of the American south-west. More dangerous, but fortunately very rare, are the Arabian hooded cobra, found in well-vegetated areas of the mountainous west, and the all-black hoodless cobra in the central and north-eastern deserts. Harmless snakes are more common, among them the *malpolon*, which spreads its neck into a hood when cornered and is often mistaken for a cobra. Potentially dangerous, but shy, sea snakes are found in the Gulf.

There are no poisonous lizards in Arabia, although two species are imposingly large, the sixty-centimeter long, plant-eating *dabb*, and the even longer, whip-tailed *waral*, or monitor lizard. Skinks, agamids, geckoes and lacertids are other kinds of lizard frequently encountered in Arabia.

Marine Life

Brilliantly coloured and exotically shaped tropical fish such as butterflyfish, angelfish and parrotfish, fill the seas and

Arabia's famous hunting dog, the saluki.

A kitten of Arabia's rare sand cat.

The oryx – saved from extinction.

The spiny hedgehog is well defended.

Many species of reptiles are found in Saudi Arabia – most remarkable of the lizards being, perhaps, the dabb (right), *which can absorb its moisture by breathing (the only animal in the world to do so), allowing it to live in a waterless desert.*

Both the Red Sea and the Gulf abound in garish marine life, of which the banded bluefish (above), the red speckled angelfish (below) and the furry sea spiders (right) are typical examples. Brilliantly coloured fish haunt the protected coral reefs along Saudi Arabia's Red Sea coast.

reefs of Arabia – unparallelled underwater paradises for the naturalist, diver, and photographer. Extraordinary coral structures provide homes not just for the spectacular fish, but also for a wealth of urchins, anemones, starfish, squid and crustaceans. Here also lurk some of the more dangerous inhabitants of the deep: the moray eel, the stonefish and scorpionfish, both of which use their camouflaging abilities to avoid detection by unsuspecting prey.

Sharks are common in the Gulf, but they are not a threat to bathers. The deeper waters of the Red Sea are better shark territory. Sea mammals include the porpoise, the dugong and the occasional whale. Several species of turtle still breed on offshore islands.

Insects

Saudi Arabia is remarkably free of insect pests. Mosquitoes and malaria have been wiped out by Government campaigns in most districts.

Among the more common desert insects are the dark-hued ground beetle and the scarab beetle. Not strictly insects, but arachnids, are the scorpion, the large, non-venomous camel spider, and the crimson velvet mite.

A wide variety of butterflies and moths can be seen in Arabia, including the beautiful Painted Lady, the African Lime Swallowtail and the Oleander Hawk-moth.

Conservation

The Saudi Arabian Government has adopted an enlightened policy towards the conservation of the country's flora and fauna. Realizing that many of Saudi Arabia's animals were nearing extinction, it outlawed hunting except under strict conditions. Next, recognising that the preservation of animals can only be undertaken in the long-term by the conservation of habitat, it set up the Environmental Protection Coordination Committee under Prince Sultan ibn Abdul Aziz, to streamline efforts towards creating marine and wildlife reserves. The emphasis at first was on the creation of protected areas to save the fragile ecological balance of the unspoiled coastlines from the pace of industrial progress, and on the creation of national parks. The first of these, the Asir National Park, has been in operation since the mid-1980s.

This approach has now been extended to the Kingdom at large. In 1986 the

Arabia's larger mammals now protected by conservation policies include (left to right, from the top): the Arabian ibex, believed to be the progenitor of the domestic goat; the Arabian gazelle, found in the mountains and foothills of the west and south; the caracal lynx, still to be seen in remoter corners of the country; and the fleet-footed cheetah, whose speed over short distances of semi-desert can reach 60 mph. Today all hunting is banned by law, and a programme for the establishment of National Parks is being implemented. The first, the Asir Park, is already in operation, and studies for parks at Billasmar, Namas and Bilqarn are under way.

National Commission for Wildlife Conservation and Development was established, again under Prince Sultan. Under its auspices the Harrat al-Harrah reserve has been set up in the Kingdom's north-west: the ban on hunting and grazing has already transformed the landscape, with dramatic results for the flora and fauna. In accordance with this forward-looking range-management policy, several other smaller reserves have been set up to protect the flora of other important habitats.

Experimental breeding stations have been established near Riyadh and Taif. Oryx, gazelles, ibex and houbara bustard are bred for return to the wild. The oryx is being re-introduced between Riyadh and Taif, and a herd flourishes on the late King Khalid's reserve at Thumamah north of Riyadh, where it has been increasing since its successful establishment there in 1980 as a result of international action under "Operation Oryx".

Ibex are being returned to the wild in southern Najd and in the Tubayq region in the north-west. Research is being conducted into the famous Hamadryas baboons of Asir.

By the 1990s, as a consequence of these expanding efforts to conserve habitats as a whole, the oryx will be once more established in the wild, the ostrich and cheetah may resume their ancient grounds, and herds of gazelles may roam the interior plains again.

Mounded basalt characterizes the surface of part of the Jabal Hashahish Quadrangle (immediately above).

Mineral Wealth

The Kingdom's precambrian Arabian Shield is a classic site for mineral wealth, and extensive geological investigations have revealed the deposits to found a mining industry, including gold, silver, copper, zinc, lead and tin-tungsten.

ANCIENT MINE-WORKINGS have always hinted at Saudi Arabia's natural mineral wealth. Up until 1986 the country was intensively prospected by geologists from the Deputy Ministry of Mineral Resources with help from

The top picture shows complex folding of precambrian shield rock in the south-west. Nickel gossan, and gossan from pyrite (above left and left) *of the Arabian Shield point to exploitable deposits; copper and gold mining has already begun at Mahd al-Dhahab* (above), *Arabia's most historic mine.*

American and French geological departments and British mining companies. Having determined the geologic and tectonic position of the major deposits, prospecting continues more slowly.

Most of the modern discoveries have been in central and western Saudi Arabia in rocks of the precambrian Arabian Shield, although some finds have also been made in the much younger rocks along the Red Sea coast. Palaeozoic rocks which overlap the Shield in the north and east continue to be investigated.

The precambrian metallic mineral deposits fall into four major types: stratiform iron-nickel deposits; massive polymetallic base-metal deposits; gold-silver deposits; and disseminated molybdenum-tungsten deposits. Other metal deposits occur on the coastal plain, and in hot brines and sediments of the deeps in the axial trough of the Red Sea.

Known occurrences of metal deposits form regional belts of mineralization which relate closely to structural rock formation. Seven principal mineral belts and/or zones have been delineated in the precambrian rocks of the Arabian Shield. These include the Bidah, Sabya, Nuqrah and Al Amar copper-zinc zone; and the Hijaz and Najd gold-silver belts. Recent exploration has also assessed several massive sulphide deposits, although the main economic metal is copper, with lesser amounts of zinc, gold and silver.

Many of the reported gold-silver deposits in the Shield appear to form belts that parallel the dominant north-west trend of the Najd fault system or trends of related subsidiary shears. Hundreds of ancient gold-silver prospects have been located and examined, and current exploration suggests that these mines have future potential.

Important iron deposits, large massive and disseminated strata-bound pyrite deposits and massive stratiform nickel-bearing sulphide deposits discovered in the Arabian Shield approach economic size, grade and access requirements.

Of the economically significant non-metallic mineral resources to be found, phosphate, magnesite, glass sand, gypsum, salt, and structural and cement materials are all being mined in increasing quantities.

Structural materials including clays, shales and perlite are being investigated for the production of light weight aggregates. Marble in pleasing colours and patterns is quarried from many localities in the Arabian Shield and eight cement plants in Saudi Arabia are utilizing the abundant cement materials indigenous to the country.

So far, all estimates of the size, quality and variety of metallic and non-metallic mineral resources confirm that Saudi Arabia's natural reserves can be relied upon to provide much future wealth.

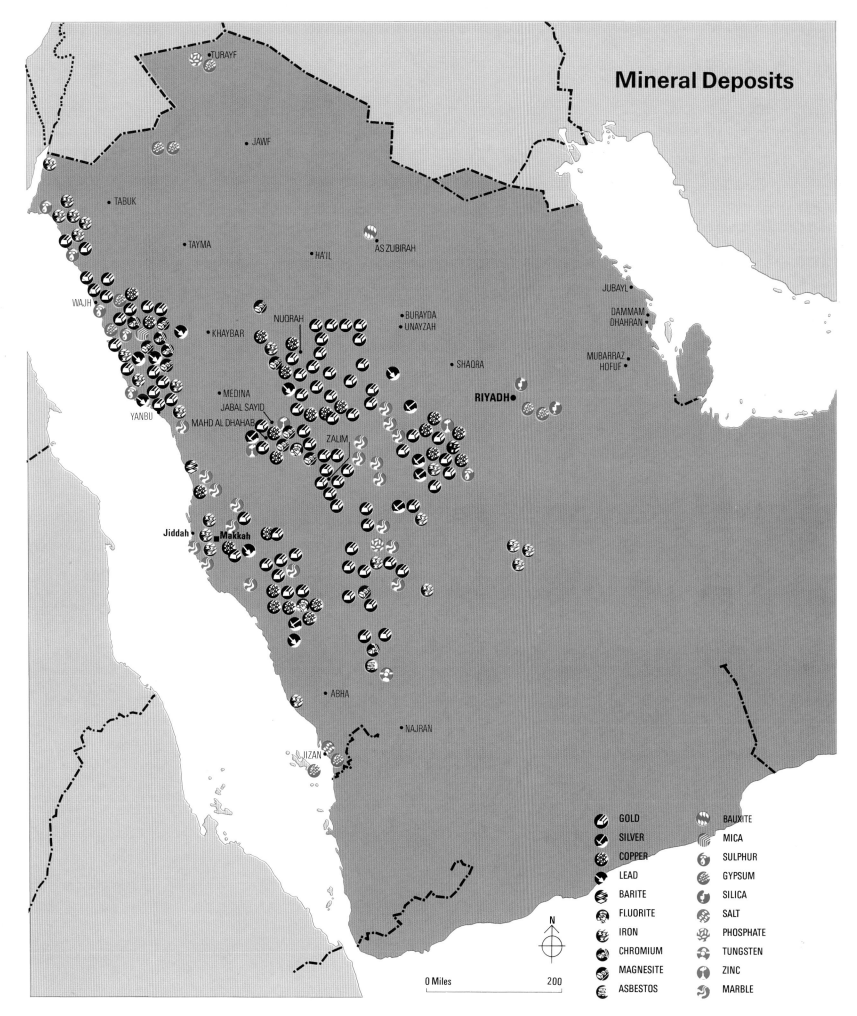

Mineral Deposits

GOLD
SILVER
COPPER
LEAD
BARITE
FLUORITE
IRON
CHROMIUM
MAGNESITE
ASBESTOS

BAUXITE
MICA
SULPHUR
GYPSUM
SILICA
SALT
PHOSPHATE
TUNGSTEN
ZINC
MARBLE

TURAYF

JAWF

TABUK

TAYMA

HA'IL

AS ZUBIRAH

WAJH

KHAYBAR

NUQRAH

BURAYDA
UNAYZAH

JUBAYL

DAMMAM
DHAHRAN

MEDINA
JABAL SAYID
MAHD AL DHAHAB

YANBU

ZALIM

SHAQRA

MUBARRAZ
HOFUF

RIYADH

Jiddah
Makkah

ABHA

NAJRAN

JIZAN

N

0 Miles   200

25

2 The Cities

Saudi Arabia's vibrant cities may be modern but are seldom new. Settled people have since earliest times outnumbered the nomads.

Makkah and al-Madinah's scholastic pre-eminence has at times been rivalled by Jerusalem or Damascus, Baghdad or Cairo, but never their spiritual role.

Expanding from 8.5 square kilometres in the 1940s to 1,600 square kilometres today, Riyadh has seen the fastest growth of any city in the Middle East. The skyline of Saudi Arabia's capital is dominated by many massive and distinctive modern buildings. The life of the city is as vital and thriving in this new context as it was in the traditional city of old. The map (below) shows the sites of the other major cities.

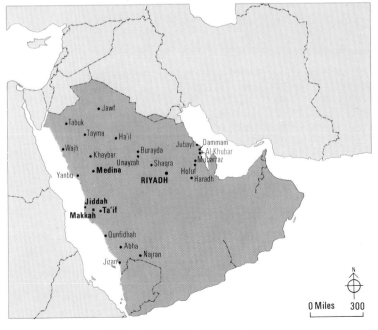

Cities~an Introduction

SURPRISINGLY – in the light of popular belief – the greater part of the people of Saudi Arabia have in the past lived the settled life, rather than the nomadic one. Many of these, it is true, lived in villages, whose size would be determined by the quantity of fresh water available. On the other hand, links with and awareness of their major cities have since ancient days belonged deeply to the patterns of thought and life in the Arabian hinterland.

The first city of Saudi Arabia must always be the Holy City of Makkah, spiritual capital of all Islam. Though Makkah's permanent population is much less than that of modern Riyadh or

Jiddah (both with populations of 1.5 million and more), at the height of the annual pilgrimage of Muslims to Holy Makkah it contains over two million people. Makkah's founding is attributed to the presence of the well opened in the desert by God to save the lives of Hagar and her son, Isma'il, from whom – with his father Abraham – the Arab race traces its descent. Other stories tell of Abraham labouring with his son Isma'il to rebuild the Holy Ka'bah as a stone structure and site of worship. The Ka'bah, of course, remains, though it has been reconstructed from time to time throughout the centuries.

Although Makkah boasts many fine

modern buildings, including its splendid Islamic conference centre, determined efforts have been made to preserve its traditional Arabian character. The same is true of Arabia's other Holy City of al-Madinah al-Munawwarah, the "shining city", which to the delight of the pilgrim or Muslim visitor has remained a small city of some 100,000 souls, and whose life centres round its magnificent green-domed mosque and famous library, and its Islamic University.

By contrast, Riyadh is today an ultra-modern metropolis, spaciously laid out as the centre of government and, now, the home of the Diplomatic Quarter. It has grown fast over the last two decades

Lively oriental imagination is displayed by the Ministerial edifice in Ta'if (below) and by buildings along the approach to Makkah (bottom).

The sequence of historic photographs shown here portrays the changing face of Jiddah as the city has developed and expanded. The fortified wall of old Jiddah – captured by the forces of Abdul Aziz in 1925 – is still visible (below) in an aerial photograph from the 1930s. It had been pulled down by 1950 to allow Jiddah to

on the basis of imaginative city planning. Restored in 1902 by King Abdul Aziz as the Saudi capital, with its plentiful water and site by the Wadi Hanifah, Riyadh's history is ancient. As the historic city of Hajr, it was in ancient times capital of the Yamamah region. It is the centre of a relatively fertile area.

Jiddah – the "Bride of the Sea" – founded by Caliph Uthman ibn Affan in 647 CE but certainly a fishing settlement before that, is today the largest port on the Red Sea, with a magnificent modern harbour. Much of the picturesque Jiddah of traditional Arab architecture was pulled down to make way for modern office blocks, banks and apartments, but

much also remains and is undergoing restoration. Jiddah was until the early 1980s the Kingdom's window on the outside world, housing all the diplomatic missions.

While the new towns of Yanbu and Jubayl continue to expand as major industrial centres, several other cities are developing fast – in every case under town planning which controls population density, the use of land for residential, industrial or agricultural purposes, the development of public utilities and road traffic systems. The summer capital of Taif, in the highlands south of Makkah, has experienced similar growth. Expansion is occurring too in Buraydah and

Unayzah in the Qasim region, and further north in Hail and Sakaka. In the east, Dammam and its neighbours al-Khobar with Dhahran have taken on the aspect of a veritable megalopolis which is still extending its embrace to include Sayhat, Qatif, Safwa, Tarut Island (linked by causeway), and Ras Tannurah. This conurbation is now linked to Bahrain by a 25-kilometre causeway. In the south-west, the chief sites of continuing expansion are: Jizan, the region's port, the military town Khamis Mushayt, and nearby Abha, the administrative capital of Asir, Najran and Bahah. In the north-west Tabuk has grown steadily as the regional centre.

begin its expansion (bottom left). *The spacious planning of today's city first emerges in the aerial shot taken in 1968* (below), *showing the first version of the main roundabout, and the edge of the lagoon. In the early 1990s* (bottom middle) *the heart of Jiddah has become a gleaming international city.*

The Dhahran Mosque located in the Saudi Aramco complex includes a prayer hall and minaret. There are 34 one-metre calligraphic panels carrying the 99 names of God legible from both inside and outside the mosque.

Riyadh

NO PAVED ROADS led to Riyadh at the beginning of the century. Indeed, until the 1940s, it was still a desert city of mud-brick buildings and heavy mud walls. Then came the boom years and this city, the very symbol of Najdi culture and the Wahhabi reform movement, began to alter, the thriving capital at the heart of the modern Kingdom.

Riyadh's original reason for settlement was its potential for cultivation – hence its name *al-riyadh*, "the gardens". Situated in the heart of central Najd, on a sedimentary plateau 600 metres above sea level, at the confluence of Wadi Hanifah and its tributaries Wadi Aysan and Wadi Batha, it has a very dry climate and low rainfall, but a good underground water supply makes it one of the few natural fertile areas in the Kingdom outside the south-west.

When the name Riyadh first occurs in the Najdi chronicles it referred to the villages on the ancient site of Hajr with their gardens in the seventeenth century. Once established as a desert city in the middle of the eighteenth century,

Riyadh under its chief Diham ibn Dawwas vied with Diriyyah for supremacy. After it joined the Wahhabi cause in 1773, it was just one of the many towns in the First Saudi State. But the fall of the nearby capital Diriyyah in 1818 to the invading Ottoman-Egyptian army focused interest on Riyadh as the centre of efforts to revive the power of the House of Saud. In 1824 it became the capital of the Second Saudi State. But, at the end of the century, Riyadh's star waned as the House of Saud lost control of its domains.

The Riyadh of January 1902, which the young Abdul Aziz Al Saud so daringly captured, was no more than a few hundred yards across. It was surrounded by a thick mud wall about seven metres high, punctuated at intervals by bastions and gates. Inside it was a maze of twisting alleys, some so narrow that it was difficult for two men to walk abreast.

In the centre was the market with, on one side, a large mosque and, on the other, the great fortress-palace which served as the seat of government. All the buildings were made of the same adobe as the walls. About half were single-

The United Nations building in Riyadh reflects the city's Najdi heritage.

storey buildings while the rest had an upper floor. Built round courtyards, their outside walls were blank except for occasional tiny windows.

Riyadh's subsequent history has remained closely linked with the reformed faith and the House of Saud. Its recovery by Abdul Aziz marked a turning-point in Saudi fortunes: he used it as the base from which he re-unified Najd and most of the rest of the Arabian Peninsula. While the new Saudi state was growing, he began re-building Riyadh as its capital.

The basic character of Riyadh changed after 1930 as the city – along with the country itself – entered a period of very rapid growth. By the early 1950s the population had quintupled; concrete, cars and asphalt were widely used; and the old mud town was engulfed by an increasingly modern city. The railway from Dammam and the first airport were built. Then it was decided to assemble most of the Ministries in Riyadh.

Its governmental role forever transformed the city. Very few of the original mud-brick structures have survived the comprehensive modernization of Riyadh which was instituted by the 1974 city plan and is scheduled to continue into the

new millennium. In the late 1980s Riyadh's population holds steady at around 1.8 million, and every inhabitant enjoys as standard such amenities as water and sewerage, while consumption of electricity peaks at around two megawatts. Since 1986 the Riyadh Development Authority has utilized a computerized urban intelligence system for mapping, planning and anticipating trends in demography.

As the capital, Riyadh is home to thousands of government officials, and the large number of government buildings give the city its distinctive appearance. As it grew, Riyadh also became a centre of commerce and industry; villagers and tribesmen from all over the country were attracted by its many opportunities, which have long been international in scope. Arab immigrants and temporary residents from all over the world were admitted to assist in the capital's development and functions. Today in Riyadh, as in many another world capital, the majority of the population was not born there.

For short periods the strain of its exceptionally swift development told on the city. In the early 1970s the old and the new were jumbled together, and the cars and trucks of Batha Street moved in a cacophany of horns, stirring up dust from the broken pavements. In those days it was still a city in search of its proper identity. Down came the old buildings and up went the new. And down came some of the new to be replaced by the newer and finer edifices which stand today.

But vigorous and coordinated planning and architectural control told in the end and finally shaped the city. From the start, land use was carefully defined to ensure that there were areas for schools, hospitals, mosques, gardens and playgrounds. Planners and architects alike created an elegant and efficient modern capital whose characteristics both in concept and detail recalled Riyadh's history. The 1990s see Riyadh as the mature international capital with confidence and pride in its civic identity. Stark Najdi simplicity in some of its modern buildings is complemented by some of the most avant-garde and creative structures ever designed to meet the administrative and technical needs of a modern state.

The successful transformation of a traditional sedentary and nomadic society into a modern urban one finds no more effective example than in Riyadh today. With its flyovers and tree-lined boulevards, its first-class hotels and its long patronage of fine twentieth century architecture influenced by local conditions and Islamic design, Riyadh has come into its own. Although most of the palm-groves of a century ago no longer exist, Riyadh has been carefully cultivated as a garden city in the desert. One hundred and twenty children's playgrounds and twelve parks have been laid out and planted.

It is no longer the "secret city" to which intrepid nineteenth century travellers journeyed. It has its own radio and television production complex, satellite telecommunications facilities, the largest and most modern university campus in the Kingdom, colleges, schools, hospitals, clinics and specialist health care centres. The 170 metre television transmission tower at the Ministry of Information is the major landmark of the city. The conference Palace in Al Nasiriyah is the largest in the Middle East. It has proved itself a sophisticated host-capital for the move, now under way, of the entire diplomatic corps from Jiddah: between 1983 and the new century, buildings and amenities will expand to accommodate some 90 diplomatic missions and 22,000 people.

In 1983 commercial air traffic was transferred to the magnificent new King Khalid International Airport, among the world's largest. It is designed to cater for 15 million passengers by the year 2000, and its air cargo facilities are the most modern in the Middle East, able to handle over 140,000 tonnes of cargo per year. A great new complex houses the King's Office, the Council of Ministers and the Consultative Assembly. Together with the continuing programme to expand the Kingdom's highway system, such developments have put an end to Riyadh's traditional isolation. Traffic systems include a 93 kilometre, six-lane ring road which girdles the city and links it to the inter-peninsula highways.

As an important world capital, Riyadh receives an annual stream of heads of state and public figures from Western, Arab, Islamic and developing countries – further underlining the city's increasingly pivotal role in Arab affairs and world affairs generally.

Riyadh Landmarks

The transmission tower of the television centre dominates the skyline.

King Abdul Aziz' favourite Palace was the Qasr al-Murabba, built in 1936.

The Al-Tuwaiq Palace in the diplomatic quarter.

Gulf Cooperation Council (GCC) headquarters close to the diplomatic quarter.

31

Jiddah

SITUATED HALFWAY DOWN along the eastern coast of the Red Sea, Jiddah is an Arabian city-port of great age: gateway to Holy Makkah and Western Arabia, this ancient "Bride of the Red Sea" is today one of the most cosmopolitan cities ever. But confined as it was for several centuries by its desert hinterland and an uncertain water supply within massive walls of bleached coral, its core is still traditionally Arab.

Ever since the profitable Red Sea spice trade, Jiddah has been the main port and commercial centre of Arabia. But with the mounting sea power of Europe, Jiddah ceased to be a commercial *entrepôt* of importance, subsiding into its other role as a pilgrim port, and in 1517 the town fell under the sometimes interrupted power of the Ottoman Turks, as part of the domain of the Sharif of Makkah. However, the opening of the Suez Canal in 1869 proved a boon for Jiddah with its merchants handling a regular volume of commerce with other Arabian ports, India, Egypt, Africa and even Liverpool and Marseilles.

From this period date the many fine

merchant family houses that survive in the old city. The most celebrated is Beit Nassif, home of the Nassif family for over a century until the house was passed to the care of the Government in the mid-1970s. Designed by a Jiddah master-builder of the day, it is built of coral limestone tied by teak beams, and contains fifty high-ceilinged rooms, including a famous library of 6,000 volumes.

The character of the town had changed little over the years. Pilgrims came, and,

Beit Nassif (above) *is one of the finest examples of traditional architecture preserved in the heart of Old Jiddah* (left).

if they could afford it, went; ships still edged through the dangerous gateways between the three coral reefs; sweet water remained the perennial problem. T. E. Lawrence described the Jiddah of 1916 in *Seven Pillars of Wisdom*:

> "It was indeed a remarkable town. The streets were alleys, wood-roofed in the main bazaar, but elsewhere open to the sky in the little gap between the tops of the lofty white walled house . . . housefronts were fretted, pierced and pargetted till they looked as though cut out of card-board for a romantic stage setting. Every storey jutted, every window leaned one way or another; often the very walls sloped."

The town surrendered to Abdul Aziz and his Saudis in 1925. But its modern history does not begin until May 1933, when his Finance Minister signed an oil concession with the Standard Oil Company; thirty-five thousand pounds in gold sovereigns were counted across a table in Jiddah. Five years later oil began to flow in the Eastern Province and Jiddah's days as a walled city were numbered.

From 1850 to 1945 the population had

32

Jiddah Landmarks

been stable at about 25,000; in the forty-five years to 1990 it leapt sixty-fold to 1.5 million. During the 1970s, the number of vehicles in the city multiplied twenty fold, and has since increased to 600,000. Far more serious in the eyes of the Municipality was the city's haphazard growth to the north and along the Makkah road as prices of land and property spiralled. But the greatest challenge to Jiddah was met by the harbour, which has become the country's gateway for building materials and consumer goods. Whereas cargo offloaded in 1946 was 153,000 tonnes, in the late 1980s imports through Jiddah Islamic Port averaged 30 million freight tonnes annually, with export cargoes at 2.5 million tonnes.

The Pilgrimage remained a priority and has been managed with increasing skill. The King Abdul Aziz International Airport, which covers over forty square miles, provides for one and a half million pilgrims (as well as six million other passengers) each year, and is capable of handling 6000 passengers per hour at its two regular terminals. Pilgrims are handled at the special Hajj terminal, a magnificent open-air structure with 210 tent-like roof units forming the largest fabric roof in the world – it can accommodate 80,000 pilgrims at any one time.

Jiddah has suffered from a rare contradiction: although architecturally and infrastructurally the richest city in the Kingdom, its commercial importance left it prone to the developer's mercy. Many felt that the glittering shops and apartment blocks had lost the city its traditional sense of direction, that it was turning its back on the sea, the source of all its prosperity, and that the new town lacked the solidity and permanence of the old. The authorities, in particular,

The telephone exchange (above left); *Monument to the Unknown Cyclist; King Abdul Aziz International Airport* (above right); *Jiddah's fountain throws the highest jet in the world* (right); *and El-Wakil mosque, winner of the Aga Khan Award* (bottom right).

became concerned to keep the town's appearance in accord with Jiddah's place, in Islam and history.

Jiddah's climate, its humidity, will always be harsh, but planning has made it bearable. Until the 1920s, Jiddah boasted but a single tree, still standing under Beit Nassif. Today, with desalination having solved the city's water problem, the whole of Jiddah has grown green with some eight million trees, and some thirty areas of former waste ground have been transformed into parks. More importantly, the city's splendid Corniche provides twenty miles of coastland for the sole purpose of providing recreation: it has been developed into a unique and imaginative blend of road, promenade, parking area, trees and sculptural monuments that has decisively brought the sea back into the life of the city.

It has begun to capitalise on the flair displayed in its city beautification programme by embarking on an ambitious scheme to increase its appeal as a city of tourism, leisure and recreation. Among projects planned are a zoo, an aquarium and marine life sanctuary, a central park with an artificial lake, restoration of the remaining parts of the old city, a motor racing track, restaurants and art galleries. The Abdul Raouf Hasan Khalif Museum provides a spectacular setting for the display of Jiddah's traditional past. Recreation projects are also planned for the mountains in the hinterland.

Traditional Architecture

In Makkah, a determination to preserve the ancient character of the spiritual centre of Islam has dampened tendencies to tear down the glories and intimacies of the past. Only Muslims are allowed to enter holy Makkah, whose foundation dates from God's miraculous provision of a well for Isma'il, son of Abraham, and his mother, Hagar.

URBAN communities are nothing new in Saudi Arabia; in certain areas they have existed for centuries. Between them is desert inhabited by a now dwindling number of tent-dwelling Beduin. Isolated by great distances and with different social conditions, climates and building materials, these settled areas have evolved distinct regional styles of architecture.

Extant buildings in a traditional style are rarely more than two hundred years old: but until the recent and almost total transformation of Saudi Arabia by determined modernization there was no stimulus to change the indigenous styles, so

that buildings erected not long ago adhered completely to the old techniques and designs. Today, several fine traditional buildings have undergone restoration by the Department of Antiquities and Museums.

Four main Saudi Arabian architectural styles are characteristic of four regions – eastern Najd, central Hijaz, southern Hijaz and Asir, and the Arabian Gulf coast.

Eastern Najd

The main building material is unfired mud-brick; the completed wall is made smooth by the application of mud-plas-

ter. These walls are very thick, and provide insulation against the extremities of the local climate. The roofing consists of wooden beams, usually of tamarisk, with palm matting or twigs spread above. This is covered with a layer of mud. Stone is used only as the foundation of a house or in fortifications.

The Najdi mosque consists of a walled enclosure around an open courtyard, with a covered sanctuary built against the *qibla* wall. Cut into this wall is the *mihrab* niche, which projects beyond the back wall of the mosque; an arrangement common in both ancient and modern mosques in Saudi Arabia. The roof of the

The preservation of ancient architectural techniques is officially encouraged. The traditional architecture of southern Najd and Najran has survived particularly well in many small villages like the one below. The characteristic thick mud-brick walls provide effective insulation against the harsh extremities of the local climate.

the privacy of family life. The buildings have one, two or three storeys depending on their importance. The entrances to the houses are closed by large rectangular wooden doors, and the windows by wooden shutters. Both shutters and doors are decorated with incised geometric patterns picked out in colour, or by geometrics burned into the pale wooden

The Central Hijaz and its Coast

Makkah, al-Madinah, Taif and Jiddah all have a similar type of architecture. This local conformity is attributable to common influences brought about in the area by the *hajj*, by trade and by trading connections further afield, particularly with Egypt.

The buildings common to all these

sanctuary rests on colonnades with keel-arches, the number of colonnades depending on the mosque's size and importance. Some mosques have underground prayer-chambers for use in winter. In the Riyadh area and Southern Najd, one or two staircases nearly always give access to the roof; in this area the mosques are either without minarets, or have only a diminutive tower over the staircase to the roof. In Sudayr and Qasim, however, minarets are tall and cylindrical.

Najdi houses are often built around a central courtyard, with only a few openings on to the street, thus maintaining

surface. The only other external decorations are rows of V-shaped mouldings on the walls, and crenellations which vary in design from area to area. Elaborately shaped mud finials stand at the corners of the houses.

The position of the reception rooms varies. In most larger houses the lower rooms are used for storage, and visitors are received upstairs. However, rooms designed to receive guests appear in Sadus and Unayzah on both the ground floor and upper storey. In a corner of these receptions rooms there is usually a small hearth for coffee-making, with shelves above.

cities are two, three or more storeys high, with level roofs. The entrance is often vaulted by a round-headed or pointed arch, and the wooden doors are decorated with rather stiff and stylized carving. The outer walls are frequently, but not always, whitewashed.

Decoration is concentrated in the elaborate wooden screens which face the upper storeys of the building around windows and balconies, with an effect recalling the *mashrabiyya* screens of Cairo. These screens guard from view people standing at windows or on balconies. They are arranged on the facade of the building in various ways; in some houses

The tremendous impact of the petroleum industry has by no means destroyed the traditional character of all ancient towns of Arabia's eastern region – as witness the view of Qatif (below). *Like Hofuf, it was the site of a Turkish fortress until captured by Abdul Aziz in 1913, in the drive for unity. The map indicates architectural areas.*

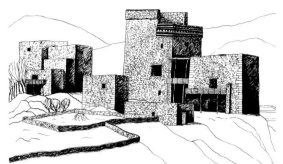

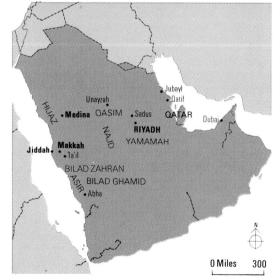

Traditional architectural techniques are illustrated by (from the top) *a typical village of the south-east (Ghamid), palaces and houses in Riyadh, Jiddah houses with slatted balconies, and a pavilion-style house in Tarut, eastern Saudi Arabia.*
(Drawings are by Geoffrey King)

36

The unique charm of Saudi Arabia's Red Sea coast is illustrated by such fishing settlements as Wajh (below), where peaceful communities linking Red Sea trade and fishing with the interior have survived for centuries. Offshore, parts of this coast are skirted by coral reefs, breeding grounds of varieties of brilliantly coloured fish.

one or two rectangular towers are a constant feature of the village architecture. These have inward-sloping walls, slight crenellations and small apertures, but they vary in height and proportion.

The houses of the Abha area are built of mud or stone or a combination of both. In those buildings constructed of mud, layers are applied successively and each

summer. Also as on the Red Sea coast, the building material is coral aggregate and wood. The walls are of pier and beam construction with rubble infill, made smooth with plaster. The roofing system employs palm thatch and wooden beams.

Although there is no single local form of building, technical and decorative devices, such as arches in carved plaster-

they occupy the whole of the upper area, while in others, two very high screens are set to right and left of a small central screen. Yet other houses have much smaller screens around the windows alone, occupying a lesser area of the whole façade.

Southern Hijaz and Asir

From Bilad Zahran and through Bilad Ghamid, north of Abha, the standard building material is rough-cut stone. These villages are often defensively positioned on hilltops, especially in Bilad Zahran, and the continuous faces presented by the outermost houses give the effect of a fortified wall. Elsewhere, in valleys and plains, the villages are in less defensible positions. In both regions

layer is left to dry before another is added. Horizontal rows of protruding stone slabs are placed between each mud-layer to break up the flow of rainwater, which would otherwise dissolve it. The mud areas of the houses are often white-washed, thus emphasizing the horizontal division of these tower-like structures. On the Tihamah, the coastal plain of Asir, can still be found villages of circular huts of brushwood with elaborately decorated interiors.

The Arabian Gulf coast

The eastern towns of Saudi Arabia are situated between the desert and the Gulf. The climate is similar to that of the Red Sea shore, with a high rate of humidity and persistent uncomfortable heat in

work, recur in structures otherwise quite different. All of these eastern buildings are distinguished by fine proportions, both in dimensions and decoration.

The wind-towers of Bahrain and Dubai do not appear on the Saudi coast. Instead, on the Saudi shore, certain rooms are arranged to benefit from the slightest breeze, while other rooms are better suited to cooler winter conditions. Thus in the centre of Qatif the houses are of several storeys. The lower rooms have small windows, whereas the uppermost storey has large arched openings piercing the walls for ventilation.

This eastern architecture bears no significant relationship to buildings inland, but has a marked similarity to those found in Bahrain, Qatar and Dubai.

3
The People, their habitat & way of life

The interplay of the hard, disciplined, wandering life of the desert and the settled life of farmers, craftsmen, merchants and teachers in the scattered towns has for countless centuries formed the character of the people. Today, well tested values stand remarkably firm among the challenges of modern city life.

A boy from Diriyyah in Najd demonstrates his Arabian desert heritage no less by his fine clear-cut features than by his characteristic red headdress, the ghutrah. *The people of the Hijaz, by contrast, have effortlessly accepted intermingling as a result of fourteen centuries of Muslim pilgrimage and trade. Settlers have arrived from China and Islamic Central Asia, from South-East Asia and the Indian Subcontinent, and from Africa and the Eastern Mediterranean.*

Arabian Faces

Variety in apparel and headdress can indicate the influence of locality, profession, or social standing. The red and white check ghutrah *(as below) is as a rule worn in winter months, for it is warmer, and the* ghutrah *of light white cotton (top row) in summer.*

Top row, left to right: *Saudis from the south-west, east coast, and Qasim.* Centre: *A coppersmith, and an oilworker.* Below: *While the majority of Saudi Arabia's traditionally nomadic population has now chosen to settle, desert disciplines and the lifestyle that accounts for the dignity and serenity of the Saudi character still prevail among a substantial minority.*

The Unity of the Saudi Arabian People

IT IS THE TOWN CULTURE – rooted in Islam – which brings together the various strands in Arabian society, to form a complex but harmonious whole, combining the virtues of Beduin life with merchanting acumen and a high standard of literacy and education.

Both archaeology and the ancient pre-Islamic records of Arabia provide evidence of a tribally organised, camel-herding society which already by 1000 BCE spanned the spectrum of nomadic and settled lifestyles. During the centuries of the high civilisation of the ancient south-west, nomad and settler were already interacting in much the same way as they did until recent times. The familiar patterns of conflict and interdependence, in which each relied upon the other for essential goods and services but could at the same time come into conflict over water and grazing rights, have thus marked their relations for some 3000 years and probably more.

It is the interdependence of nomads and settlers which gives the lie to the notion that nomadism, because it is in some sense more "primitive", must pre-date the emergence of settled life. In fact, the archaeology of the region suggests that both lifestyles evolved in parallel as ways of exploiting scarce resources to the full. It is clear that there are not, and never have been, nomads in Arabia who had complete economic independence. They have always relied on the settled areas for a proportion of their food.

There has always been interchange between the desert and the town, with settlers adopting a nomadic or semi-nomadic lifestyle and nomads taking over settlements and becoming farmers and traders, in response to prevailing environmental, social and political conditions. Hence settlements in what is today Saudi Arabia have always reflected their tribal origins: towns were often organised in quarters corresponding to the tribal origins of their inhabitants. The same tribe could frequently include both settled and nomadic components. But the conditions of settled life tended to produce a more sophisticated culture than that of the nomadic tribes.

In one sense the rise of Islam can be seen as a clash between the aspirations of the town and the customs of the tribal nomads, whose religion had been polytheistic and animist. The early Muslims were essentially townsmen who sought to replace the limited loyalties of the tribe with a greater one to the Islamic state under God, and with the idea of the brotherhood of all Muslims.

Tribal attitudes are embodied in the oral Arabian poetry of pre-Islamic times which has come down to us. Recited in the earliest surviving form of Classical Arabic, it describes an heroic society demanding heroic virtues. The heroes are the symbol, the poets the voice, of their tribes.

To these people the word had real power. The poet was regarded as inspired; he acted for his tribe in negotiations, and could bring shame on opponents by his wit, skill and the force of his ridicule. The tribe which possessed the best poets was held to be thereby strengthened. Verbal pre-eminence was established at annual reciting competitions, the most famous of which was held at Ukaz near Taif.

Some of this reverence for oral poetry survives to this day in the desert, where poets are still held in high esteem. But, with the Dawn of Islam, the old tribal virtues were replaced by a divinely inspired ethical code. Many of the customs of early tribal life were banned, such as the exposing of unwanted female children, and the veneration of certain rocks and trees. The exacting of revenge was discouraged, to be supplanted by the administration of law. Oral poetry lost its special character and, in any case, was soon outshone by the multifaceted glories of Arabic literature.

However tribalism itself persisted down the centuries in Arabia in a counterpoint to the efforts of enlightened settled rulers and jurists to broaden its scope. By the twentieth century, some of the values of nomadic life had changed very little, with Beduin often placing their tribal obligations over their duty to Islam. The economic changes of recent times have, more than any other factor, wrought a change in the tribal scene. The motor car spelt the end of Beduin wealth based on camel and horse breeding, and

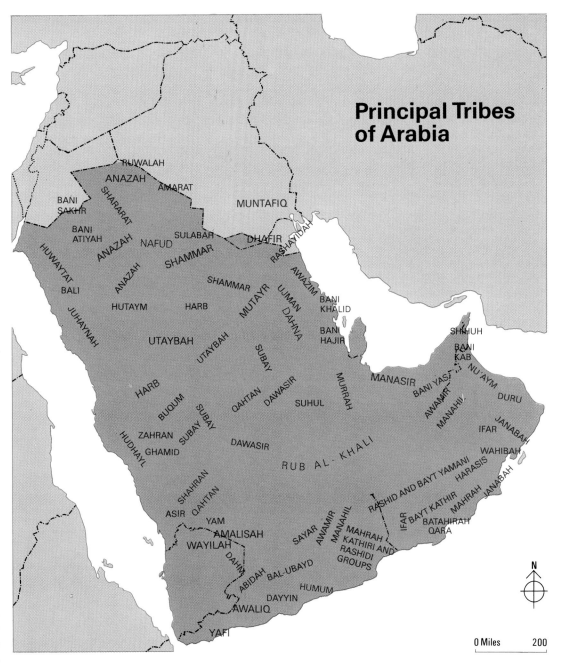

Principal Tribes of Arabia

Tribal allegiance gives both character and meaning to life among Saudi Arabians, ensuring a sustained loyalty to locality, while allowing for the prevailing national unity.

the rise of the oil industry has attracted them into new occupations, giving them skills and education in the process.

But the subordination of tribal values to those of Islam, and the triumph of settled values over nomadic ones which were its inevitable accompaniment, traces its real origin in Saudi Arabia to the rise of the Wahhabi reform movement in the eighteenth century and the establishment of the First Saudi State under the leadership of the House of Saud. King Abdul Aziz's achievement in the early part of this century in unifying much of Arabia was but the latest, if the most far-reaching, manifestation of this process.

The People of the Central Province

THE Province of Najd is the heart and cradle of Saudi Arabia. Its inhabitants – Najdis – are a gifted and remarkable people. Adapting easily to the furious rate of change which has prevailed in Saudi Arabia, they have proved their aptitude for jobs which were completely beyond the purview of their ancestors. Yet their basic conservatism and their attachment to traditional ways and ideals remains strong; they believe in treasuring the fundamental principles they have inherited, knowing that if they fail to do so, they will be left rootless. They cling to the flowing robes and headgear of their forefathers as an outward

Najd, a secure and geographically isolated centre, was never a strong magnet for foreign invaders.

manifestation of this belief. Family allegiances are as strong as ever. Marriages arranged by parents for their offspring prove more durable and contented than marriages in the West. The spirit of Islam continues to permeate Najdi thinking.

Fully to appreciate their charm and strength of character, an outsider must visit them in Najd, and see how they rejoice in, and delight to share, the simple pleasures of life – love of the desert and the exhilaration of the chase, with falcons flashing down on the prey; horse races and camel races, the sword dance exalting the old martial prowess of the Arabs; the flow of conversation, spiced with cardamom-flavoured coffee and sweet tea; the banquet spread on a rug, with succulent mutton crowning a mound of rice, the poet reciting his rhymes; and the passing around of the incense burner when the time has come for guests to take their leave.

Najd (that is, "highland") has never been easy to reach from the outside. The mountain barrier of the Hijaz towered above the land to the west, and on the other three sides lay a wilderness of sand. But trails did thread their way into the interior, and resolute men followed them. Members of tribes calling themselves sons of Qahtan or southern Arabs moved northwards and intermingled with the sons of Adnan or northern Arabs they found there.

The chiefs of Kindah, a southern tribe, founded a kingdom in the late fifth century of the Christian era, the first organized state known to have existed in Najd, but it was doomed to fall after only a few decades. Men of Tayy, another southern tribe, went even further north to what is now called Jabal Shammar. The Najdis of today are in the main the offspring of these northern and southern stocks. In other parts of the Arab world, Arabs have blended themselves with the indigenous peoples, but in Najd they have maintained a thorough Arabness which is perhaps their most distinguishing characteristic. In a sense they are Arab aristocrats, although their pride in this respect is tempered by the Islamic doctrine which proclaims piety and the brotherhood of Muslims rather than blood to be the truest touch-stone of nobility.

Najd had little to offer beyond the bracing air of the uplands, the stark beauty of landscapes, pastures for the grazing of herds of camels and flocks of sheep and goats, and scattered springs and wells. The nomads roamed from pasture to pasture and from source to source, while the denizens of the oases clustered together in spots where water flowed abundantly enough to irrigate their date palms and other plants. Although economically interdependent, there were times when neither element had much understanding of or sympathy for the other, and brawling often broke out between them.

The people of Najd have always loved

eloquence, especially when cast in the form of poetry. During the century before Islam, there was an outpouring of magnificent verse in classical Arabic, much of it composed by men and women of Najd. This literature resembles a gorgeous tapestry depicting the life of that time and the ideals of Arab society. The poets held manliness and fortitude and honour to be supreme virtues. Men showed tenderness towards women, whom they pledged to protect with their lives. Frequent wars and feuds called for courage on the field of battle; death was never to be feared. Leaders and elders deserved respect, but could not and did not act autocratically. The harshness of existence in a largely barren land and the need of wanderers for food and shelter fostered the traditions of hospitality and generosity. Hatim, a poet of the tribe of Tayy, is still the paragon of open-handed giving throughout the Arab world.

As the new religion of Islam advanced in the Arabian peninsula, it met resistance in central Najd where, soon after the death of Muhammad the Prophet, a false prophet, Musaylimah the Liar, preached a heretical creed. To overcome him, Abu Bakr, the first Caliph, had to call upon his finest general, Khalid ibn al-Walid, the Sword of God. Once the Najdis came to understand the spiritual message and values of Islam, however, they devoted themselves enthusiastically to its cause. As warriors and mis-

sionaries, countless Najdis left their homeland, many never to return. Carrying the gospel as far east as China and as far west as the Atlantic, these Najdis contributed largely to the expansion of the faith. Their old pagan fearlessness was now reinforced by the promise of eternal life in Paradise for those martyred in the path of God.

Najd, relatively secure in its geographical isolation and possessing few riches to be plundered, was not a strong magnet for foreign invaders. The bane of the region, however, remained for centuries civil strife and almost incessant feuding, town against town, tribe against tribe, nomadic bands against settled communities. This feuding militated

Coffee in the majlis, *the men's meeting tent* (left), *is a ritual of desert hospitality; women remain in the* mahram, *the female quarters* (right), *where they are protected from gaze.*

The ancient skills of falconry represent one of the most sophisticated sporting activities in the world. Skilled falconers are found around the country, outside the major cities. The game most often sought is Mac-Queen's bustard (hubara), sand grouse and stone curlew, dove, quail and courser. Falcons are kept hooded unless they are being worked. A skilled man will train a falcon in under three weeks. Of several varieties of falcon, the peregrine – shahin – is probably commonest: they are swift, bold and persevering. The saker falcon - hurr – is also favoured.

Men of Unayzah gather for a dignified but spirited traditional dance, com- *bining skilful sword play with complex drumming.*

against the formation of a powerful and durable state, and the absence of such a state meant that there was no authority to enforce effectively the Sacred Law of Islam and hold the people of Najd to orthodoxy. As time went by, backsliding became common. Many Najdis embraced innovations and beliefs abhorrent to the true spirit of Islam.

In the eighteenth century a religious scholar of central Najd, Sheikh Muhammad ibn Abd al-Wahhab, determined to bring Najd and the rest of Arabia back to the original and undefiled form of Islam as revealed through the Prophet Muhammad and upheld by the first generations of pious believers. To achieve this purpose he allied himself with Muhammad ibn Saud, the ruler of the oasis of Diriyyah not far from Riyadh. This alliance survived in the person of the late King Faisal, who was descended on the paternal side from the ruler and on the maternal side from the Sheikh.

The Reform Movement inaugurated by the Sheikh relied for support principally on the townsmen. Contrary to the misconception common in the West, the townsmen in Najd far outnumber the Beduin; this appears to have been true during the past several centuries at least. Despite some checks in the nineteenth century, the Reform Movement is still alive and vigorous, commanding the allegiance of the people of Najd, who thus stand out in the Islamic world as being among the foremost champions of conservative Islam.

In the twentieth century the late King Abdul Aziz, popularly known as Ibn Saud, found himself confronted with a problem of far-reaching implications. The Reform Movement, of which he was a devoted proponent, had as a cardinal objective the weeding out of all reprehensible innovations from Islamic society. So which new things were acceptable and which were not? Ibn Saud

took the liberal view that modern devices such as the automobile and the telephone, as long as they were useful to the community and not harmful to its religious beliefs, were acceptable. Various fanatical tribal chiefs rejected this view. They also chafed under the restraints Ibn Saud placed on their raids against those Arabs they regarded as infidels in the neighbouring states of Transjordan and Iraq. Finally, they rose in revolt against their sovereign. After much bitter fighting Ibn Saud, who secured an even larger measure of help from the townsmen of Najd as the revolt went on, succeeded in crushing the rebellion. Since then tribalism has died out as a political force in the Kingdom.

Today the loyalty of the Najdis to the House of Saud, a house sprung from the heart of their own region, is unswerving. At the same time, the old provincialism of the different parts of the Kingdom has been steadily waning. In the past Najdis

45

Traditional Najdi House Styles

Traditional methods of building in Saudi Arabia are highly efficient. The unfired clay bricks, finished in plaster, which provide the basic material, give excellent insulation against the heat of the sun. Roof structures are usually of tamarisk. Mouldings, crenellations and finials beautify the exteriors, executed with grace and restraint.

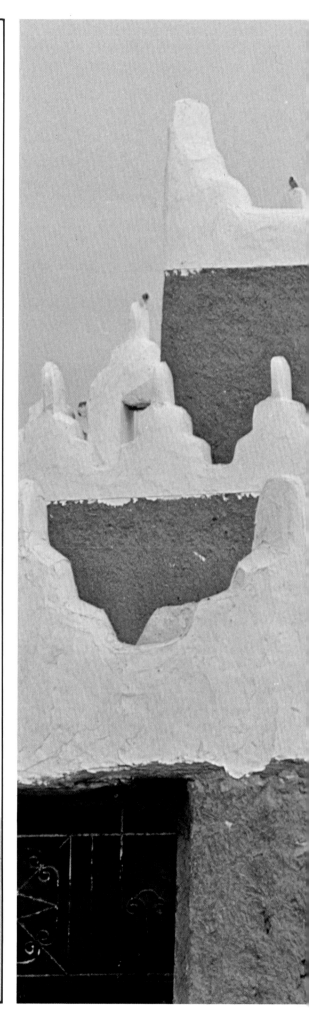

An instinctive sense of design prevails among the country's builders of traditional houses – as these examples from Burayda, in the Qasim area indicate. Crenellations and rooftop edges are picked out in white. The windows and air vents, peepholes and hatches, by which occupants of houses can look out or inspect the arrival of visitors, are worked into the overall design. The triangular decorations of the doorway (centre picture) are widely found throughout the country. Family and social life may proceed at three levels – in the street, within the house itself, and on the level of the complex of roofs, parapets, and alfresco stairways.

and Hijazis often looked at each other with a jaundiced eye, and Sunnite Najdis tended to disdain their Shi-ite neighbours in Hasa and Qatif to the east. Now they are all coming to think of themselves primarily as Saudi Arabs, fellow citizens of a state created, held together, and built up by two families of genius, the House of the Sheikh and the House of Saud.

The prevailing of Ibn Saud's liberal view meant an era of great changes in Saudi Arabian society. The pace was slow at first. In the 1940s, two decades after the suppression of the recalcitrant chiefs, Riyadh was still a walled town built of mud-brick. The country had only a handful of paved roads, and modern airports were just beginning to be constructed. Since the 1950s the rising production of oil has helped to make the pace increasingly rapid and in recent years almost impossible to catalogue.

Yet life among today's people of the Central Province does retain its profundity and society its balance. The impact of modernism, the explosion of opportunities, the infusion of new wealth, have created strains, but manageable strains. The illiteracy of former times which was widespread in Najd, with the only formal instruction being in the religious sciences and the ancillary discipline of the Arabic language, has been eradicated by the government's anti-illiteracy campaign. Primary and secondary schools abound in the towns and villages. In Riyadh universities for both men and women, with their *curricula* largely shaped on western models, are complemented by Islamic Studies at al-Imam University. Young Najdis doing postgraduate work both at home and abroad have demonstrated their ability to compete successfully with students from all parts of the world.

Not only in the sphere of education but in other spheres as well, Najdis have mastered new techniques and acquired new outlooks. In the government of Saudi Arabia and in private business Najdis have proved their aptitude for callings which a generation or two ago would have been unthinkable – a tribute to the versatility of this people who for long were cut off from the mainstream of mdoern industrial civilization, but who now play a leading role in the modern world.

(See also Sections 8 and 9)

The Arabian Horse

The legendary Arabian horse originated in the deserts of Saudi Arabia and through the centuries has been highly regarded for its extraordinary stamina and endurance.

The Najd pure-bred Arabian horse variously coloured bay, chestnut, grey or brown, stands from fourteen to fifteen hands in height. The head is larger in proportion than that of the English thoroughbred, the chief difference lying in the depth of the jowl. The ears are quite large but beautifully shaped, the eyes large and mild, the forehead wide and prominent, and the muzzle fine, sometimes almost pinched. The crest is slightly arched and the neck strong; the head is held high, the shoulders oblique, and the hoofs are round, large and very hard. The back is short and the croup longer and typically more level, with the tail set higher than in most other saddle breeds; indeed, Arabs have boasted that they could use them to hang their cloaks on.

For cross-breeding, the Arab stallion is notable for the transmission, to inferior stocks, of constitution, quality, intelligence and style.

It is written in the Qur'an that every man shall love his horse, while according to the *Hadith* the Prophet is said to have owned fifteen mares in his lifetime and to have quoted the following about them: "After woman came the horse, for the enjoyment and happiness of man."

Traditionally, the people of western Arabia have linked the world of Red Sea and Mediterranean with the interior.

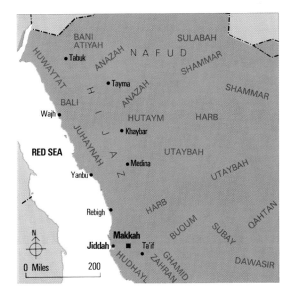

The People of the Western Province

OF all the natural divisions into which the Kingdom may be reduced, the Western Province is the most diverse. It approximately corresponds to the region known immemorially as the Hijaz. It is an area of about 80,000 square miles extending approximately 200 miles inland from Haql in the north to Qunfidhah in the south.

It is a land of great variety where cultivated hilltops give way to seemingly endless desert, where steamy heat yields to bracing winds and frosts, and where townsmen live cheek by jowl with nomads. Over the whole area, the ebb and flow of many civilizations has left its impress on the people. Yet, out of all this diversity it is possible to identify a Hijazi, not by physical appearance or by way of life, but by a bond of historical and cultural associations. For centuries, the settlements have been linked by the passage of caravans bearing precious cargoes and communities of the devout performing the *hajj*, the years spent as an outlying province of the Ottoman Empire and fourteen centuries of provisioning and serving the *Haramayn*, or Holy Cities.

The origins and distribution of the Hijazi peoples have been strongly influenced by geography. North of a line from Jiddah to Taif is a land of deserts: arid mineralized mountains or great

Though water is relatively abundant in the mountainous west, the lore of the desert prevails among the tribesmen and makes men hardy and devout.

sweeps of sand and stone. Where the fortunes of geology have yielded water near the coast or at a few points inland, settled communities of farmers, traders, fishermen or sailors have formed. But where aridity prevails then man has adapted to a way of life based on movement. In consequence, the northern Hijaz has never been able to support significant densities of population, with the one striking exception of al-Madinah, where water gushes out from beneath the great lava field of the Harrat al-Rahah.

To the south of the Jiddah-Taif line is another world entirely. There, high above the foetid heat of the Tihamah, the ascending winds of the summer monsoon bring regular rains which have permitted the development of many hundreds of tiny farming hamlets. Outward and downward from the mountains aridity prevails, and settlements become fewer until the wandering way of life prevails once more.

Although the word "Hijaz" means

"barrier", the history of the area and its peoples belies the term. The barrier referred to is the Great Escarpment which runs along, rather than across, the Hijaz, dividing it only from the interior plateaux. This same escarpment transforms the arid Hijaz into a natural corridor between the frankincense and myrrh country of Arabia Felix and the rich markets of the Fertile Crescent. Along this route a number of resting places and trading centres developed such as Makkah, al-Madinah, Khaybar and Tabuk, where water was available to sustain a settled population. Into these settlements came the merchant adventurers of the past: the Nabataeans in their rock-cut city of Madain Salih; the Jews in their fortress towns of Yathrib and Khaybar; the Babylonians with their palaces at Tayma.

From later pre-Islamic times the city of Makkah held a special place as a centre of pilgrimage and culture: a role which was greatly emphasized after the *hajj* brought new racial and cultural strains into the Hijaz and, as the word of the Prophet spread, so the diversity increased. Many who came stayed, while others brought their skills to the service of the pilgrimage: from India came the grain merchants to Jiddah; from the Hadhramawt, the traders and importers; from Java the descendants of Muslim missionaries, and, from Turkey and Egypt, the soldiers to police the desert trails. Sometimes, as in Makkah and Jiddah, the ethnic types congregated into district *haras* or quarters of the city such as the Nusla Yamaniyya of Jiddah. Often, however, the individual groups were absorbed into the cosmopolitan embrace of the Hijazi way of life, only their names distinguishing their origins:

Al-Ula village near Madain Salih is typical of Western province architecture.

the Tunsis (Tunisia), the Daghestanis, the Yamanis (Yemen) and the Misris (Egypt).

Such are the demographic origins of cities like Jiddah, Makkah, al-Madinah, Taif and Yanbu. In the smaller towns and oases of the north, a lasting symbiosis developed between, on the one hand, the itinerant Beduin such as the Bili, Huwaytat, Juhayna and the Harb, and on the other hand, the settled farmers of the agricultural oases. Very often the oases were dependencies of one or other Beduin group and were peopled by slaves and their descendants brought from Somalia, Eritrea and the *Swahili* coast of East Africa. This introduced a negroid

trait into the ethnic diversity which already existed, but, in general, brought none of the more pernicious aspects which accompanies slavery in the European Empires and Dominions.

In the south, along the coast, the African strain is strong and the Takarinah retain their distinctive thatched dwellings and racial features, though their African dialects have yielded to a universal use of Arabic. In the stone hamlets of the highlands, however, a Semitic homogeneity prevails, possibly because the farmers, pressed hard upon their pocket-handkerchief-sized farms, could neither use nor support a slave population.

The variety of landscape and habitat is reflected in the traditional social organization of the peoples. The Beduin form a complex skein of relationships based on common ancestry, so that lineage is not only a matter of great pride, and prodigious feats of memory, but also an entrée into a system of territorial rights, privileges and obligations. Binding this loose hegemony is a structure of often hereditary sheikhs wielding an even looser form of control. The villagers, on the other hand, may have some form of affinity by residence, but, in general, they belong to a wider community such as the Ghamid or Zahran tribes south of Taif. In the cities the situation is much more fluid. Some traditional sheikhly families are afforded their customary respect, but now they must compete with the great businessmen and traders, and an emerging group of technical and professional men.

Recent trends have accelerated many of the forces which shaped the population of the province. Most significant is the wealth created by the oil industry and the economic impetus it has given to the Hijaz, traditionally the commercial heart of the country. During the 1960s and 1970s, prosperity attracted increas-ing numbers of people into the Hijaz in several well-defined streams. At the same time, a clearly differentiated pattern of internal movement established and reinforced itself.

From Syria, Palestine, Egypt, Lebanon, Iraq and Pakistan came the skilled and semi-skilled workers needed to fill the gaps created by sudden and rapid growth. They concentrated mostly in the cities and towns, but some, notably doctors and teachers, were sent into rural areas. This was seen by the Saudis as a stop-gap measure while the country

Intricate latticing and wood carving pay tribute to the skills developed over centuries of settled life in the Western highland city of Taif (below).

trained its own qualified staff. For years, unskilled Yemenis poured north to work on the building sites, while women from Ethiopia and Somalia came seeking domestic employment.

Within the Hijaz the economic take-off had no less an impact on the indigenous population. The Beduin largely quit their traditional pastoral wanderings and exchanged the camel caravan for the Mercedes truck, the goathair tent for a breeze-block house on the outskirts of a town or city. Here, too, job and origin remain allied: find a taxi driver and you have found a Beduin. The hill villages, however, just about held their own while the cities continued to grow.

Now urban Jiddah has stabilised at around 1.5 million. Of the total Hijaz population of more than 2 million, over 70 percent are resident in the five main historic towns. The romance of the desert, if it ever existed, has yielded to the opportunities of the town. But, while subsistence farming in the mountains has failed to compete with the security of paid employment and the comforts of an urban environment, generous agricultural subsidies have helped to keep the people on the land.

All of the five major cities of the Western Province are of ancient foundation. Jiddah, commercial and industrial focus of the Western Province, has been an active port, certainly for 1,200 years, probably much longer. It is increasingly cosmopolitan. Yanbu, the region's second port, features as al-Madinah's port on the earliest maps of the Red Sea Coast but has for centuries been Jiddah's inferior. Since the mid-1970s Yanbu has boomed as a vital petrochemical centre; its population is planned to grow to 130,000 and is increasing as the port develops into an industrial complex of world importance.

Makkah, "the Blessed", lying at 610 metres in its hollow among the hills, is truly of the area, yet as the most venerated shrine in all Islam, is cosmopolitan in its spiritual role. So, too, is al-Madinah, also at 610 metres, centre of religious learning and site of the Islamic University's three colleges of Basic Religion, Shari'ah (Law), and Missions. The abundant wells of both cities have secured their survival over the centuries: both have seen rapid growth recently.

Lastly, Taif, by virtue of its high elevation (1,500 metres), became increasingly the annual refuge of those trying to escape the stifling summer heat of the lowland. Monarch, court and cabinet move to Taif in summer, making it for these months the second capital. For centuries Taif and its fine surrounding uplands have been the provider of fruit for the Hijaz, and of rosewater (*attar*) distilled from its vast acres of rose gardens, for the whole of Arabia, and, indeed, for Europe too.

(See Sections 8 and 9)

The People of the Eastern Province
THE coastal strip of the Eastern Province is low with relatively plentiful water; it was here that oil was first discovered. The shore is sandy, with sand flats occuring in depressions. Sandy plains from Jubayl to Kuwait Bay, drifting sand and dunes from Jubayl southward, a great belt of sand known as the Dahna and a rock plateau called the Summan are the region's other main features.

Educational and career opportunities for citizens of the Hijaz multiply.

Inland, migrations from Najd into the eastern Province, and regular communication between the great Hasa Oasis and the tribes and towns of the Riyadh area and southern Najd, ensured a homogeneity of tribal culture. On the coast, by contrast, favoured locations such as Qatif and Tarut Island attracted people into the region from the sea. Enterprising individuals came wherever social conditions allowed travel routes to develop, thus adding non-tribal sectors to the population and building up coastal centres. This polyglot population became socially integrated with other groups but remained politically subordinate to the tribal factions of the interior.

Today, that subordination has been overtaken by the wealth and power of the coastal cities and petroleum towns

into which people from all over the country, but particularly from the region itself, have flooded. The recent expansion of the complex of towns encompassed by the port city of Dammam, al-Khobar and Dhahran (which wholly consists of the adjacent compounds of Saudi Aramco and the King Fahd University of Petroleum and Minerals) has been phenomenal. The recent completion of the causeway linking this area to Bahrain will be a spur to further development. Reflecting the planned diversification of the Saudi economy, the industrial city of Jubayl is now in its second decade of development. Covering an area of 360 square miles, sixteen miles north of the historic fishing port

Football is the core of the Kingdom's new sporting endeavour.

of Jubayl, its population is planned to grow to 280,000. Its production facilities are designed to use the Kingdom's-

Herd of camels near Abqaiq (above). *The Ruwalah* (left) *range the North.*

petroleum and other mineral resources as feedstocks to generate domestic and export products.

Inland, the oil drills, pipelines and infrastructure of the petrochemicals industry pinpoint where industrial man has intruded upon the traditional lands of the tribe. Even so, there is always a "beyond" in Arabia; and beyond this intrusion the nomad does indeed pursue his life. The experience of the Murrah tribe, for example, along the northern edge of the Empty Quarter, is one of inescapable heat and shortage alleviated by space and freedom of movement. These tribesmen move their entire household in pursuit of grazing for their animals every few days throughout most of the year. They live largely on their animals' milk products and to a lesser extent on their meat, on dates, and on small amounts of rice and unleavened bread. Their inherited independence makes it difficult for them to fit into schemes of modern development.

The agriculturalist is generally better fed and better sheltered. The tribes of Bani Khalid and Bani Hajir live in the Haradh and Hasa Oases. Hofuf is the capital of Hasa Oasis, which is one of the largest oases in the world, its abundant natural artesian waters having supported settlement here since ancient times. The gardens of Hasa Oasis are magnificent, well tended groves amid colonnades of palms, which number in the millions.

The oil industry has brought increasing prosperity to the whole province. Even deep in the hinterland tribesmen dress better and live more safely and satisfactorily than their grandfathers did. Oil turned the port of Dammam into the thriving centre of the region, and its neighbour al-Khobar – once a fishing village whose inhabitants supplemented their living with pearling – into the expanding centre of business. Fairly copious underground water is today supplemented by desalination plants (e.g. at Jubayl, Ras al-Khafji, al-Khobar, and al-Uqayr). The coastal population, amid their extensive groves of date palms, thrive. It is a region of very ancient settlement, at one time controlled from the islet of Tarut, now linked by a road to the mainland.

The People of the North

NORTHERN Saudi Arabia is part of the great Syrian Desert of rock, gravel plains and lava beds. For thousands of years one of the most important trade routes connecting the Mediterranean and central and eastern Arabia passed through Wadi al-Sirhan and the oases of Jawf.

Northern Arabia is typified by the Nafud, a great expanse of rolling red dunes which cover 22,000 square miles and reach almost to the Jordan border; their deep orange-red at dawn and dusk is offset by the grey-green of tamarisks here and there. Otherwise it contains few watering places, but it affords good grazing for camels, sheep and goats in winter and spring.

Chief amongst the tribes of northern Saudi Arabia, the Anazah, from whom Al Saud are in part descended, comprises many distinct tribal units, of which the largest is the Ruwalah, the most powerful tribe in the north Arabian desert for centuries. Rivalling the Anazah – and once a challenge to Ibn Saud's power – is the great tribe Shammar, with the headquarters of its paramount sheikhs, the Ibn Rashid, at Hail. And to the west range the Huwaytat, with a tradition of enmity towards both; it was their paramount sheikh, Audah Abu Tayi, whom Lawrence called "the greatest fighting man in northern Arabia."

Amid the warring of these noble Beduin tribes, lesser shepherd tribes were left to rear their flocks in peace, providing they paid for the privilege. Below these in the social hierarchy of the desert in times past were the Sana, a blacksmith tribe, and the semi-gypsy Sulubba, a tribe of tinkers and trackers. Only the neutral Sulubba stay in the desert all year, for with their small donkey herds, they are able to use shallow wells.

Along with poems, stories and songs, camel-raiding was a favourite occupation for enhancing the reputation; herds that were too big to be guarded properly were attacked and spare camels were thus distributed about the desert.

King Abdul Aziz put a stop to the feuding and raiding of the Beduin in the late 1930s. He was the first ruler for centuries to be able to enforce his will on the Beduin tribes, who respected their powerful desert leader and became his most devoted subjects. Many have now abandoned their nomadic life to settle in the oases and cities. They are proving very adaptable, both in their willingness to settle to city life, and in their acceptance of new ways in the desert. Many families have abandoned herding camels. Sheep are more profitable, and grazing and water can be provided for them thanks to motor transport.

The tribes of northern Arabia believe that Beduin ways are best, and that the desert made the Beduin what they were: God sends the rain so that the herds will have pasture; from the herds they have milk to drink, hair for their tents, and young to sell for grain and coffee. Only in the desert is man truly free.

The slight winter rains fall in a different location every year and, after the star *Canopus* is visible in the night sky (October-November), everyone wants information on rain. From reports, which they check with everyone they meet, the herders can tell where the grazing will be, its quality and quantity.

Traditionally the Ruwalah have divided men into *hadhar* (permanent house dwellers) and *arab* (people who live in the movable black tent); of the latter, the true Beduin are those who breed camels and for ten months live in the interior of the desert (see Beduin Life, Section 10). They eat twice a day, the main meal in the evening, a diet based on milk and supplemented by bread, coffee, dates and sometimes locusts. As the various tribes differ in dialect, so do they in dress. They all wear the same basic *thobe*, but of varying colours, cut and ornament. If a *Rweli* sights a troop of riders in the distance, he can tell at once whether they are Ruwalah and of what clan.

A single family can manage forty to fifty camels, but it can survive on fifteen. Summer encampments on the high ground have been known to exceed 10,000 tents. The sheikh is the head of the tribe, chosen from the leading family for his courage, generosity and mediating skill. Today they deal with the government over concessions for the drilling of new oil wells, rents payable for pipelines crossing their grazing, jobs at the new administrative centres and vehicle licensing.

But northern Arabia is not all great red Nafud desert, and its people are not all nomadic Bedu. The main town in northern Arabia is Tabuk, whose busy main streets are modern dual carriageways taking the heavy traffic of container trucks bringing goods overland from Europe to the Kingdom. Graceful eucalyptus trees grow in Tabuk, and a Turkish fort, nearly 300 years old, stands on its edge. Then there are the oasis towns, founded on sources of perennial water, and supported by an economy of date palms and tribal markets, with a cultural life of their own. Dates were the staple food of the oases, and all other plants – fruit trees, vegetables, and alfalfa – were cultivated in their shade. And many oases established links with a local Beduin tribe who would defend them, and who may indeed have made their headquarters in the oasis town.

Typical of these is the ancient wellwatered town of Dumat al-Jandal in Jawf, some 220 miles north-east of Tayma and linked to it by a new asphalt road. The old town is sited on the slopes of a great basin surrounded by cliffs. Beside it stands the new town and both are dominated by a great castle, Qasr Mared. Its mosque, believed to have been founded by Caliph Umar, is one of the oldest in the land, and has a particularly beautiful minaret.

Beyond the crumbling stone walls of the old town, and the white concrete buildings of the new, stretch the palm groves, orchards, and even meadows of the oasis. Amid fields of grazing cows one might easily forget one was near the great Nafud.

It is now linked by road to the next oasis way-station, Sakaka, famous for its lively rock carvings on the Jebel Burnus, an outcrop projecting from the near-vertical rock which is crowned by the Zabal fort. Continuing north from there, the next oasis town is Badanah, which is only thirty miles from the Iraqi border.

The People of the South-West

THE traditional name for the south-west, Asir, means "the difficult region" – and so indeed it is, for the outsider. The range which, as one moves southwards, becomes the south-western massif of peaks and terraced valleys and plateaux at over 6,500 feet, actually begins with the hills to the north of Taif and includes the hill of Arafat, known to all pilgrims to Makkah. But the route southwards through the foothills was indeed a difficult one, until the building of today's highway, and more difficult still from the west, where the great block of mountain rises precipitously from the low coastal plain, the Tihamah.

To the east, the Asir slopes gently down into the largest sand-sea in the world, the Rub al-Khali. Southwards, these highlands of Saudi Arabia are

In the settled and agricultural south-west, traditional veiling of women has not taken hold, and vivid colours and jewellery characterize the apparel. Right: a similarly vigorous sense of colour is exploited in the interiors of lowland homes.

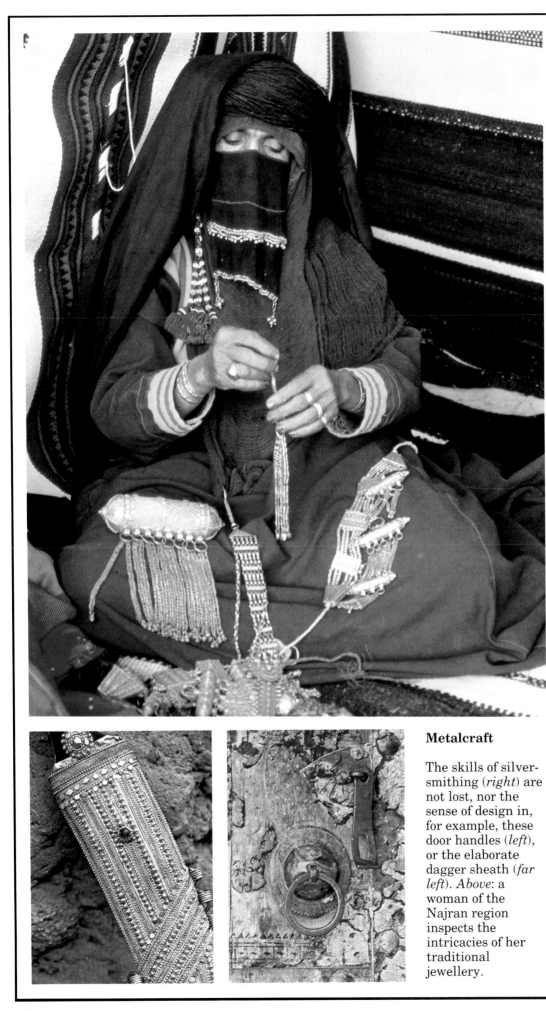

*The heat of the charcoal is intensified by the bellows worked (*above*) by the craftsman's knee. The tradition of patterning by rows of fused beads (*bottom left*) is one that has survived from the Ancient World, and for which the Etruscans were famed. This technique of granulation is highly skilled, since it requires fusing minute metal beads at great temperature (*below*).*

Metalcraft

The skills of silver-smithing (*right*) are not lost, nor the sense of design in, for example, these door handles (*left*), or the elaborate dagger sheath (*far left*). *Above*: a woman of the Najran region inspects the intricacies of her traditional jewellery.

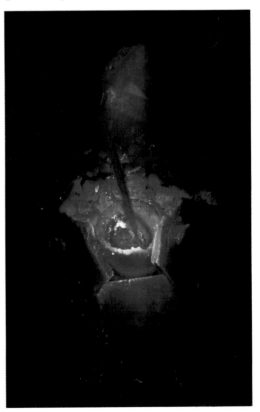

These pictures from the early 1970s (above) *show traditional methods of extracting oil from sesame seed in a mortar turned by a blinkered camel. Modern equipment and new farming methods eliminated this practice.*

separated by deep valleys and a rugged causeway of uplands from the mountains of northern Yemen. The people south of the border are different in appearance, custom, temperament and religious attitude from their Saudi neighbours. But both regions catch the monsoon rains.

The south-west is the one well-watered region of Saudi Arabia. The annual rains have cut deep gorges beneath the high peaks and valley walls. To hold the soil from the ferocity of the rains, the farmers have – for thousands of years – turned the valleys and bowls into beautifully contoured walled terraces. In this ancient terrain grow every manner of cereals, fodder crops and fruit.

Likewise, to protect their dwellings, the people in some areas have evolved the unique practice of mortaring into the outer walls row upon row of shale louvres. In so fine a natural setting, a sense of design prevails. Homes are washed outside with colours that intensify the upland sunlight. Smithing abounds, as does the wearing of jewellery. Strong colours are prevalent amongst the women's dress. There is a celebrated grace and confidence among

the highland people.

The south-west is not all highland. To the west, beneath the steep, sometimes vertical escarpment, lies the lowland Tihamah. And the Tihamah in turn presents two different aspects, the valleys, and a shady plain stretching towards the Red Sea. Generally speaking, the people in the highlands are taller than those in the lowlands.

The heavier and relatively dependable rainfall has allowed south-westerners, for the most part, to live a settled life as cultivators of the soil and as herdsmen. The different regions are identified according to the tribal groups which inhabit them. The most important groups, from north to south, are Zahran, Ghamid, Bajr, Asir, Shahran, and Qahtan. When referring to a particular area one says for example, Bilad Zahran, "the land of Zahran," or Bilad Asir, "the land of Asir".

In the highlands, villages are found in clusters and the appearance of these differs often significantly from area to area. Thus between Bilad Zahran and Bilad Hajr, the houses are built of stone, while southwards towards Asir, both stone and mud houses are found, the latter being more numerous. Before the expedition of the late King Faisal (then a Prince) some two generations ago, which brought it into the Kingdom of Saudi Arabia, this south-western area was a warlike region where feuds between villages were com-

monplace. The disused watchtowers which dot the landscape everywhere are witnesses of that period.

Because of their altitude the highlands are cool in the summer with plentiful rain. This makes a good region for agriculture. Indeed, the highlanders are an agricultural people, growing barley, millet, vegetables and fruit, but the date palm is not grown in the highlands. The terraced field, to be seen everywhere on the mountain slopes, is commonest of all. To ensure a better yield, irrigation is used in both orchards and non-terraced fields generally found in the drier and flatter areas. The water may come either from a water course swelled by rain, or from a well. In many areas where irrigation is mechanized, wells are drilled directly on the farm land, and pumps are placed in the old wells to replace muscle power.

The highland farms are compact, orderly and highly productive. Sophisticated marketing and excellent road and air communications today enable produce from the high Asir to reach Jiddah, Riyadh and the Gulf coast. The farmers enjoy a high standard of living, many of them owning cars or trucks or mechanized agricultural equipment. Yet, as is refreshingly true elsewhere in Saudi Arabia, new techniques and rising expectations and the advent of schools, hospitals, modern roads and dams, have not destroyed the respect for traditional values and styles. For example, while some "functional" modern buildings have gone up in Abha, in the Asir as a whole, homes are built in highly distinctive styles, with the encouragement of an enlightened regional administration.

Inevitably – and desirably – the highland people will be brought increasingly into contact with the "outside" world as a result of the certain growth in the tourist trade. Now that major roads have been opened from both north and south, and with the expansion of already efficient airline services to Khamis Mushayt, the flow of visitors escaping the summer heat of the lowland plateaux will swell year by year, affecting both the economy and the outlook of the indigenous people.

At the southern end of the south-west region lies the oasis of Najran, below the highland chain. Although linguistically it must be considered part of Najd, geographically it is part of the south-west. The architecture, of mud and straw, belongs to the south-west and not to central Najd. Furthermore, the half-moon shaped windows of tinted glass above the main windows of the houses in Najran are Yemeni in style.

The fertile oasis of Najran lies in the lower reaches of a wadi debouching into the lowland to the east, and so is in easy contact with the Beduin tribes of the Rub al-Khali and southern Najd. Beduin thus come into close contact with the settled people of Najran, with whom they have ties of commerce and kinship. The main agricultural products of Najran are dates, as the climate allows the growth of the date palm, and grapes, for which Najran is famous. Today cultivation of various fruits and vegetables for the domestic market is encouraged.

The clothing of the men consists of long shirt-like robes, like those of their counterparts in Najd, but here the width of the lower edge of the garment is greater. They may be white, blue or olive in colour. The headgear is usually a red and white checkered headcloth. The women wear long, waisted colourful

dresses, often heavily embroidered. Stress is on individuality. In the Asir region the peasant women wear broad brimmed sombrero-type hats. Women rarely veil the face.

In the Tihamah the population is of two types, sedentary people living in villages, and nomads. The sedentary population of the valleys is in close contact with the highlanders. There are dirt roads winding up the steep mountain passes separating the two regions. The impressive Jizan highway is the most used link between these valleys and the flatter lands bordering the Red Sea.

A good example of a village of the valleys of the Tihamah is Rijal, west of Abha. The village is of stone and built on two sides of a narrow valley. The way the houses rise on the slopes gives the impression of skyscrapers. Rijal used to be a trade centre, but the shops are now closed down as the Abha-Jizan road has diverted their trade. But the village is still renowned for gold-smithing.

The interiors of the houses in Rijal are attractive. Even more than in Abha the walls are decorated with gay, stylized designs painted by the women. For more decoration colourful imported enamelware adorns the shelves of the walls.

In the Rijal area agriculture is restricted to the sides of the valley. There is little terracing. The fields in the bottom of the valley have high retaining walls to protect them from the violence of flash floods. Higher up the slopes towards the highlands, where the climate is cooler, coffee has become a successful crop.

The other type of population found in the valley are the nomads who raise sheep and goats. They are unlike the Beduin of central Arabia. The men often

The influence of Africa is seen in the conical homes of the southern Tihamah coast (below), *where villagers wear distinctive hats, rather than the ghutrah, while characteristic Yemeni features* (far left) *are found on the highland borders of Saudi Arabia's neighbour.*

go bare-chested, wearing a length of colourful cloth around their waists. Their side-arm is a sword-like curved dagger just under a metre long, a protection against leopards. Often their headgear is a tall, black, brimless hat with a flattish backward-sloping top. The women wear tall straw hats with brims, similar to the hats worn by South American Indians.

Coastal Tihamah is flat and sandy. The majority of the population is agricultural, growing mostly millet. In Wadi Baysh, about forty miles north-east of Jizan, is a vast expanse of millet covering about six hundred square miles. Much of this region is newly watered by rain floods stored in the massive Jizan dam, which is transforming a former wilderness into a significant grain-producing area, including an extensive experimental farm run by the Government. The visual impression of so much millet is strongly reminiscent of the endless maize fields of the American Mid-West.

Southwards down from the Red Sea coast, the influence of Africa is clearly to be seen among the people and their style of life. Conical houses are built in clusters behind high reed palisades. On the flats inland from Jizan, these villages present remarkable toothed silhouettes on the horizon. The single-chamber houses, lined with mud, are brilliantly painted inside with imaginative designs that reach to the pinnacle of the under-roof. Fishing is a major local industry, the Spanish mackerel being a principal source of protein food. The traditions of seamanship have maintained links with the Eritrean coasts across the Red Sea.

In the extreme south-west where the mountains rise sharply out of the plains, the lowland markets on the Saudi side of the frontier are frequently thronged with Yemenis with produce to sell. Higher Saudi standards of living bring higher prices.

In both the highlands and the lowlands the many markets constitute an important part of the people's life. The market in a village may be open every day or only once a week. If the latter is the case, market day is on a fixed day of the week, and, like anywhere else, that day is a social occasion for the people of the neighbouring villages. Often the name of the village incorporates the name of the day on which the market was customarily held. Thus: Khamis Mushayt, "the Thursday of Mushayt", Ahad Rufaydah, "the Sunday of Rufaydah", Sabt Tanumah, "the Saturday of Tanumah". Such places are usually referred to by the people of the region only by the name of their market day: Khamis, Ahad, Sabt. In some towns, where the market nowadays is open all week, as in Abha and Khamis Mushayt, market day sees more wares on display than other days of the week. On market day one may find nomads travelling up from the

Tihamah to trade with the highlanders. In the markets, in addition to food and modern goods, one finds local products, such as straw baskets and hats, keys and nails made of locally mined iron, or, as in Najran, salt mined in the Empty Quarter.

The people of the south-west pride themselves on their hospitality. When a guest arrives, he is feasted by his host and various other members of the family who, on a more prolonged visit, take turns to entertain the guest. Besides the standard fare of lamb and rice, a dish offered to the guest is *arikah*, half-baked bread dough served in a big circular dish covered in brown honey. The guest fashions pieces of dough between his fingers into the shape of a spoon which he then dips into a side dish filled with white honey.

Weddings are a most important social occasion. Guests come, often from far away, to participate in the festivities.

There is dancing and singing on two separate days, one day for the men, and the following day for the women. On the men's day the guests dance in public in lines or circles, singing to the accompaniment of drums. There are also dagger dances.

On the women's day there are similar songs and dances performed in a marquee to the accompaniment of drums and pestles and mortars which serve as percussion instruments. The women put on all their jewellery on such an occasion. Such ceremonial reflects the rich oral traditions of song and poetry of the people of the south-west.

The highland South-West is today a sought after resort during the heat of the lowland summer. A bluish wash gives a jewel like quality to an Abha farmstead (opposite). *Slate louvres ensure weather-proofing* (left and below).

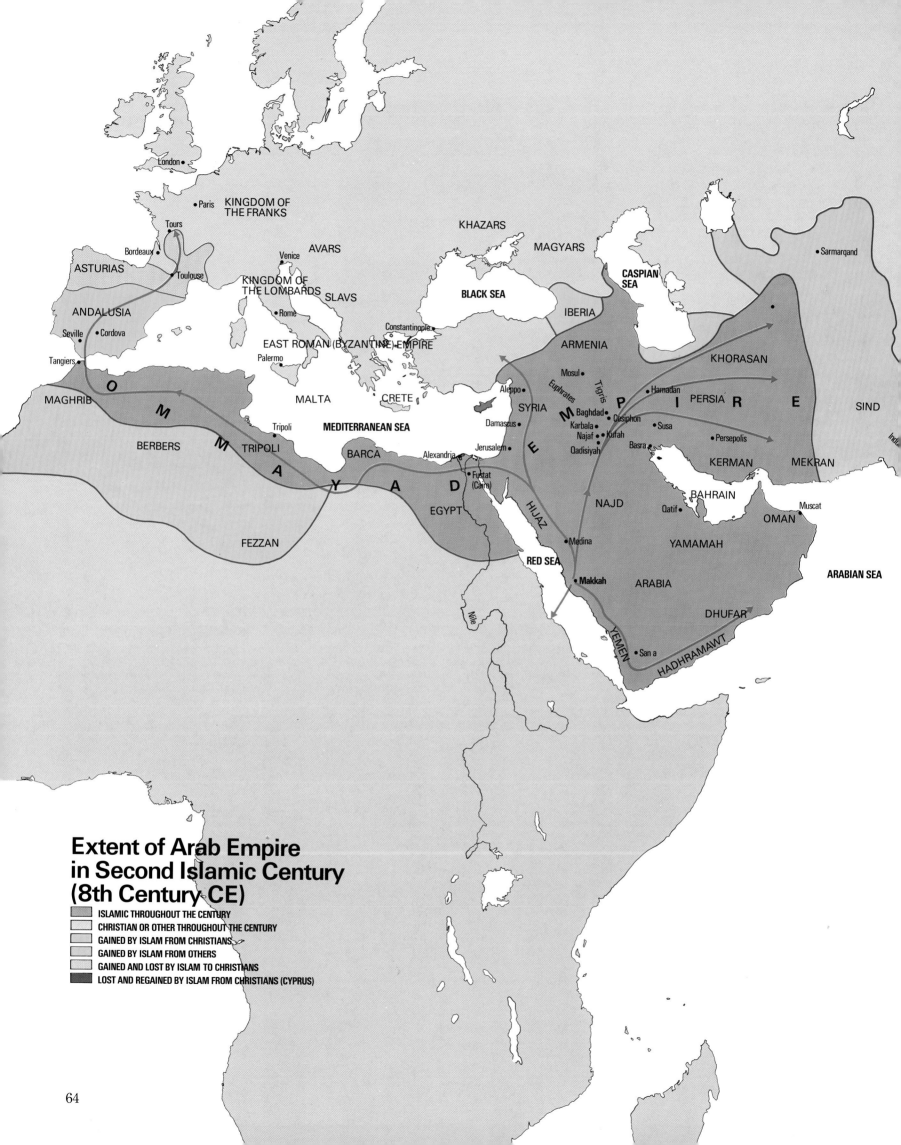

London •

• Paris

KINGDOM OF
THE FRANKS

KHAZARS

MAGYARS

AVARS

CASPIAN
SEA

ASTURIAS

Bordeaux •

Tours

Venice

Toulouse

KINGDOM OF
THE LOMBARDS

BLACK SEA

IBERIA

ANDALUSIA

SLAVS

ARMENIA

KHORASAN

• Sarmarqand

Seville •

• Cordova

• Rome

EAST ROMAN (BYZANTINE) EMPIRE

Constantinople •

Mosul •

Euphrates

Tigris

Hamadan •

PERSIA

Tangiers •

O

Palermo

Aleppo •

M

Baghdad •

Susa •

SIND

MAGHRIB

M

M

MALTA

CRETE

SYRIA

Ctesiphon

E

P

I

R

E

BERBERS

A

TRIPOLI

MEDITERRANEAN SEA

Damascus •

Karbala •

Najaf •

Kufah •

• Persepolis

Y

Tripoli •

Jerusalem •

E

Basra •

KERMAN

MEKRAN

A

BARCA

Alexandria •

Qadisiyah

Indu

D

Fustat
(Cairo)

BAHRAIN

EGYPT

HIJAZ

NAJD

Qatif •

OMAN

• Muscat

FEZZAN

Nile

RED SEA

• Medina

YAMAMAH

ARABIAN SEA

• Makkah

ARABIA

DHUFAR

YEMEN

• San a

HADHRAMAWT

Extent of Arab Empire
in Second Islamic Century
(8th Century CE)

ISLAMIC THROUGHOUT THE CENTURY

CHRISTIAN OR OTHER THROUGHOUT THE CENTURY

GAINED BY ISLAM FROM CHRISTIANS

GAINED BY ISLAM FROM OTHERS

GAINED AND LOST BY ISLAM TO CHRISTIANS

LOST AND REGAINED BY ISLAM FROM CHRISTIANS (CYPRUS)

64

PUNJAB

4 History

Saudi Arabia has a rich pre-Islamic past, the civilizations of which are only today being uncovered by archaeologists. It was here that Islam was revealed to the Prophet Muhammad, and the country then became the focus and the centre of the swiftly spreading new religion.

However, Saudi Arabia as we know it today was created only at the beginning of the twentieth century, through the vision and daring of the young Ibn Saud – later King Abdul Aziz. He restored the fortunes of the House of Saud which, since the mid-eighteenth century, had ruled much of Arabia.

Aramaic inscriptions have been found in Tayma (left). Other inscriptions excavated in parts of Arabia are in pre-Islamic scripts peculiar to the Peninsula, as that in Himyaritic and Lihyanite from the south-west and north-west (above). They yield evidence of sophisticated civilizations reaching back some three millennia. The function of these fragments was votive.

Old Babylonian Empire, 1700 B.C.

Babylonia-Assyria, 1450 B.C.

Assyrian Empire, 7th Century B.C,

Pre-Islamic Datelist

Involving Arabs and Related Peoples of the Near and Middle East

	BC
2350	Sargon builds Akkad
2300	Ascendancy of Ebla (Tell Mardikh)
2270-2233	Reign of Naram-Sin of Sumer
2200	Decline of Pharaonic Old Kingdom
2000	Zenith of civilization of Dilmun in Eastern Arabia
1991-1792	12th dynasty of Middle Kingdom of Pharaohs
1728-1686	Hammurabi reigns (founder of Babylon)
1700	Abraham leads migration to Palestine from Ur
1570-1545	18th Egyptian dynasty founded in Thebes by Ahmose
1545-1525	Amenhotep of Egypt moves capital to Akhetaton (Tell al-Amarna)
1530	Hittites sack Babylon. End of first Amorite dynasty
1502-1448	Egyptian conquest of North Nubia and neighbouring Mediterranean coast under Thutmose III
1361-1352	Tutankhamun reigns
1300-1200	Rise of Sabaeans under the Queen of Sheba in South Arabia
1280	Treaty signed. North Syria recognized as Hittite, South Syria (Palestine) as Egyptian
1234-1215	Hebrews' exodus from Egypt
1200	Damascus gained by Aramaeans
1100-888	Rise of Sidonian state
1020	Saul anointed. First King of the Hebrews
945	Shishak of Libya ousts Pharaohs
936-923	Reign of Solomon
900-842	Rise of Damascus
884-859	Rise of Ashur-nasir-pal and an initial Assyrian conquest successful
875	Israel becomes a vassal of Damascus
814	Carthage founded by Phoenicians
806-732	Decline of Aramaean Damascus
733	Tiglath-Pileser of Assyria defeats Israel
732	Tiglath-Pileser overthrows Damascus, centre of Aramaean power
727-722	Shalmaneser V of Assyria conquers Tyre
722-705	Sargonid dynasty. Ascendancy of Assyria. Campaigns against "Arab" tribes in N. Arabia.
705-681	Sennacherib destroys Babylon
671	Tirhaka of Ethiopian dynasty in Egypt defeated by Assyrians.
600-593	Phoenicians under Pharaoh Necho circumnavigate Africa
605-562	Reign of Nebuchadnezzar II. Restoration of Babylon and creation of the Hanging Gardens.
586	Nebuchadnezzar destroys Jerusalem.
572	Nebuchadnezzar conquers Tyre
550-540	Nabonidus adopts Tayma in Arabia as Babylonian royal residence.
550-529	Cyrus of Anshan in Elam founds Achaemenid dynasty in Persia
546	Cyrus overthrows Croesus and seizes Sardis

539 Babylonians under Belshazzar defeated by Persians
539-332 Phoenicia under Persian rule
529-521 Cambyses of Persia conquers Egypt
521-485 Darius I establishes Persepolis
490 Darius loses Battle of Marathon to Athenians
480 Spartans defeat Persians at Thermopylae
480 Xerxes of Persia routed by Greeks at sea battle of Salamis
446 Artaxerxes I makes peace treaty with Greeks
330 Alexander the Great burns Persepolis
323 Alexander the Great conquers Babylon and dies there
312-280 Seleucus I founds the Syrian Kingdom
300 Petra becomes Nabataean capital
226 Parthians defeated by Sassanids
218 Hannibal of Carthage crosses the Alps
202 Hannibal defeated by Romans
169 Antiochus IV of Syria defeats Ptolemy IV of Egypt
133 Attalid Kingdom creates extensive province of Asia
85 Nabataeans take Coele-Syria from Seleucids
69-83 Tigranes of Armenia makes conquests in Macedonian Kingdom
64 Romans conquer Syria
51-30 Rule of Cleopatra in Egypt
48 Julius Caesar conquers Pompey at Zela
44 Caesar murdered
30 Roman annexation of Egypt
37-4 Rule of Herod the Great of Judaea
6 Birth of Jesus (as calculated by scholars)

CE
0-100 Himyarites migrate to Axum (Abyssinia)
27 Death of Jesus
70 Titus, Roman Emperor, starves Jerusalem into surrender
106 Romans destroy Nabataean Petra
114-116 Rome at war with Parthia
123 Hadrian renounces Euphrates territory
195-199 Severus conquers Mesopotamia
226 Foundation of the new Sassanid Persian Empire
268-273 Palmyra conquers Syria, Mesopotamia and parts of Egypt
330 Constantinople becomes seat of Eastern half of Roman Empire
354-430 Life of Augustine
433-453 Attila, ruler of the Huns
525 Abyssinians conquer Yemen
568-572 Fall of Rome
571 Birth of Muhammad
575 Khosrau I of the Sassanids expels Abyssinians from the Yemen
596 Muhammad marries Khadijah of the Quraysh tribe
610 Muhammad's first revelation outside Makkah
614 Persians conquer Damascus, Jerusalem and Egypt
622 Muhammad flees from Makkah to al-Madinah, the *hijrah* and official beginning of the Muslim era
632 Death of Muhammad

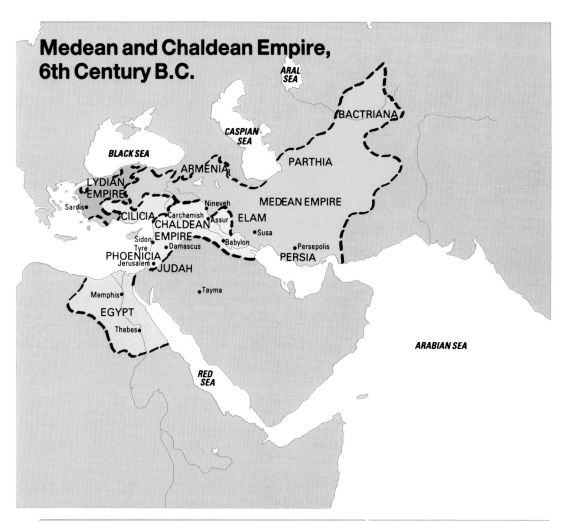

Medean and Chaldean Empire, 6th Century B.C.

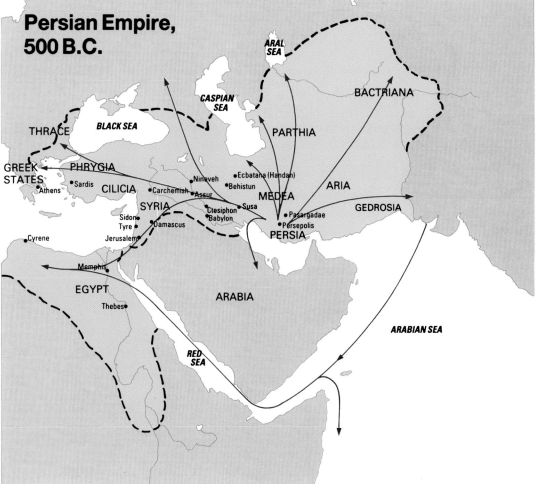

Persian Empire, 500 B.C.

The "Age of Darkness" to the Coming of the Prophet

SCHOLARS may disagree about the location of the cradle of the human race, but about the cradle of civilization there is no disagreement. It lies in the area called the "Near East" and is composed of the Fertile Crescent – Mesopotamia (modern Iraq), Syria, Palestine, Egypt, Anatolia (Asia Minor, Turkey) and Persia (Iran). At one time most of Europe and much of the Middle East was covered in ice, but to the south of this ice-sheet, Africa and Arabia were fertile with grass and streams flowing in what are nowadays dry *wadis*. The climate gradually changed, the ice-sheet retreated and the grasslands advanced.

International highways have always linked Africa, Europe and Asia, and these continents provided the stage not only for the world's three great monotheistic religions but also for some of the earliest, most spectacular and enduring discoveries and achievements of man. The civilizations which developed in this area passed on to later generations a matchlessly rich heritage of science, art, literature and philosophy.

Civilization as we recognise it probably began in the vicinity of the basins of the Rivers Tigris and Euphrates in Mesopotamia, the River Nile in Egypt and the River Indus valley. From here it spread over the Middle East, while men in the rest of the world still lived in a primitive state. The area of the Middle East, originally a European geographical term loosely used to designate that part of south-western Asia nearest Europe, has a recorded history filled with drama – the rise and fall of empires, the growth and decline of great cities, the ascendancy and decline of great peoples, wars, invasions and deportations, kings and emperors, treachery, and disasters.

More than 5000 years ago, the people of the Middle East had developed urban life, with ordered governments, religions, and social and economic institutions. Earlier still, those who occupied the Fertile Crescent had discovered metal, realized its potential and worked it into tools and weapons which replaced the more primitive stone implements of preceding generations. Civilization first developed where it did because this was the one area of the globe which provided the climate, vegetation, and fauna necessary for the transition from a life of nomadic grazing and hunting to a

The exceptionally well-preserved rock tombs and dwellings of Madain Salih in north-western Saudi Arabia give vivid

settled existence. Through migration, invasion or cultural osmosis these remarkable accomplishments eventually found their way into the Eastern Mediterranean and the Aegean islands, and thence to the European mainland where they formed a prelude to the classical civilizations of Greece and Rome, parents to all Western civilizations. The full extent of the debt that Greece and Rome owed this area was hardly appreciated until recently, a debt which does not make the glory that was Greece less glorious, or the grandeur that was Rome less grand. In fact, it was not until the early nineteenth century that scholars began to rediscover the empires of Egypt, Babylonia and Assyria and to reconstruct their cultural institutions. As for the Hittites and their empire in Anatolia, the rediscovery began as late as the twentieth century. Historians and archaeologists disagree about some of the detail of pre-Islamic history but

evidence of the Nabataean civilization which flourished two thousand years ago on the rich spice trade.

during the last century a great deal has been ascertained by exploration and excavation. Only since the 1960s has the role of what today is Saudi Arabia begun to be revealed by the discoveries of archaeologists.

The Sumerians created one of the earliest civilizations, in an area adjoining Arabia. By 3000 BC they occupied their new homeland of Sumer at the head of the Arabian Gulf, at the junction of the Tigris and Euphrates rivers. The principal city was Ur. Other cities founded then were Erech, Lagash and Nippur. Eridu was a burgeoning port on the coast, although its site is now some 130 miles inland, and the other cities are just mounds in the desert. Irrigation, trade, the use of money and codes of laws were all developed by the Sumerians, and their clay tablets of pictorial and syllabic writing became the cuneiform script widely used in the ancient Middle East. Our modern science of astronomy is derived from their advanced knowledge of the stars, supplemented by Babylonian, Greek and Islamic influences. They used wheeled vehicles, and built beauti-

ful and imposing arches with dried bricks as a feature of their tower temples, known as *ziggurats*. Archaeologists have found good examples of utensils, sculpture and other remnants of the Sumerian way of life in the tombs which were constructed for each dead leader, and which habitually included all the men and women who had been his close servants in his lifetime.

But contacts between the rich lands of Mesopotamia and the coast of eastern Saudi Arabia were already vigorous during the preceding two millennia, the earliest traces beginning in 5500 BC and continuing through the rise of Dilmun (today's Bahrain and neighbouring mainland) during the third millennium when the Arabian Gulf ports were of great importance, as excavations inland from Abqaiq have proved.

Traditionally the people known as the Semites are thought to be descended from Shem, the eldest son of Noah. Their languages, belonging to the closely related Semitic group, were unrelated to Sumerian, but they also lived in the Fertile Crescent and, as early nomads, on its

arid borderlands in the Syrian and North Arabian deserts. Over the centuries they gradually filtered into central and northern Mesopotamia. Gradually they built up their own city states such as Kish and Mari, having for many years plundered their more advanced neighbours, the Sumerians. About 2360 BC the first empire of recorded history emerged, that of Akkad, in the area which became known as Babylonia. Akkadian influence spread beyond Mesopotamia to Arabia. This empire was destroyed after a couple of centuries, and, although Akkadian Semites continued to be one of the main elements in the population, other Semitic powers gained ascendancy, notably the invaders of Mesopotamia, the Amorites, who came from the present area of Syria.

The ancient city of Babylon was ruled in the eighteenth century BC by the Amorite, King Hammurabi. Basic laws were formalized and great progress was made in the fields of scholarship and science, especially mathematics and astronomy. The Hittites overwhelmed Babylon in approximately 1600 BC. These tribes from Asia Minor absorbed Syria and made treaties with the Egyptians before they too were overcome by an invasion of barbarians from Europe in 1200 BC. The Kassite dynasty ruled Babylonia successfully for four hundred years. Thereafter it came to be ruled by Assyria.

The Assyrians had settled in northern Mesopotamia; their capital was Assur on the Tigris, named after their national god. Nineveh later became the imperial capital, and the cultural ideas of the Babylonians and the Sumerians were developed by the Assyrians with their own characteristic variations. Very active commercially, they used stamped silver bars for money, employed letters of credit

Though strongly influenced by the architecture of Greece, Madain Salih was built by Nabataean Arabs to forestall the Romans' attempt to take over the spice trade, which they controlled until the early second century CE.

and originated the practice of lending money to neighbouring people at an interest rate of twenty or thirty per cent. They constructed libraries for cuneiform documents and great palaces and temples. From the tenth to the seventh centuries BCE they remained powerful,

Nabataean life was strictly controlled by an elaborate priesthood, occasionally depicted in stone relief (below) among other images drawn from daily life (below right). The Nabataeans, of the same stock that built Petra in Jordan and among the ancestors of today's Arabs, were masters at collecting water from precipitation in the most forbidding of arid territories, and preserving it in underground cisterns hewn out of the rock. Pinnacles of hewn rock (opposite) with their hollowed-out interiors (right) provided chambers for burial; temples also served as palaces. Architectural details (above) show the influence of Greece.

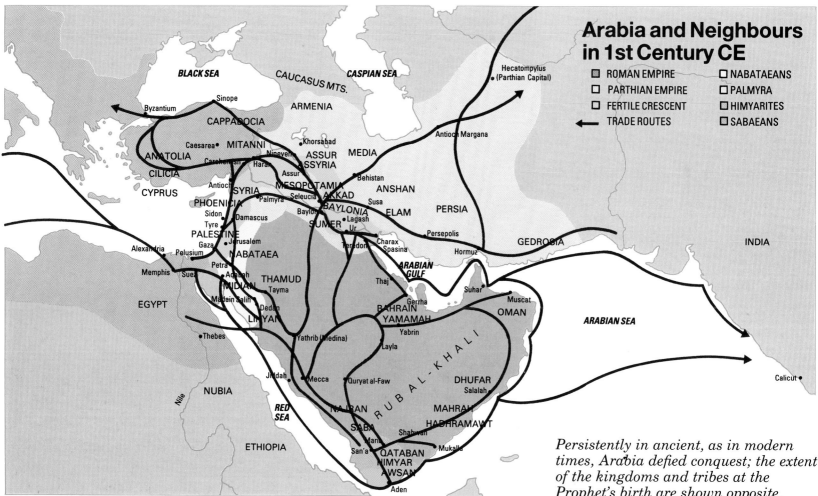

Arabia and Neighbours in 1st Century CE

- ■ ROMAN EMPIRE
- □ PARTHIAN EMPIRE
- □ FERTILE CRESCENT
- ← TRADE ROUTES
- □ NABATAEANS
- □ PALMYRA
- □ HIMYARITES
- □ SABAEANS

Persistently in ancient, as in modern times, Arabia defied conquest; the extent of the kingdoms and tribes at the Prophet's birth are shown opposite.

employing iron weapons to arm their bellicose formations of infantry, cavalry and archers. Eventually in 612 BC the Assyrians were over-thrown by a combination of Medes, Babylonians and Persians, and Nineveh was destroyed.

Babylon continued to be powerful and remained a centre of scholarship. The city was destroyed by the Assyrian conqueror Sennacherib as a punishment for rebellion, but was rebuilt by his heir, Esarhaddon. It later became the capital of an empire known as Babylonia, which was created by the Chaldeans, who included both Aramaeans and Arabians. Nebuchadnezzar was the greatest of its kings; he conquered a reviving Egypt, destroyed Jerusalem in 586 BC and rebuilt Babylon with greater grandeur. The famous Hanging Gardens became one of the seven wonders of the world. Two chariots could race abreast on the city walls. Palaces and temples combined to make Chaldean Babylon one of the most remarkable capitals the world has ever seen. Nebuchadnezzar carried many of the people of Judah into exile in this city. His successor Nabonidus, for religious reasons, abandoned Babylon in c.550 BC and moved his royal residence

to Tayma, in north-west Arabia, where he stayed for some ten years. In 539 BC Babylon fell to Cyrus, the Persian conqueror.

The Persians had a number of great emperors – Cambyses, Darius, Xerxes – and their strategies conquered a vast region extending from Asia Minor and Egypt as far east as India. These conquests and the ensuing advance of the Persian empire were finally arrested at Marathon, in 490 BC, by the Greeks, who after a setback at Thermopylae and the sacking of Athens in 480 BC forced the Persians to return to Asia.

An efficient and stable administration enabled the Persians to perfect a system of fast communication by horse. They spoke an Aryan language and practised a version of Zoroastrianism. Some two centuries later, Alexander the Great finally conquered the Persian or Achaemenid Empire in 334-323 BC. Having conquered the whole of the civilized world from Macedonia to India, he died in Babylon in 323 BC. Greek culture was influential in other Middle Eastern countries through the Seleucids in Syria and the Ptolemies in Egypt, and through the later Byzantine and Roman Empires

until the dawn of Islam.

The Persian Empire was revived by the Parthians between 250 BC and 226 CE, and afterwards by the Sassanids from 226-650 CE. There was at this time a close relationship between the Arabian Gulf and Mesopotamia, and in the latter fertile area was the site of Ctesiphon, the Persian capital when the Sassanids were conquered by Muslim Arab armies in the *jihad* or holy wars of 637-650 CE.

The Hebrews as well seem to have developed first as semi-nomadic tribes, brought together under a common traditional patriarch, a system characteristic of some Beduin tribes today, for whom the desert life has only recently begun to change. The Old Testament was probably finished while the Hebrews were in captivity in Babylonia. They were much influenced by the Canaanites of Palestine, part of whose land they conquered and inhabited. The time of Moses and the Exodus from Egypt is thought to have been early in the thirteenth century BC. The Hebrews were never an important people politically and the great empires of Egypt, Mesopotamia, Greece and Rome ruled them successively, although occasionally the

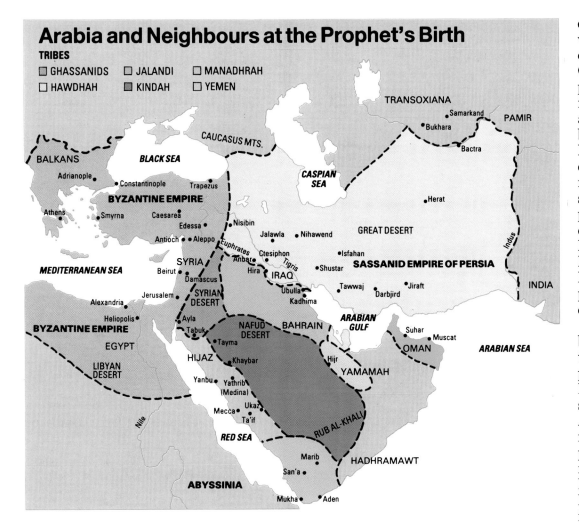

Arabia and Neighbours at the Prophet's Birth

TRIBES

☐ GHASSANIDS ☐ JALANDI ☐ MANADHRAH
☐ HAWDHAH ◼ KINDAH ☐ YEMEN

dynastic era in which the two kingdoms were consolidated and Egyptian power expanded into Syria and Palestine. The Old Kingdom saw the building of the pyramids, followed by further conquests in Nubia during the Middle Kingdom, although there was some disintegration between these periods. Then came the Empire, during which the Hebrew Exodus from Egypt took place. Under Akhnaton father-in-law of Tutankhamun, sun-god monotheism was practised temporarily. Sovereignty over Egypt changed hands from a Libyan to a Nubian Dynasty, but was returned to the Egyptians during the Lower Empire. Rome and Byzantium were the last powers to rule Egypt before the Arab conquests of the seventh century CE.

Although the Arabian Peninsula has been increasingly arid since ancient times, its oases and steppes have been populated for many thousands of years. During the last Ice Age which rendered so much of Europe uninhabitable, the Arabian region seems to have enjoyed a mixture of aridity and more temperate periods, from which evidence remains of numerous watercourses and shallow lakes. Until the fourth-third millennia BC the Peninsula supported a developing Neolithic hunting and gathering society with, in favoured spots, emergent farming communities. With the gradual domestication of the camel in the third and second millennia BC, the people of Arabia were able to evolve the nomadic and settled tribal culture which is first recorded in the Assyrian records of the ninth-seventh centuries BC.

In the meantime the settled civilization of south-west Arabia was emerging. Its cities were to grow into great agricultural and trading centres, exporting indigenous frankincense and myrrh, together with aromatics and other luxury commodities from India and East Africa. As this trade increased, so the Arab tribes and oases in Arabia came to provide the overland link between the Indian Ocean and Mediterranean worlds throughout Classical times. By the sixth century BC several favoured locations in western, central and eastern Arabia were beginning to develop into the great caravan towns only now being uncovered by archaeologists – Tayma, Dumat al-Jandal, al-Ula/Dedan. By the fourth century BC others had come on the scene: Najran, Qaryat al-Faw, Layla/Aflaj, Kharj, Thaj and the legendary Gerrha in the Eastern Province.

Hebrews gained independent control of their so-called "promised land" for brief periods between their arrival there under Joshua, in the thirteenth century BC, and their final futile rebellions which were cruelly put down by their Roman overlords in 66-70 CE and 132-135 CE.

The Phoenicians, the northern Canaanites who originated in what is now the Lebanon and the coast of Syria, became the greatest Semitic seafarers and traders during a period of growth which started in the twelfth century BC. Through their far-flung voyages they disseminated their cultural influence. Their alphabet, and the resulting great improvement in communication, was a major development which took place in the Semitic territory between Sinai and Syria, the homeland of the Phoenicians. This became the basis of the European alphabets and those of India and Mongolia. The Minoans of Crete had led the civilized world in seafaring but were replaced by the more adventurous Phoenicians, who traded in tin from Western Europe, silver from Spain, and Tyrian purple dye from the Mediterranean and tropical seas. Carthage was their great

colonial possession, situated in north Africa, not far from present-day Tunis. Other homeland cities included Tyre, Sidon and Jubayl. Carthage almost defeated Rome in the three Punic (Phoenician) Wars of the third and second centuries BC, but was finally destroyed by the Romans in 146 BC.

Parallel with the existence of the Hebrew Kingdom was that of Syria, whose capital was Damascus. The Syrians, known earlier as Aramaeans, fluctuated between alliance and war with the Hebrew people. Their close links with the Phoenicians included a similar alphabet and language, Aramaic, which survived as the language of the people of Palestine until it was replaced by Arabic after the Dawn of Islam. They were equally successful in spreading their commerce abroad.

Of all the very early civilizations the one which left the most splendid cultural legacy was Egypt. The predynastic period had its beginnings in the days of the rise of Mesopotamia, when its provinces, known as *nomes*, were united into northern and southern kingdoms. During this time the 365 day calendar was devised. This was followed by the

Acceptance of the Prophet's message transformed the Eastern world from the Atlantic shores to the Indus and, later, beyond. The threads of earlier cultures were drawn together and under the inspiration of Islam a new and confident civilisation flowered.

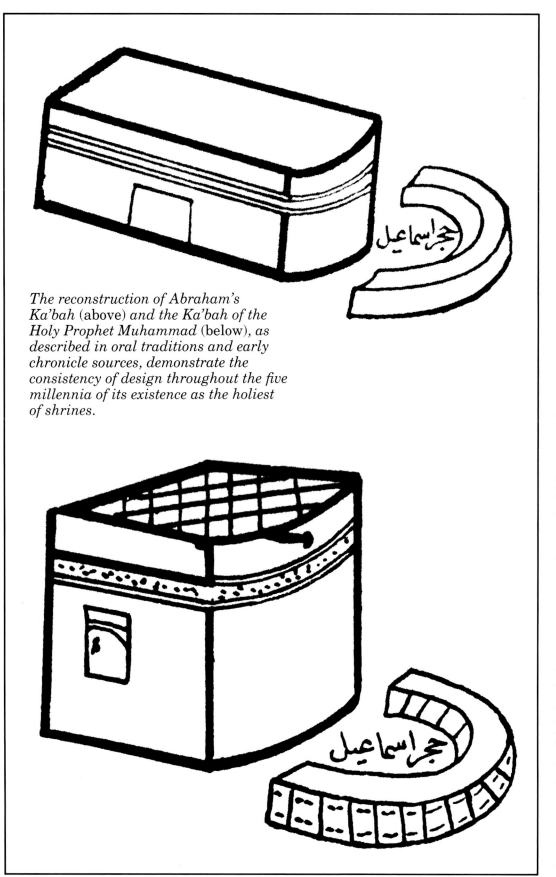

The reconstruction of Abraham's Ka'bah (above) and the Ka'bah of the Holy Prophet Muhammad (below), as described in oral traditions and early chronicle sources, demonstrate the consistency of design throughout the five millennia of its existence as the holiest of shrines.

By 300 BC this overland trading network had become prosperous. The cities of the Yemen exported its frankincense and myrrh, silks, spices and jewelry, ivory and precious metals, across Arabia into the Fertile Crescent, Egypt and the eastern Mediterranean in unprecedented quantities. A quantity of copper and gold seems to have been mined in Arabia itself. The Peninsula was criss-crossed by caravan routes – some of them still in use by pilgrims to Makkah and al-Madinah, although the camel is no longer used for transport. Agriculture was difficult, but a sophisticated system of irrigation included the building of dams to retain flood water for the dry season. One such dam was at Marib, built of limestone and so well designed that it stood intact almost up to the birth of Muhammad.

The kingdoms of south-west Arabia were subject to frequent change and internecine warfare. Ma'in and Saba, the probable domain of the Queen of Sheba, were two of the earliest which rose to power. Others included Awsan, covering approximately the area now known as Aden, Qataban to its north-east and Hadhramawt to the east of Qataban. The powerful tribe of Himyar in the south-west gave its name to contemporary civilisation there. In south-east Arabia, Oman had been a centre of trade and ship-building for centuries, and Dhofar the source of frankincense.

By the second century BC the north-western portion of the country had fallen under Nabataean control. The Nabataean capital was at Petra, but their southernmost stronghold at Madain Salih, in north-western Saudi Arabia, was of great importance in controlling the trade routes. The influence at Madain Salih evident in the fine facades of the tombs, with their pilasters and pediments, is wholly Hellenistic. The Nabataeans, too, controlled the trade route to the Greek and, later, Roman worlds from the northern Gulf through al-Jawf. Their remarkable technology involved the construction of dams, rock cisterns and irrigation systems, some of which are usable today. With the rise of Rome, the peninsula's commercial wealth came under military threat, but an invasion launched by Aelius Gallus in 24 BC ended in failure. Having overcome one hurdle, however, south-western spice trade routes based on such cities as Dedan, Yathrib (modern al-Madinah) and Najran, fell at another: trade began to decline when the Greeks and Romans discovered how to sail to India on the monsoon winds. Their trade thus in decline, once-prosperous towns along the trade routes that withered include that of Qaryat al-Faw, recently excavated by the University of Riyadh, on the way from the south-west to the east.

In the fourth and sixth centuries, south-western Arabia fell under Abyssinian rule, and it was in about the year 571, when Makkah successfully rebuffed an attack by the Abyssinian Abraha, that the Prophet Muhammad was born in the Holy City.

The birth of Muhammad was a momentous event in history. The followers of Islam today number some nine hundred million. Muhammad was the son of Abdullah and Aminah, of the tribe of Quraysh; he became an orphan when still young and spent part of his boyhood among the Beduins of the desert. At twenty-five years of age he married Khadijah, also of the Quraysh tribe, and entered a life of meditation. Soon after, in 610, he experienced his first revelation and began his role as a prophet spreading the message of the one, all-powerful God and the day of judgement to come.

The early converts were few and slow to follow his teachings, but the turning point came in 622 when two hundred followers eluded the vigilance of the Quraysh and slipped into Yathrib, to be known as al-Madinah. Seventeen years later the *hijrah* migration was described by the Caliph as an essential part of the Muslim experience. The Prophet assumed the role of warrior, judge and civil administrator, winning several victories against the Qurayshis and their supporters, among them the Madinese Jews. From being a religion within a state Islam became the State itself.

Although an unschooled man, Muhammad was the vehicle through which God chose to reveal the Holy Qur'an, regarded by Muslims as their spiritual and moral guide. Within his life-span Muhammad established a religion that replaced Christianity in most of Asia and Africa, and laid the foundations of an Empire that was soon to embrace a large part of the then civilized world.

Early Islamic cartography

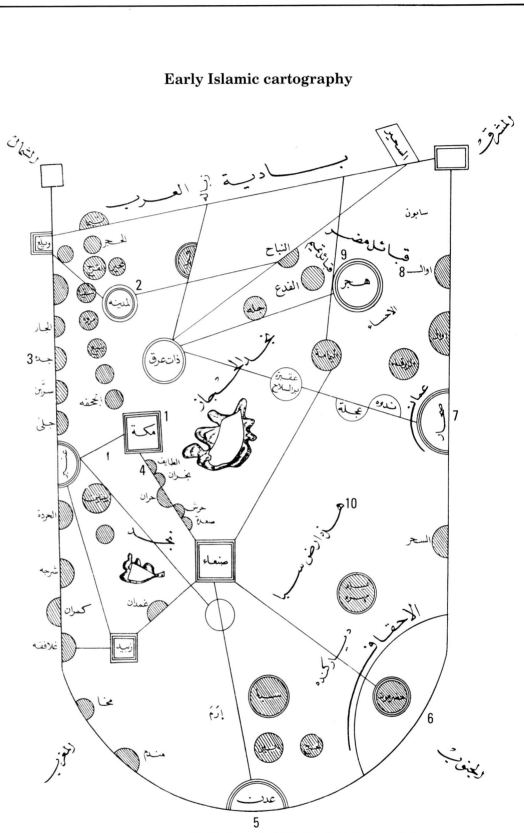

The emphasis upon Makkah and al-Madinah (1 & 2) and the relative unimportance ascribed to the port of Jiddah (3) by the 6th century AH map above, shows the significance of the Holy Cities and Arabia to the cartographers of the Arab world during the mediaeval period. The Hijaz is shown as thickly settled, especially around Taif (4), while the coastal regions of Aden, the Hadhramawt and Oman are clearly marked as important (5, 6 & 7). The inland areas of Hasa and Hajar (8 & 9) share equal note with the famous land of Sheba (10). The map was probably commissioned and made in the mercantile city of Baghdad.

The Rise of Saudi Arabia to the Mid-20th Century

THE modern state of Saudi Arabia began to develop in the Najd region of central Arabia some two hundred and fifty years ago. From the start of the Islamic era to the middle of the eighteenth century CE Arabian history is made up of the separate stories of a number of individual regions. Despite contacts between these regions and the unifying force of Islamic civilization, the political and religious development of Arabia was by no means uniform. More information is available about the important coastal areas – the Hijaz, Yemen and south Arabia, Oman and Hasa on the Gulf – than about central Arabia, the heartland of the future Saudi state.

Until the European expansion into the Indian Ocean after the fifteenth century, the Hijaz – the region containing the two main sanctuaries of Islam, those of Makkah and al-Madinah – was the area of significance to the outside world. For reasons of prestige, as well as for the financial benefit which accrued from control of the annual pilgrimage, powerful Muslim rulers frequently sought to establish their ascendancy over it. In the tenth century CE a descendant of the Prophet declared himself Sharif of Makkah, and the Sharifate thus founded survived, sometimes independently, sometimes under outside control, until Ibn Saud conquered the Hijaz in 1925. Most frequently it was the ruler of Egypt who controlled the Sharifate, and after 1517, when Egypt became part of the Ottoman Empire, the governor of Egypt was recognized as having authority over the Hijaz on behalf of the Ottoman sultan.

Yemen too, because of its position at the mouth of the Red Sea, was of interest to the rulers of Egypt, who on occasions exercised political control over the area. From the early ninth century CE a number of independent dynasties established themselves in the Yemen, and at the end of the century two competing schools of thought in Shi-ite Islam, Isma'ilism and Zaydism, won support among some sections of the population. The Makramid dynasty of Najran, which arose in the eighteenth century and with whom the Saudi rulers came into conflict, espoused a form of Isma'ilism, but ultimately it was Zaydism which prevailed in most of Yemen. In 1636 CE, following an Ottoman withdrawal, the Zaydi Imam occupied San'a and united the greater part of Yemen under his authority. Despite the breakaway of the southern part of his territories, including the port of Aden, at the beginning of the eighteenth century CE, the Zaydi Imamate in the Yemen survived into the twentieth century.

Oman has a similar history, being ruled for much of the period by a non-Sunni Imam, and subject to tension between the tribes of the interior and the towns of the coastal region. The Imams followed the Ibadhi form of Islam. They established their power in the ninth

Venerated Places

Almost equal in sanctity to the two Saudi Arabian cities of "Makkah the Blessed" and "Madinah the Radiant" is Jerusalem, and its Qubbat al-Sakhra, the Mosque of Omar *pictured here*, and al-Aqsa Mosque. Sites in Damascus and in Baghdad, both seats of the Caliphate, are also revered. It was in Damascus and Jerusalem that the Umayyads built their mosques. Apart from its very ancient Arab association, Damascus was associated with the relic of John the Baptist. Jerusalem is associated with Solomon, Jesus and Muhammad's Night Journey to Heaven.

century and, ruling from the interior, managed to maintain it with interruptions down to the sixteenth century. In 1507 CE the Portuguese captured Muscat, the main port, but in the middle of the next century the Omanis recovered it. In the succeeding period the division between the coastal region, centred on Muscat, and inner Oman intensified. The Saudis were sometimes able to establish their authority in inner Oman by way of Buraymi.

The region of Hasa on the Gulf came at times under the authority of powerful rulers in Iraq, and at other times had independent rulers. From the late ninth to the late eleventh century Hasa was the centre of the heterodox Qarmatian state which, at its height, became involved in Iraq and Syria and for a while even removed the Black Stone from the Ka'bah in Makkah. In c.1550 CE the Ottomans brought Hasa under their control but, in 1669, a local clan, the Banu Khalid, drove them out, and between 1694 and 1709 actually extended their influence into Najd, bringing Uyaynah, Diriyyah and the House of Saud under their sway. By the end of the century, however, the tables had been turned, with Hasa becoming part of the First Saudi State.

Information about the pre-Saudi history of Najd and inner Arabia is fragmentary. For the outside world Najd was important because of the pilgrim route which crossed it from the Gulf to the Hijaz, but the area remained largely independent. The population was mainly nomadic, but here and there conditions did allow the growth of sizeable settlements. One such area was that of Wadi Hanifah, including Diriyyah and Riyadh, where, by the fifteenth century CE, a number of independent emirates or principalities had established themselves. Here the Saudi state had its origins.

The Saudi family traces its descent from Mani ibn Rabia al-Muraydi, who came in 1446 CE from Hasa to settle in Wadi Hanifah. By the beginning of the seventeenth century his descendants had established themselves as rulers of a small emirate centred on Diriyyah to the north of Riyadh. Shortly before 1720, Saud ibn Muhammad, the eponymous founder of the family, became ruler. He was succeeded, on his death in 1725, by his son Muhammad. It was under Muhammad that the Wahhabi form of Islam was espoused, and the expansion of the emirate began.

Wahhabism takes its name from Muhammad ibn Abd al-Wahhab, who was born in 1703 CE into a family of religious scholars at Uyaynah, the centre of another emirate in Wadi Hanifah, to the north of Diriyyah. He was brought up to follow the Hanbali Law School, the most rigorous of the four law schools of Sunni Islam, and from an early age was noted for his strictness. In the course of his education he became influenced by the ideas of Ibn Taymiyya, a theologian and jurist who died in 1328 CE and who had argued for a purification of Islam from what he considered to be accretions to the primitive faith. His ideas had some influence, especially among followers of the Hanbali Law School, and Ibn Abd al-Wahhab came to believe that the essential monotheism of Islam had been compromised by excessive veneration of the Prophet Muhammad and other "saints". This veneration was most commonly expressed in pilgrimages and visits to minor sanctuaries and to the tombs of holy men; so Ibn Abd al-Wahhab preached against these. He also insisted on the stricter implementation of penalties – such as death for adultery – fixed in the Qur'an, and he forbade certain innovations, notably the smoking of tobacco.

In 1745, after setbacks elsewhere, Ibn Abd al-Wahhab settled in Diriyyah, where he was favourably received by Muhammad ibn Saud. This event marks the beginning of a seventy-year period of expansion for the Diriyyah emirate, the first of three distinct phases in the history of the Saudi state. Modern Saudi Arabia is the product of the third of these phases. Wahhabism seems to have provided the Saudi power with an ideological basis for expansion which the competing emirates lacked. It appealed equally to the tribes and to the settled population – the latter provided the main support for the dynasty in the first two phases, and the tribes were crucial in the third.

By the end of the eighteenth century CE the emirate of Diriyyah had extended its authority over Najd, finally gaining control of Riyadh in 1773. This extension of politiclal power was accompanied by the spread of Wahhabism and the implementation of its teachings. Tombs of holy men raised above the ground more than about thirty centimetres and other minor sanctuaries were destroyed. By 1792 when Ibn Abd al-Wahhab died, his ideas had already proved more directly

influential than those of Ibn Taymiyya ever were.

The rapid expansion of the Saudi emirate inevitably provoked fear and hostility in neighbouring non-Wahhabi states. The Sharif of Makkah undertook a series of expeditions against the Saudi state which now bordered his in the Hijaz, but these expeditions were unsuccessful, and in 1803 CE, shortly before the death of Abdul Aziz, who had succeeded his father Muhammad in 1765, a Wahhabi army brought Makkah under Saudi control. Two years later al-Madinah was taken. In the north the Ottoman governors of Iraq supported the anti-Wahhabi tribes on the border between Iraq and Arabia, but they too were unable to hold back the Wahhabi forces. In 1802 Wahhabi raids into Iraq reached a climax when the tomb at Karbala of Husayn ibn Ali, the Prophet's grandson, whom most Muslims regard as a martyr, was sacked, together with its neighbouring town. However, the Wahhabis were not strong enough to take and hold the towns of Iraq.

The sack of Karbala provoked the hostility of most Muslims, Sunni and Shiite, and the occupation of the Hijaz brought the Saudi state into direct conflict with the Ottoman sultan, who regarded himself as the guardian of the Holy Places for the whole Muslim world. At first the sultan was unable to act, but in 1811 CE the Albanian, Muhammad Ali, having secured control of Egypt, organized, at the sultan's command, an expedition against the Wahhabis. In 1812 forces from Egypt, led by Muhammad Ali's son Tusun, took al-Madinah and in the following year Makkah. Abdul Aziz had been assassinated in 1803, probably by a Shi-ite Muslim seeking vengeance for the sack of Karbala, and was succeeded by his son Saud. Saud himself died in 1814, and his successor, his son Abdullah, had to conclude a truce with Tusun, ceding control of the Holy Cities to Muhammad Ali. In 1816, however, fighting began again, an army from Egypt invaded Najd, and in 1818 CE Diriyyah was taken. Abdullah was sent in captivity to Istanbul, where he was executed. This was the end of the First Saudi State.

In 1824 CE Turki, the son of Abdullah ibn Muhammad, seized Riyadh from Muhammad Ali's forces. From then until the last two decades of the nineteenth century, when the Saudi state was taken over by the Rashidi rulers of Hail in

Jabal Shammar, Riyadh was the capital of the Second Saudi State. From there Turki extended his authority over the whole of Najd, inner Oman, and Hasa, which had been occupied for a time by Muhammad Ali's forces. Abd al-Rahman ibn Hasan, a grandson of Ibn Abd al-Wahhab, was appointed by Turki to be *qadi* of Riyadh, and he, together with his

agent in Riyadh. Faisal himself was taken prisoner to Cairo, but escaped and re-established his rule with the help of Abdullah ibn Rashid.

Faisal's death in 1865 CE was followed by a struggle for power between two of his sons, Abdullah and Saud; a conflict which enabled the Ottomans to win back Hasa and the ruler of Hail, Muhammad

the Saudi state, lasting from the beginning of the twentieth century CE until the present day. In 1902 he was able to take advantage of the weakness of Rashidi power, following the death of Muhammad ibn Rashid in 1897, by recapturing Riyadh with the help of what was really no more than a raiding party from Kuwait. The following ten years were

---

Western Travellers in Arabia

The dangers of desert travel and Arab caution towards foreign intruders deterred Westerners until quite recently. In 1761 Carsten Niebuhr, a German in the service of Denmark, travelled in portions of Western Arabia. So, too, did the Swiss J. L. Burkhardt in 1814. The British explorer Richard Burton, setting out in 1853, like Burkhardt followed the *hajj* route. Starting in Alexandria, he landed at Yanbu. Later he travelled in Midian. At much the same time another Englishman, Charles Doughty, was travelling in north-western and west central Arabia (1875-78). First to enter the "cradle of the Arab race", as Lady Anne Blunt called the Najd, was the Finnish professor Wallin, reaching Hail in 1848. The Levantine Italian Guarmani started from Jerusalem in 1863, with a commission to buy horses, and reached Tayma, Buraydah, Hail and Jawf. The Jesuit missionary Palgrave travelled to Hail and Riyadh in 1862. The Blunts reached Hail in 1879. Of all the subsequent outstanding travellers in Arabia – Alois Musil, T. E. Lawrence, Gerard Leachman, William Shakespear, Bertram Thomas, Wilfred Thesiger among others – none covered half as much territory as St. John Philby.

Richard Burton's (1821-90) famous journey on the pilgrim route took place in 1853.

Charles Doughty (1843-1926) wrote his Travels in Arabia Deserta *after travels in the Hijaz and Najd.*

Bertram Thomas (1892-1950) crossed the Rub al-Khali in 1931, from Salala to Qatar.

Gertrude Bell (1868-1926), a fine Arabist and tribal expert, reached Hail in 1914.

St. John Philby (1885-1960) explored and mapped more widely than any other.

Setting off in 1917, he crossed Arabia from Uqayr in the east to Jiddah, travelling the following year through the Aflaj to Sulayyil. From then on he travelled extensively, journeying through the Rub al-Khali in 1932 and south from

the Tihama to Mukalla in Hadhramawt in 1936. His last journeys in the early 1950s took him north through Wajh and Tabuk.

Wilfred Thesiger (b.1910) made several journeys in the Rub al-Khali in the 1950s.

---

son, Abd al-Latif, was largely responsible for the continued development of Wahhabism in the nineteenth century.

In 1834 CE Turki was assassinated in a dispute between members of the Saudi family, but his son Faisal managed to wrest power from the rebels who had seized Riyadh. In the following year Faisal appointed Abdullah ibn Ali ibn Rashid to be his governor in Hail. Ibn Rashid's descendants were eventually to extend their power and establish their own rule over the Saudi state. Between 1838 and 1843 CE Faisal's rule in Riyadh was interrupted when Muhammad Ali again sent a force to invade Najd and set up another member of the Saudi family as ruler under the supervision of his

ibn Rashid, to extend his power over the Saudi state, while ostensibly seeking to uphold the rights of Abdullah. By the time of Abdullah's death in 1889 CE, the Saudi state was no more than a province of the territory ruled by the Rashidis from Hail. Two years later Abdullah's brother and successor, Abd al-Rahman, was expelled from Riyadh by Muhammad ibn Rashid who appointed a puppet governor there. Abd al-Rahman and his family, including his young son Abdul Aziz, who had been born about 1880, fled to Kuwait, which was at this time an independent sheikhdom.

It was Abdul Aziz ibn Abd al-Rahman, usually called simply Ibn Saud, who initiated the third phase in the history of

spent in ousting the Rashids from Qasim and in inconclusive fighting against the tribes. It was not until 1912 CE that Ibn Saud took a step which was to prove decisive – the inauguration of the *Ikhwan* movement. During his exile in Kuwait and the fighting with the Rashidis, Ibn Saud had come to see the military potential of the nomadic tribes if their customary resistance to state control could be overcome. Realizing that he must settle the tribesmen and give them a motive for uniting, he organized them into a religious brotherhood (*Ikhwan* means "brethren"), the aim of which was the militant expansion of Wahhabism. The members of the movement were to settle in military encampments called *hijrahs*,

The House of Saud

1 From whom the Jiluwi branch of the House of Saud derive their name

2 From whom the Abdullah al-Turki branch of the House of Saud derive their name

3 Known as "al Kabir", a name retained by his descendants

FAHD The Seven Sons of King Abdul Aziz by the late Hassa bint Sudairi, who are known as the Al Fahd

Note: This Family Tree, though the result of meticulous research, does not attempt to be comprehensive.

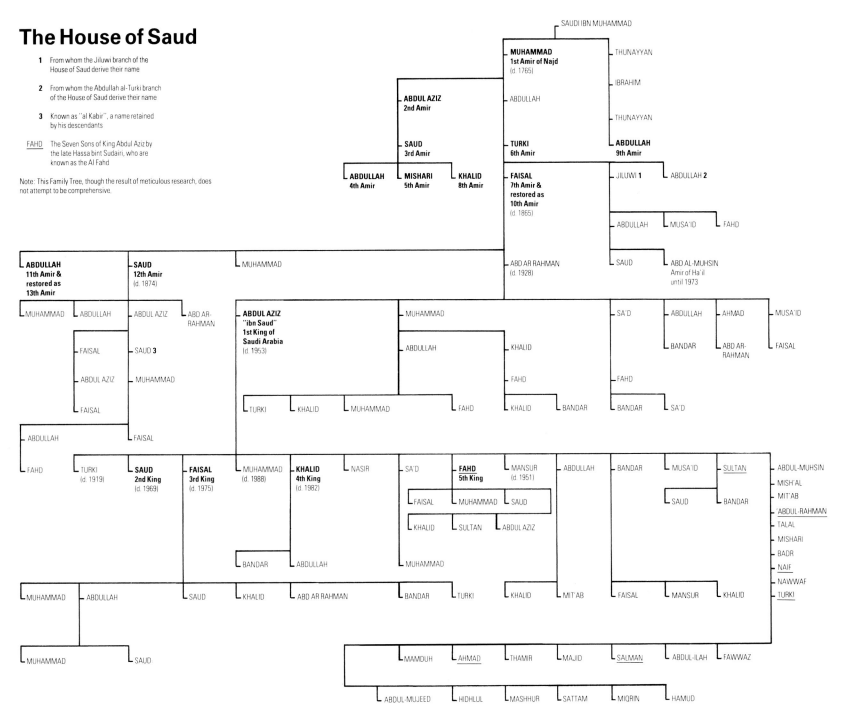

just as at the time of the Arab conquests the tribesmen had abandoned their nomadic way of life in Arabia for the garrison towns of the conquered territories. The first *hijrah* was founded at Arta-wiyyah in 1912. Nobody knows the exact number of *hijrahs* which were established, but it was some two hundred or more. The warriors in each of them varied between ten and ten thousand.

With the help of the *Ikhwan*, Ibn Saud took Hail in 1921 CE and the whole of the Hijaz including Makkah, in 1924-26. Any further expansion in Arabia or its border areas would entail a clash with Great Britain, which was involved as protector or mandatory power in all of the territories now bordering the north-

ern Saudi state. Indeed clashes had already occurred. To the *Ikhwan*, such political considerations appeared a betrayal of the doctrine of holy war against all infidels (i.e. non-Wahhabis) with which they had been inculcated. Relations between Ibn Saud and the *Ikhwan* deteriorated rapidly in the late 1920s as the *Ikhwan* began to act more independently. In 1929 they massacred a party of Najdi Wahhabi merchants, and the revulsion which this act aroused among the settled population of the Najd, as well as among several of the tribes, strengthened Ibn Saud's hand sufficiently for him to take action against the *Ikhwan*. At the battle of Sabalah in March 1929 Ibn Saud put the *Ikhwan* to

flight, and their power collapsed. Early in 1930 a number of their leaders surrendered to the British authorities in Kuwait, whence they were extradited by Ibn Saud. He spared their lives but imprisoned them in Riyadh. This marked the end of the power of the *Ikhwan* as a force independent of Ibn Saud. Some of their *hijrahs* continued to exist, but were now under government control. Eventually the *Ikhwan* were incorporated in the National Guard.

After 1930 Ibn Saud began the transformation of the state which is still continuing. The battle of Sabalah marked the end of the era in which the history of Saudi Arabia can be discussed only in traditional terms.

From Abdul Aziz to the Present Day

Saudi Arabia's stability owes much to the fact that a single dynasty has governed since Abdul Aziz ibn Saud formally established the Kingdom in 1932. King Fahd succeeded his brothers, Khalid, Faisal and Saud in 1982 to become the fifth king. Born in 1921, he too is the son of the kingdom's founder, Abdul Aziz.

TODAY'S Saudi Arabia under King Fahd – energetic, swiftly developing, yet profoundly respectful of tradition – is the direct heir of the Saudi Arabia created by Abdul Aziz ibn Saud. King Fahd is the fifth king in the present dynasty of Saudi rulers, succeeding his brothers Khalid, Faisal and Saud. It is easy to overlook the fact that he is only one generation away from the founder of this stable, forward looking state.

King Fahd's father, Abdul Aziz ibn Saud, is remembered by all who knew him for characteristics which distinguished him among the Arabs of his generation. Physically, he was outstandingly tall; self-disciplined to be hardy, he relished battle and was indifferent to injury. Spiritually, his faith dominated his life; he was deeply devout, and steadfast in upholding the puritanism preached to his forbears by the eighteenth century Islamic reformer, Ibn Abdul al-Wahhab. Mentally, he was a master of politics; his appraisal of men and their capacities was shrewd, and his grasp of world affairs astounding in one who during his long life paid only three brief visits outside his native Arabia, and never left the Arab world. Lastly, his basic instincts – integrity, a sense of honour, of justice, of humour – added up to a nature that brought him success despite early vicissitudes in his chequered life.

He was born in or about 1880 CE into a family – the Saudis of southern Najd – that had formerly been great but was then in decline, shortly to go into exile after defeat by its northern rival, the Rashids of Hail. He spent his childhood in Kuwait, dreaming of restoring his family's fortunes. At twenty-one, he took advantage of some leisurely skirmishing between Kuwaitis and Rashidis to slip inland with forty picked companions and, in a night of surprises and sharp sword thrusts, to recapture his home town, Riyadh. This exploit brought him his first acclaim, and to this day Riyadh, in all its other buildings fashionably modern, preserves at its heart the old mud fort that is his people's memento of his daring. In 1902 his father, glad to reward determination allied to piety, named him Emir of Najd and Imam of its puritanical brand of Islam.

Thereafter, he simultaneously spread religious reform and Saudi power, sometimes in battle, sometimes in the name of Wahhabism (a movement which appealed for a return to the true teaching of Islam), sometimes through persuasiveness or through respect for his military success. By 1926 he had captured the Holy Cities of Makkah and al-Madinah and the whole Red Sea coastal province of the Hijaz. He declared himself King of Hijaz and Najd, and in 1932 renamed his kingdom Saudi Arabia.

As always happens, conquest brought complications. He owed to his belligerent *Ikhwan* the conquests that enabled him to dominate Arabia, yet was obliged to suppress them, because he could not condone their wish to carry Holy War abroad. Again, although Wahhabism had become a matter of course in the austere climate of Najd, it was less acceptable in the more sophisticated and easy-going Hijaz. In overseas Islam, too, the thought of Wahhabi fanatics in charge of Makkah and al-Madinah caused deep disquiet. These misgivings he was within two or three years able to dispel, partly by ensuring the safety of the pilgrimage, partly by his handling of the *Ikhwan*, partly by the tact and moderation that he showed to anxious visitors. Equally tactfully, he slowly introduced his own people to innovations that they saw as heresies, but which he knew must come if his country was to grow great – concessions sold to infidels, the telephone, pilgrimage by motor transport,

The great Abdul Aziz ibn Saud (right) *was swift to perceive the potential of his country's oil wealth and to encourage prospecting by foreigners like the early American oilman* (above), *robed for the desert.*

wireless telegraphy. But it was in his dealings with great powers that he best showed the acumen, and the awareness of Arab limitations, which made him an outstanding diplomat. For instance, though he hated the two Hashemite brothers whom the British had installed as rulers in neighbouring Iraq and Transjordan, he punished tribal or religious forays into their territory. Again in 1934 when armies led by his sons were

on the verge of conquering Yemen, to their chagrin he ordered them to withdraw, because he realized that their approach to the confines of Aden and the coast of Eritrea was antagonizing both Britain and Italy. He was always circumspect with the British, surrounded as he was by their sea power, their mandates and their dependencies. Yet he was friendly; even during the darkest days of the Second World War, he warned them of local pitfalls and backed them to win in the end. Only on the subject of Palestine did he censure them, then and later. As he listened, conscious of Arab impotence, to broadcasts about the British handling of Palestine's dismemberment, tears, it is said, poured down his cheeks.

At home, the greatest boon that he gave his people was internal security. Until his reign, all towns were walled, all gates barred at nightfall, all desert journeys undertaken at risk from raiders or feuding tribes. At the sight of strangers, friend could be told from foe only by some conventional gesture such as waving a headcloth or throwing up sand; if no such sign were given, the safest course was to gallop out of sight. Ibn Saud put an end to these hazards. His ways of doing so were to appoint trusted Najdis as regional governors, usually members of his vast family or of related stock – the Sudayris, Jiluwis or Thunayyans; these outposts he furnished with the mobile wireless trucks that enabled him to keep a watch – miraculous to the tribes – on desert behaviour; he also travelled widely and frequently among them, often cementing loyalties as he went by arranging a marriage between some sheikhly family and his own. By the time of his death, town walls were a thing of the past; he had induced the *Ikhwan* survivors to settle in agricultural colonies, and a traveller could stop and pray at the lawful hour or camp at nightfall without fear of molestation, as he can today.

When Ibn Saud won his kingdom, it was pitifully poor. It produced only the bare necessities of life; its so-called roads were tracks; it had no ports; its sole source of foreign exchange was pilgrimage dues. Religious learning apart, education was scanty; he had to resort to foreign Arabs as his advisers. All but one

A memorial of Abdul Aziz's capture of Riyadh's Masmak Fortress remains in the spear-tip lodged in the woodwork of the door (right).

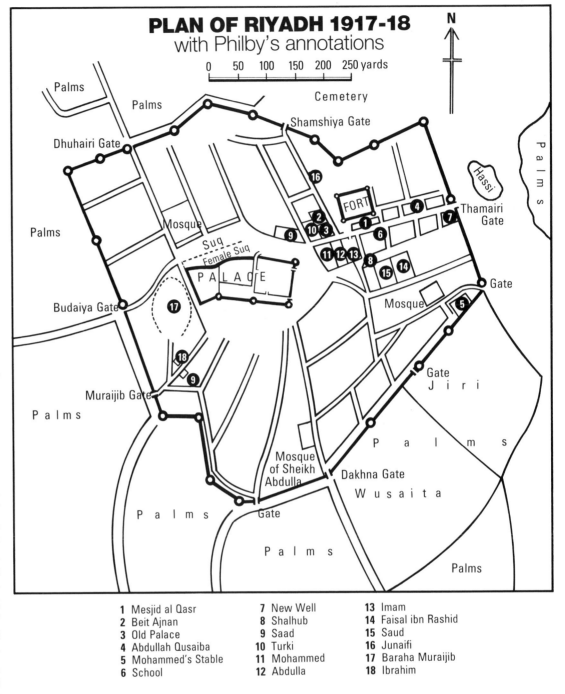

PLAN OF RIYADH 1917-18
with Philby's annotations

N

0 50 100 150 200 250 yards

Palms
Palms
Cemetery
Shamshiya Gate
Dhuhairi Gate
Palms
Hassi
Palms
Thamairi Gate
FORT
Mosque
Palms
Suq
Female Suq
PALACE
Budaiya Gate
Gate
Mosque
Muraijib Gate
Gate
Jiri
Palms
Palms
Palms
Mosque of Sheikh Abdulla
Dakhna Gate
Wusaita
Palms
Gate
Palms
Palms

1 Mesjid al Qasr	**7** New Well	**13** Imam
2 Beit Ajnan	**8** Shalhub	**14** Faisal ibn Rashid
3 Old Palace	**9** Saad	**15** Saud
4 Abdullah Qusaiba	**10** Turki	**16** Junaifi
5 Mohammed's Stable	**11** Mohammed	**17** Baraha Muraijib
6 School	**12** Abdulla	**18** Ibrahim

of his immediate entourage were literally advisers, for though he listened to information, he took all decisions, however trivial, himself. The exception was the one Najdi among them – his Minister of Finance, Abdullah Sulayman. Ibn Saud, though the equal of anyone in political skill, negotiation or paternalistic power of decision, hated administration and was not good at it. As the business of his kingdom swelled and paperwork piled up, he was fortunate in having at his elbow for over twenty years one Najdi possessed of executive ability. When the outbreak of the world economic crisis of the early 1930s seriously reduced the numbers making the pilgrimage, the repercussions magnified beyond management his kingdom's endemic poverty. At this moment of crisis, a stroke of fortune relieved his plight.

In 1932, oil was discovered in Bahrain, an island visible from the Saudi mainland. Mining geologists suspected that oil deposits might underlie the mainland also. An American oil company, offering to pay gold for prospection rights, enabled the desperate King and Finance Minister to round a tight corner. So began the exploration and discovery that, once the Second World War was over, turned Saudi Arabia's oil production into the most promising and wealthiest venture in an oil-rich peninsula.

Ibn Saud was abstemious throughout his life. His tastes were simple. Prayer and reading the scriptures took up many hours of each day; late in life he composed his own anthology of religious wisdom, sayings and proverbs. He rejoiced in family life; children and grandchildren were his delight; a cluster of them surrounds him in every informal photograph. Since at his death he left behind him forty-seven living sons (the youngest under seven) and unnumbered daughters, children were always in plentiful supply. He could be irascible, but not for long. Among his greatest pleasures were desert life and pursuits, camping for part of every year, hunting, hawking, tests of horsemanship, camel racing. Whether in tent or palace, his mornings were spent giving audience in a majlis open to all his subjects, hearing grievances, righting wrongs, dispensing reward and punishment. Duty done, he

The fort wall in Hofuf (right); it was walls such as these that Abdul Aziz and his Saudis scaled in 1913 to found their Kingdom.

liked to spend his afternoons in the peace of the desert, on some restive horse when in his prime, travelling by car in old age. A tremendous talker, his evenings were spent in discourse; topics on which he liked to dwell were theological niceties, such as the distinction between pure and impure belief; desert genealogies, which he had at his fingertips, and the details of old campaigns. He was a devout man who consistently relished the gift of life.

Legend and anecdote sometimes tell more of a man's character than a recital of fact. It is said that when he captured Hail in 1921, a traitorous defender let him into the town by one of its five gates; he honoured the captains of the other four and punished the traitor. He handed out judgement with assurance and well-remembered imagination – summary execution for a villain, coupled with compassion for the victims of his crime, the shaving off of the beard and moustache of a young man who had simply been pert. Until crippled by arthritis, he liked to join in fun or horseplay; part of his personal success with his subjects was the spontaneity with which he rubbed shoulders with a crowd or joined in a war-dance. He loved an apt quip. Once, chatting tête-à-tête with a British envoy, he

health had deteriorated. An old eye trouble worsened; old wounds generated arthritis; unwillingly, he took to a wheel chair; inch by inch he lost his grip as he fought a long last illness. He grew un-equal to controlling leaks of revenue. He had named his son Saud as Crown Prince. When the old king died in 1953, Saud became king. It was a difficult period for the Middle East. It was charac-terised by a fashionable republicanism and wild radio propaganda from abroad. Nasser was the new hero of the market place. The sudden influx of wealth in Saudi Arabia found the country without an infrastructure to cope with its oppor-tunities. Many a ruler might have fal-tered in such circumstances. King Saud built hospitals, opened schools, initiated the education of girls. A programme of road building was begun.

Yet it was not until a decade later that the Prince fit to meet the situation suc-ceeded, as King Faisal, to the throne.

Statesmen blessed with Ibn Saud's moral stature, high principles and com-mon sense are rarities; by any standards, he must be reckoned among the greatest in the first half of our century.

"From log cabin to White House" was a phrase once coined by an American

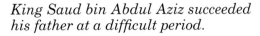

King Saud bin Abdul Aziz succeeded his father at a difficult period.

mentioned the contrariness of his English friend, St. John Philby. The en-voy countered with the story of the British mum watching the Guards march by: "Everyone's out of step but my Johnnie." The king laughed till his sides ached. Philby, often described as his "British adviser", was never this, but rather his walking encyclopaedia and verbal sparring-partner.

By 1950, in which year Petromin and Aramco recorded that oil production topped twenty-five million tons, his

Up to the First World War, Turkey claimed a sovereignty over Arabia that was never more than nominal, and not even that so far as King Abdul Aziz was concerned. The war affected Arabia principally in the Hashemite area of the Hijaz, where T.E. Lawrence came to fame – not least in his role in the destruction of the Turkish-controlled Hijaz railway, of which some relics (left) survive in the desert to this day. Hashemite rule did not long survive the Great War. By December 1925 al-Madinah and Jiddah were Abdul Aziz's, and in January 1926 the principal citizens of Makkah offered their allegiance to Abdul Aziz.

84

author to epitomize the life of Abraham Lincoln. From desert obscurity to world status is no less a shift of fortune, and perhaps the more remarkable of the two in that it sums up the career not of one man – the late King Faisal of Saudi Arabia – but of a whole nation.

Changes of this magnitude within the span of a lifetime are seldom wholly due to the worth or character of a single individual. Outside agents such as a freak of timing, or the unwisdom of others – or a simple stroke of luck – often play their part. Yet King Faisal ibn Abdul Aziz ibn Saud made a great personal contribution to his own rise to fame and power. When historians come to assess him, they will refer first to the spiritual reserves underlying the inner calm which enabled him to bide his time when things were not going his way, and secondly to the cautious reasoning and balanced judgement that made him a first-class negotiator. Add to these assets a presence marked by a fine bearing, inborn dignity and grace of manner, and you have the outlines of a portrait that is filled in by the story of his life.

He was the fourth son of a father who had won back from a rival – the Emir of Hail – the family patrimony of Najd in central Arabia, after years of exile in Kuwait. At Faisal's birth, Riyadh, the capital which Ibn Saud had recovered less than four years before, was hemmed in by the enemies of its puritanism and its claim to spiritual superiority. The Rashids of Hail lay to its north, the Turks in the coastal province of Hasa to its east, and their myrmidon the Sharif of Makkah on the Red Sea coast to its west. Riyadh was in those days a dour place, dependent for life on dates and herding; its gates clanged shut at dusk and at the hours of prayer; at night, no glimmer of light revealed its existence except when, in Ramadan, a huge arc lamp was hoisted above the palace flagpole to signal the breaking of the fast. Faisal was educated by the customary *qadi*, and knew only family pleasures – hunting, horse and camel racing, hawking, picnics in the gardens of the neighbouring *wadi*. Desert excursions were unsafe, except for in well-armed bands, owing to the prevalence of raiders, tribe against tribe.

But before Faisal was out of his 'teens, this state of isolation had begun to change. His father the Emir Ibn Saud had chased the Turks out of Hasa province (1913), had established treaty relations with the British in the Gulf

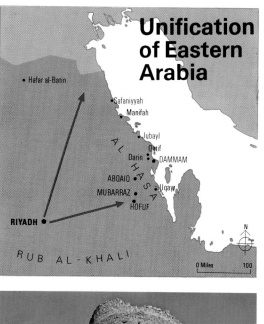

By 1920, the fortresses of eastern Arabia (illustrated) *had all fallen to Abdul Aziz. But the Turkish hold on the area had been broken on a moonless night in April 1913 when Abdul Aziz, with 600 men, scaled the walls of Hofuf and surprised the defenders.*

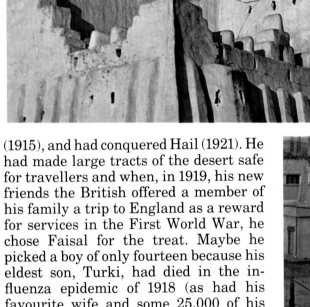

(1915), and had conquered Hail (1921). He had made large tracts of the desert safe for travellers and when, in 1919, his new friends the British offered a member of his family a trip to England as a reward for services in the First World War, he chose Faisal for the treat. Maybe he picked a boy of only fourteen because his eldest son, Turki, had died in the influenza epidemic of 1918 (as had his favourite wife and some 25,000 of his people); anyway, he reckoned Faisal to be the child most likely to profit from a new experience. Faisal justified the choice. With the dignity that was to mark him throughout his career, he exchanged swords with King George V and, in the freezing cold of a post-war December, gravely accepted the visits that were thought suitable to his years – to the Zoo, to the Greenwich telescope and to *Chu Chin Chow*.

By 1925-1926, when his father overpowered the Sharifian family and conquered the Holy Cities of Makkah and al-Madinah, he was thought old enough to command an army. He brought up the reinforcements for which his father sent in order to capture the sea port of Jiddah. Later, still only twenty-nine, he was to prove his military capacity more conclusively by commanding the most successful of the armies used by his father on the last of his campaigns – that of 1934 – by means of which he settled his frontier with the Yemen. Faisal's army, which sped down the coastal plain of the Red Sea, was the spearhead of this operation.

For all his success in the field, it was in the council chamber that Faisal's talents showed up best. Makkah and Jiddah once conquered, Ibn Saud proclaimed himself king of the Hijaz and Najd; but he could not be everywhere at once and he appointed Faisal his Viceroy in the Hijaz, with his seat in Makkah. Here the

The decisive incorporation of the southwest (top pictures: *Abha's fortress*) *into the young kingdom was assigned by Abdul Aziz to his young son Faisal* (later King), *while he himself subdued the last strongholds in Hijaz* (above) *and to the north, including Hail and Shenanah* (far right).

responsibilities were great, for the whole of the Islamic world outside Arabia was exercised, if not aghast, that its Holy Cities should have passed into the hands of unlettered desert religious reformers who might in their zeal destroy the essential features of the pilgrimage and tamper with the seats of Islamic learning at Makkah and al-Madinah. For several years after 1926 anxious delegations poured in from more sophisticated lands – Egypt, India, Indonesia, Iran, Iraq. Whenever possible, Ibn Saud received and reassured these delegations himself. When he was there, his sons, if they appeared at all, took the customary place

behind his chair. But at times he was forced to be absent because of the demands of Najd, where his warriors were champing to carry their Holy War into Iraq and needed curbing. In his absence, visitors to Makkah were received by Faisal.

Faisal was likewise his father's deputy in many dealings with non-Islamic states. In 1926, he was sent to Europe to broaden his mind in Britain and France, and five years later he embarked on a wide-ranging tour that included Soviet Russia. (Saudi-Soviet relations at the time were good, for Soviet Russia, with its own Muslims in mind, had been one of the first foreign states to recognize the new King and his Kingdom.) Ibn Saud throughout his life continued personally to handle dealings with foreigners if they came to Arabia – for instance, to negotiate frontiers or seek concessions, but abroad he left everything to Faisal, whom he appointed as his Foreign Minister.

Murabba Palace

Abdul Aziz's Palace of Murabba in Riyadh is today preserved as a memorial to his achievement – with its traditional decoration and weaponry, it is characteristic of the period.

It was here at Qasr al-Murabba that the ailing King spent the last years of his life, yet maintaining his strict routines of life.

A selection of flintlock rifles, used by King Abdul Aziz's soldiers in the early days of the unification of the Kingdom, are preserved at the Palace (above).

The Second World War changed the status and outlook of most Arab lands. They joined forces in a League; they gained admission to the United Nations; they gave new forms of expression to their nationalism. Some began to earn income from the oil that had been discovered before the war; most planned to use this new wealth for development and welfare. Looking back, it is odd to remember that, at this stage, the states which made all the running in the Arab League were Egypt, Iraq and Syria; Saudi Arabia's contribution to the League's budget was seven per cent of the total as against Egypt's forty-two per cent. Only from 1950, when it made its "fifty-fifty" arrangement with the Arabian-American Oil Company (Aramco), did Saudi Arabia throw off its image of barren desert, backward inhabitants and poverty.

Faisal, who during the war had further broadened his experience of the world by visiting the United States with his half-brother Khalid (later King Khalid), became a figure of note in world conclaves. At the San Francisco Conference which inaugurated the United Nations, at meetings of the Arab League, in the United Nations Assembly, his dignified figure and graceful robes (he never wore Western dress) singled him out for attention. His father, smitten from 1950 with the sad illness of which he died in 1953, became wholly dependent on the two eldest of his thirty-five surviving sons – Saud, the Crown Prince, who had inherited touches of Ibn Saud's humour and gaiety, and Faisal, who was more like him in his piety and austerity, and in his grasp of human foibles.

When the old King died and Saud succeeded him, the younger, graver brother became Prime Minister as well as Foreign Minister. At the time, Saudi Arabia lacked the institutions and the administrative framework that were becoming necessary if it was to handle its mounting revenue and play its potential role in Arab affairs. Faisal responded to the challenge and, with the assistance of a devout and cautious Pakistani financier, set up the Saudi Arabian Monetary Agency (SAMA).

When King Saud's health deteriorated in 1963, Faisal picked up the reins of power, and in 1964 Crown Prince Faisal became King of Saudi Arabia.

The role was not easy. To the right of him, the *ulama* and the more pious members of his family were pressing for a re-

King Faisal ibn Abdul Aziz combined inspirational leadership with sound management, and respect for the past with sagacious innovations.

turn to the austerity of his father's day; to his left, and in the forces, young men who had been abroad urged "modernization" and less rigorous adherence to the strict rules of religious extremists. Faisal, as was his wont, steered towards compromise. He permitted television but not the cinema; he promoted secular and technical education for boys, but kept girls' education under the jurisdiction of the Sheikh al-Islam – the chief religious authority. His middle way was not everywhere popular. Whatever his personal inclinations (and he cannot have enjoyed the glare of lighting for the television cameras that he permitted even during audiences) he never forgot that it was the *ulama* who had helped him to restore the Kingdom to its proper course. Foreign policy, too, presented its problems. Nasser's Egypt, the most powerful of his

neighbours, had to his consternation taken up arms in support of the republicans against the royalists in Yemen; Aden, which the British were about to leave, was a hotbed of left-wing parties fanned by Egyptian propaganda; Syria and a newly-republican Iraq were flirting with his bugbear, Soviet Russia. He sought to create for himself a new base by visiting Islamic countries and establishing an Islamic summit that would include Iran and Pakistan. But this plan foundered because the Islamic states had differing political priorities.

It won him little beyond the respect he already commanded as Defender of the Faith and guardian of its Holy Places.

The Palestine War of 1967 abruptly changed his role in foreign affairs. Egypt, till then a rival, was humiliated and truncated. So was Jordan. Jerusa-

the important decisions. On the Prophet's birthday, 1975, one of his scores of nephews, the son of a much younger half-brother, slipped into his audience chamber and fired three shots at the King over the shoulder of the Kuwaiti Oil Minister whom the King was receiving. Although the assassin's motives may never be completely understood, what is certain is that he acted to deprive his countrymen of a leader with a store of wisdom and experience.

The stability of the Kingdom stood the test of this capricious act. King Khalid, next in line, moved naturally into the role of leader of the nation. His own wide experience and the talents of the immediate family – exemplified by Prince Fahd, the Crown Prince as First Deputy Prime Minister, and Prince Abdullah, the Second Deputy Prime Minister and Head of the National Guard – ensured the smooth continuance of government. Within six months, King Khalid launched the monumental Second Plan. (He is pictured left.)

Like his father, Khalid honoured the essentially Arabian quality of his roots. He was at home in the desert and trusted by the tribes. With his father he took part in several expeditions during the unification of the country. In 1932 he was appointed Governor of the Hijaz, and in 1934 Minister of the Interior. As a young man he represented the Kingdom on various missions abroad with his brother Faisal (e.g. to Britain in 1939 and 1945, and the US in 1943).

As Faisal's First Deputy Prime Minister he moved to the centre of the affairs of state, was party to all major decisions of policy and frequently travelled abroad. When he became King in 1975, Saudi Arabia was already committed to carefully planned development on a massive scale. Fahd was by his side as First Deputy Premier, dynamic and involved in the day-to-day administration of government. Khalid's heart disease, twice alleviated by open heart surgery, precluded sustained strenuous public duties. Yet it was remarkable what he achieved, repeatedly travelling at home and overseas in his kingly role, and playing a vital personal part in Arab and Islamic affairs.

Khalid's intervention halted – for a while – the Lebanese civil war in the late 1970s; he also brought Muslims together in the historic 38-nation summit in Taif and Makkah in 1981, and that year launched the six-nation Gulf

lem, the third holiest city of Islam, fell into Israel's hands. Faisal set about providing financial support for the states on Israel's borders. Nasser's death in 1970, and the passing of Egypt's presidency to a less dominant figure, Anwar Sadat, opened Faisal's way to the leading role in Arab affairs which, with his usual dignity, he now assumed. Though in his late sixties and often far from well, he made long journeys to Arab summits in order to have his say.

To him Zionism and Communism were twin evils, and he warmly approved when, in the summer of 1972, Sadat dismissed his Soviet advisers. Now nothing stood in the way of the full-blooded alliance that was capable of dominating the Arab scene – the marriage of Saudi wealth with Egyptian manpower and technical superiority. In July 1973 King Faisal gave the world an idea of what was in his mind when for the first time he publicly mentioned his country's power to cut back oil deliveries if President

Nixon did not modify his support for Israel. The Arab oil embargo that accompanied the general oil price-rise during the October War of 1973 was applied only with his customary caution, but a repetition could be all-important since Saudi Arabia owns one quarter of the world's known oil reserves.

At the time of Faisal's death, his country was one of the richest in the world in liquid funds. Riyadh, seventy years earlier a mud town, was a city throbbing with activity, besieged by salesmen and technical experts out for contracts to fulfil the developments he had in mind, pierced by dual carriageways, humming with traffic, twinkling at night with the lights that outline mile on mile of ribbon development, yet with *suqs* that fall quiet, empty of their menfolk, at the hour of prayer.

Saudi Arabia's government is highly centralized. Though competent and well trained Saudis are now available to run it, King Faisal personally took most of

Cooperation Council.

He was a man of generosity of heart and personal modesty. He had little time for the panoply of power. When he died in Taif on June 13, 1982, at the height of Israeli aggression in Lebanon, his people mourned a wise, fatherly and devoted leader.

For many years King Fahd, his successor, had above all others exemplified Saudi Arabia's unprecedented evolution into modern statehood – as a substantial contributor to world stability and cool-headedness, and as a country shaping for its own clearly defined needs the benefits of modern technology in a strictly Islamic framework.

King Fahd was born in 1921. Recognition of his abilities came early: in 1953, in his early thirties, he took the education portfolio and was responsible for the first expansion in schools throughout the Kingdom. In 1962 he became Minister of the Interior, and Second Deputy Prime Minister in 1967.

After appointment as Crown Prince and First Deputy Prime Minister on King Faisal's death, he acted as viceroy during King Khalid's absences, and remained at the heart of the daily affairs of state throughout his brother's reign. His wide travels abroad included several official visits – twice to the United States, for example, in the 1970s. As early as 1953 he represented his father at Queen Elizabeth's coronation.

Thus he came to power as a statesman well known and profoundly respected in the world, no less than in his own Kingdom, as a man of experience, authority, and consistency of policy, much admired for his accessibility and concern for all.

During his reign, the Kingdom has played a prominent role in international affairs, through its membership of the United Nations, the Non-aligned Movement and OPEC. At a regional level, Saudi Arabia makes its voice heard at Arab Summit Conferences, at OAPEC, in the Organisation of the Islamic Conference, and at the Gulf Cooperation Council, at all of which it exerts a major influence on issues of concern to the world community such as Palestine, the Gulf War and its aftermath, Lebanon, Afghanistan, and oil pricing policy.

Domestically, King Fahd is intent on building a Saudi Arabia whose prosperity will endure by means of painstaking planning, sound education, diversification of the economy, conservation of resources, and devotion to Islam.

King Fahd was proclaimed King of Saudi Arabia on June 13th, 1982. He has established Saudi Arabia as a steadying influence in world affairs, skilful in the use of the Kingdom's economic strength to preserve equilibrium and promote confidence, even during times of recession. He has represented the Kingdom in many delegations and state visits to other countries and at international conferences.

King Fahd is widely known for his interest in education, his diplomacy and his accessibility to all.

The Islamic World

GREAT BRITAIN

ATLANTIC OCEAN

GERMANY

U.S.S.R.

FRANCE

RUMANIA

KAZAKHSTAN

ARAL SEA

YUGOSLAVIA

BLACK SEA

CASPIAN SEA

SOVIET CENTRAL ASIA

ITALY

BULGARIA

ALBANIA

PORTUGAL

SPAIN

GREECE

TURKEY

SYRIA

LEBANON

IRAN

AFGHANISTAN

SIN

MEDITERRANEAN SEA

TUNISIA

MOROCCO

IRAQ

JORDAN

ARABIAN GULF

PAKISTAN

ALGERIA

LIBYA

EGYPT

GULF OF OMAN

UAE

INDIA

MAURITANIA

RED SEA

OMAN

ARABIAN SEA

MALI

NIGER

YEMEN

SOUTH YEMEN

SENEGAL

CHAD

GAMBIA

GUINEA-BISSAU

VOLTAIC REP

SUDAN

GUINEA

NIGERIA

SIERRA LEONE

IVORY COAST

GHANA

CENTRAL AFRICAN REPUBLIC

ETHIOPIA

SRI LANKA

LIBERIA

SOMALIA

TOGO BENIN

CAMEROON

UGANDA

KENYA

GABON CONGO

ZAIRE

TANZANIA

ANGOLA

ZAMBIA

MOZAMBIQUE

MADAGASCAR

5
Islam

To Saudi Arabia, the holy cities of Makkah and al-Madinah are a sacred trust, exercised on behalf of all Islam. To the fountainhead of their faith every year flock pilgrims in their hundreds of thousands, to offer their "submission", as is the meaning of Islam, to God's will as revealed through the Prophet Muhammad.

From its foundation in the Arabian heartland, Islam today circles the globe and is the accredited faith of some 900 million people. It is constantly making new converts among those without belief.

Saudi Arabia as the Heartland of Islam

The religious pre-eminence of Saudi Arabia in the Muslim world is vouchsafed by the fact that it contains the two cities of Makkah and al-Madinah, where Islam was revealed and where it matured under the Prophet Muhammed himself. Makkah also has the Ka'bah, Islam's central shrine, while the tomb of the Prophet and his mosque are in al-Madinah. The Saudi regime earned the gratitude of all Muslims by ensuring the safety of pilgrims under the strong hand of King Abdul Aziz, who enforced the strict Shari'ah rules of law and order. The late King Faisal brought a new political dimension by pursuing a policy of Islamic solidarity, as distinct from pure territorial nationalism.

Islam is a world-wide faith. There exists today a world Muslim community about nine hundred million strong which, despite sectarian differences, feels bound together in one faith: every Muslim must recite the profession of faith, "There is no God but Allah, and Muhammad is his Prophet", with awareness of its meaning and full consent from the heart. The first proselytizers were, of course, the Arabs themselves. The Qur'an repeatedly states that it is "a Reminder *for the whole world*", that differences of tribes and peoples, of tongues and skin-colour, are signs of God's power and mercy, but that real rank in God's sight depends on piety and virtue, and that the Prophet himself was "sent only as a mercy *to all mankind*". This universal character of the Islamic teaching was also strongly underlined in the Prophet's Farewell Pilgrimage sermon, which declares the religious ideal to be indifferent to racial and other natural differences.

The fact remains that Islam's origins lie in an Arab milieu and that it has a clear Arab base. Muslim thinkers have considered this point and given explanations to rationalize it. Thus, Ibn Khaldun holds that the Prophet had to be born in Arabia, whose people were not primitive, yet were close to the natural state of man and therefore possessed of natural manly virtues and minds unencumbered by preconceived notions. Indeed he had to be born among the Makkan tribe of Quraysh, who, once converted to Islam, had the necessary power and prestige to protect and propagate it. It is, of course, historically true that when Makkah joined Islam, the rest of Arabia followed. Shah Walig Allah of Delhi adds that it was part of the divine plan to replace the older Middle Eastern civilizations with a new civilization which would have a moral freshness and virility that could be supplied only by the Arabs, once they had been nurtured by Islam.

Be that as it may, there was undoubtedly a religious ferment in Makkah and al-Madinah prior to the appearance of the Prophet. While the Jews of al-Madinah longed for a Prophet to make them victorious over the Arabs there (*Qur'an* II, 83), Arab intellectuals in Makkah, having accepted neither Judaism nor Christianity, desired a new Arab Prophet so that "they may be better guided" than the Jewish and Christian communities (*Qur'an* XXXV, 42; VI, 157; XXXVII, 168). When the Makkans opposed the Prophet, the Qur'an repeatedly reminded them that he had been raised up "from among themselves" and that they knew him well because he had lived among them for so long. Even more emphatically, the Qur'an time and time again states that it is revealed in a "clear Arabic tongue" (*Qur'an* XVI, 103; XXVI, 195; also XII, 2; XIII, 37; XX, 113), for "if We had made it a non-Arab Qur'an, they (the opponents) would have said, 'Why are its verses not clearly set out?" (*Qur'an* XLI, 44). This last statement refers to the belief of the Arabs that the Arabic language is the most expressive and eloquent.

That the Prophet, since he was an Arab himself, should communicate to his people in Arabic, and that they should be the first addressees of Islam, was, of course, natural. But the statements of the Qur'an about its own nature go much

Focus of the annual pilgrimage of hundreds of thousands of devout Muslims is the Ka'bah of Holy Makkah which pilgrims circle seven times – the first three times preferably hastening round.

The Way to Makkah
The King Abdul Aziz International Airport (*bottom*) is one of the wonders of modern aviation. The Hajj terminal's award-winning roof design (*Below*), based on the tents of the desert, is a striking reminder to millions of pilgrims of the pilgrimage's past.

further, since it regards itself as miraculous and challenges its opponents – those Arabs who were proud of their literary perfection – to produce anything like it (*Qur'an* X, 38; XI, 13; XXVIII, 49). In these verses, the Qur'an is emphasizing that its source is Divine, and cannot be the composition of a human mind, even that of the Prophet himself; and it is, indeed, clear that the speech of the Prophet, outside of Revelation, is of a different quality from that of the Qur'an. Muslim theologians early deduced the doctrine that the Qur'an is "inimitable" and hence untranslatable. Many Western scholars also think that it is not really translatable – which is why Arthur J. Arberry called his English rendering *The Qur'an Interpreted*, rather than *The Qur'an Translated*. For centuries, the religious scholars of Islam did not allow the Qur'an to be translated. This law has been quite recently relaxed in the interest of the wider dissemination of the Qur'anic teaching; but they still insist that no translation be published without the Arabic text.

The second major source of Islamic doctrine and practice – particularly in the field of Law, which stands at the centre of the entire Islamic system – is the Sunnah (Example or Model) of the Prophet – that is his precepts and conduct, both in private and public activity. The Sunnah interprets and elaborates the teaching of the Qur'an, and is embodied in certain authoritative works. These do not only include what the Prophet actually said or did. At a very early stage, the Muslim jurists decided that the entire body of Arab practices and customs to which the Prophet had not explicitly objected and *hence had tacitly approved of, is part of the Prophetic Sunnah*. This concept of the "tacit (*sukuti*) Sunnah" thus sanctified the entire gamut of Arab life – essentially Makkan and Madinan after its reform by the Qur'an and the Prophet. In its outward expansion and during its long development it was certainly modified, elaborated and changed (on the basis of the principle of *ijtihad*, or fresh thinking), but it always served as the normative base of reference.

Besides being the birthplace of Islam, Makkah is the object of the great annual pilgrimage (*hajj*) undertaken by Muslims to the Ka'bah Sanctuary (the Haram), also called the "House of God" (*bayt Allah*). A pre-Islamic Arab site, it was officially adopted by Islam in the year 1 AH (or 622), after reforms purging

By 1990 some 2 million pilgrims a year are expected to pass through the Hajj terminal (above) *at Jiddah's impressive international airport.*

it of idolatrous practices and implications. It is, for all Muslims, the most holy place, where the Divine comes into special touch with the earth. Muslim mystics (Sufis) in particular developed a mystique of the Ka'bah, regarding it as the earthly manifestation of a metaphysical Divine reality. Throughout the centuries, almost every Muslim no matter how distant his abode, has aspired to visit Makkah, thus rendering it the metropolis of Islam, and the *hajj* the greatest living religious epic on earth. Scholars and saints – side by side with common folk – have usually visited Makkah, often more than once in their lifetime, to meet scholars and spiritual leaders from other parts of the Muslim world. Many stayed on in Makkah for study, reflection and spiritual enlightenment, some earning the honorific name

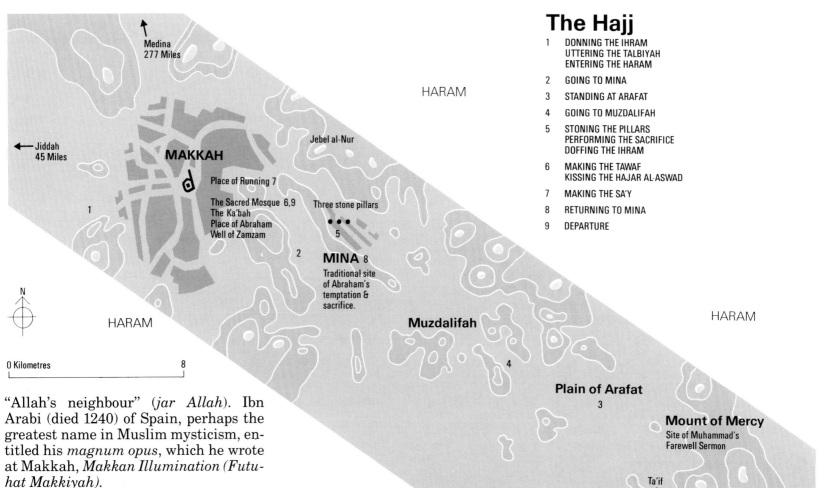

Medina
277 Miles

HARAM

Jiddah
45 Miles

Jebel al-Nur

MAKKAH

Place of Running 7

The Sacred Mosque 6,9
The Ka'bah
Place of Abraham
Well of Zamzam

Three stone pillars

● ● ●
5

1

2

MINA 8
Traditional site
of Abraham's
temptation &
sacrifice.

HARAM

N

HARAM

Muzdalifah

0 Kilometres   8

4

Plain of Arafat
3

Mount of Mercy
Site of Muhammad's
Farewell Sermon

Ta'if

The Hajj

1 DONNING THE IHRAM
   UTTERING THE TALBIYAH
   ENTERING THE HARAM

2 GOING TO MINA

3 STANDING AT ARAFAT

4 GOING TO MUZDALIFAH

5 STONING THE PILLARS
   PERFORMING THE SACRIFICE
   DOFFING THE IHRAM

6 MAKING THE TAWAF
   KISSING THE HAJAR AL-ASWAD

7 MAKING THE SA'Y

8 RETURNING TO MINA

9 DEPARTURE

"Allah's neighbour" (*jar Allah*). Ibn Arabi (died 1240) of Spain, perhaps the greatest name in Muslim mysticism, entitled his *magnum opus*, which he wrote at Makkah, *Makkan Illumination (Futuhat Makkiyah)*.

The quantity of pilgrims celebrating the *hajj* has increased vastly since 1925 when the number of pilgrims was estimated at about 100,000. The number reached 2 million in 1977, and passed 2.5 million in 1985. The key to the increase lies in the development of Saudi Arabia rather than the rising affluence of most Muslims. The Saudi regime has acquitted itself admirably as protector of the Holy Cities. King Abdul Aziz's main task was to put an end to the lawlessness which deterred Muslims from performing the *hajj* for fear of robbery and murder. Inheritor to the puritanism of his ancestors, he strictly enforced the penal law of the Shari'ah, which ordains severe punishment for theft and murder. At the same time travel was made easier, and ever since air travel, roads, water, electricity and the supply of better and more hygienic accommodation have been improved, until today the handling of what is now an influx of millions of pilgrims, all at once, in the performance of the *hajj*, is an annual feat of astonishing organization. Profiteering is non-existent. Traffic is controlled by helicopter. There are no scrums, no shortages. Yet the techniques of control do not obtrude upon the mood of devotion. The development of the area surrounding the Holy

Mosque at Makkah to accommodate 1.5 million worshippers will have completed the infrastructure for the modern *hajj* that Saudi policies have facilitated.

The Kingdom's prestige in the international Muslim community has grown gradually and lastingly. Although the Saudi regime has never made theocratic or caliphal claims, its policies represent a broad-based Islam and a robust realism which have won the respect of peoples and governments alike. Turkey, alienated since the First World War, had virtually banned Turks from making the pilgrimage for decades, but finally lifted restrictions in 1965; at the *hajj* in 1974 the Turkish contingent was the largest from outside Arabia. Due primarily to the religious basis of the state, the Saudi monarchy is the only one in the world to eschew such symbols of worldly power as the crown and throne; a practice much respected by the world's many Muslims.

King Faisal, in particular, brought a new dimension to the Saudi rule by his active policy of pan-Islamic solidarity – a policy sustained by King Khalid in his efforts to bring peace to Lebanon. The acute crisis created by Israel's occupation of Arab lands and particularly by its

takeover of Jerusalem presented King Faisal with a special challenge after the incident in 1969 which left Jerusalem's Aqsa Mosque badly damaged. He also played a central role in the Islamic summit meetings held in Morocco in 1969 and Pakistan in 1974. Under his guidance a permanent Islamic Secretariat was established with its headquarters in Jiddah, and financed by Saudi Arabia, to bring about closer cooperation among all Muslim governments. The Organisation of the Islamic Conference (OIC) holds regular summits at which it addresses itself to matters of politics and intra-Muslim development. Its most recent initiative, in 1989, has been to call for the creation of an Islamic Common Market to achieve integration of economic development. It also concerns itself with, among other things, research into and the conservation of the Islamic heritage.

At semi-official level, the Saudi government set up in 1974 the World Muslim Congress (*Rabitat al-Alam al-Islami*), with which many other Muslim organizations all over the world have become affiliated or associated. The Congress discusses religious problems and socio-political issues arising from them.

The Hajj

"And complete the Hajj *and the* Umrah *in the service of God. But if you are prevented (from completing it) send an offering for sacrifice such as you may find. And do not shave your heads until the offering reaches the place of sacrifice. And if any of you is ill or has an ailment in his scalp (necessitating shaving) he must in compensation either fast or feed the poor or offer sacrifice."*

HOLY QUR'AN II

Medical facilities (top) *and nourishment* (centre) *are available to pilgrims as they adopt the simple* Ihram *garb of two pieces of white towelling.*

AFTER belief in the one God (Allah), the performance of regular, ritual prayers, fasting during the month of Ramadan and the giving of fixed alms (*Zakah*), the *hajj* is the fifth pillar of Islam, a fundamental duty which a Muslim, male and female alike, must perform at least once in his lifetime if he or she has the material means to do so.

Long before the Prophet Muhammad began to preach Islam and summon the Arabs and all mankind back to the worship of the One True God, indeed since time immemorial, the barren valley of Makkah had been a place of pilgrimage venerated by the Arabs, both settled and nomadic. It had been associated with the Patriarch Abraham, the Friend of God, who was the first to establish there a house to the glory of God. In the Holy Qur'an (II, 122-123) we read: "And lo! Abraham and Ishmael raised the foundations of the House saying: 'Oh Lord! accept this from us. Thou art, indeed, the All-Hearing, the All-Knowing. Our Lord! and make us submissive to Thee and of our progeny a nation submissive to Thee and show us our rites and turn to us in Mercy. Indeed, Thou art the All-Forgiving, All-Merciful. Our Lord! send amongst them a Messenger of their own who will recite to them Thy signs.'"

Again we read (III, 91-92): "Indeed, the first House (of worship) established for men was at Bakka (Makkah), full of blessing and guidance for all men. In it are clear signs, the Station of Abraham. Whoever enters it shall be safe. Pilgrimage thereto is a duty men owe to God, all those who can afford the journey. But if any reject this, God is in no need of any of His creatures."

And so the ancient pilgrimage to Makkah became incorporated in Islam; the guiding lines of its performance were laid down by the Holy Qur'an (II, 193 ff.): "And complete the Hajj and the Umrah in the service of God. But if you are prevented (from completing it) send an offering for sacrifice such as you may find. And do not shave your heads until the offering reaches the place of sacrifice. And if any of you is ill or has an ailment in his scalp (necessitating shaving) he must in compensation either fast or feed the poor or offer sacrifice. And when you are in safety again, if anyone wishes to continue the Umrah on to the Hajj he must make an offering such as he can afford. But if he cannot afford it he should fast three days during the Hajj and seven days on his return, making ten days in all. This is for those whose household is not settled in the Sacred Mosque. And fear God and know that God is strict in punishment. The Hajj is in well known months (Shawwal, Dhu'l-Qa'dah and Dhu'l Hijjah). If anyone undertakes that duty in them let there be no obscenity, nor wickedness, nor quarrelling in the Hajj. And whatever good you do God knows it. And take provision for the journey. But the best of provisions is fear of God. So fear him, all you who are wise."

The pilgrimage is made to Makkah, the most sacred city of Islam, where the Prophet Muhammad was born, where his mission was first revealed to him and where he began preaching Islam. In the centre of Makkah stands the Sacred Mosque (al-Masjid al-Haram), a large open courtyard enclosed by cloisters, rebuilt and enlarged many times.

"The Pilgrimage is in months well-known; whoso undertakes the duty of Pilgrimage in them shall not go in to his womenfolk nor indulge in ungodliness and disputing in the Pilgrimage. Whatever good you do, God knows it. And take provision; but the best provision is godfearing." HOLY QUR'AN II

Roughly in the centre of the Sacred Mosque stands the Ka'bah, the House of God, towards which all Muslims turn their faces in their daily prayers, no matter where they may be. The Ka'bah, as its name denotes, is a cube-shaped building of stone, the front (north-east) and back (south-west) sides being forty feet long, the other sides being thirty-five feet and the height fifty feet.

In the east corner, about four feet above ground level, is set the Black Stone in a silver frame. This stone (eight inches in diameter) is believed to be the only remnant of the first mosque built by Abraham and to go back even before him to the time of Adam. The Ka'bah has been rebuilt many times in the course of the centuries, once in the lifetime of the Prophet, before his mission, when he was chosen by chance to place the Black Stone in its position. In the north-east wall of the Ka'bah close to the corner in which the Black Stone is set and some

seven feet above the ground is the door to the Ka'bah which is opened at special times. There is nothing inside the building, which was cleansed of its idols when the Prophet returned in triumph to Makkah early in 630 CE. The Ka'bah is covered with a black pall decorated with verses from the Qur'an. This is the *Kiswah* (garment) which from the Middle Ages was made in Cairo and brought ceremoniously to Makkah every year by the Egyptian pilgrims. It is now made by local craftsmen.

The two remaining shrines inside the Sacred Mosque are the Station of Abraham (facing the door) where the Patriarch bowed down in prayer and the Well of Zamzam, north-east of the Ka'bah, which sprang up when Hagar was desperately seeking water for the in-

Pilgrims gather on the Mount of Mercy, the site of Muhammad's farewell sermon, to watch in prayerfulness as the sun descends over the Plain of Arafat.

fant Ishmael. Just outside the Sacred Mosque is the Mas'a (running place) between the rocky hillocks of al-Safa and al-Marwah, a distance of 440 yards. The Mas'a, which was until recently an ordinary street with shops, is now covered over and paved with marble flags. It was between these two hills that Hagar ran distractedly seeking water.

Pilgrimage to Makkah is of two kinds. There is the *umrah*, the Lesser Pilgrimage or Visit, which can be performed at any time of the year and is confined to worship at the places mentioned above. Then there is the *hajj* proper, which combines the rites of the *umrah* with others outside Makkah and takes place only once a year in the first part of the month of *Dhu 'l-Hijjah*, the last month of the Islamic lunar calendar.

Again, the *hajj* and the *umrah* can be performed together (*Qiran*) or separately (*Tamattu*). The latter is chosen by pilgrims who arrive in Makkah some days before the ninth of the month, which day is the culmination of the pilgrimage. *Tamattu* entails either sacrifice at Mina or fasting during the pilgrimage and on return home.

Nowadays, with frequent and easy means of transport, the number of pilgrims to Makkah during the pilgrimage

"When you press on from Arafat, then remember God at the Holy Waymark, and remember Him as He has guided you, though formerly you were gone astray. Then press on from where the people press on, and pray for God's forgiveness; God is All-forgiving, All-compassionate. And when you have performed your holy rites remember God, as you remember your fathers or yet more devoutly. Now some men there are who say, 'Our Lord, give to us in this world'; such men shall have no part in the world to come." HOLY QUR'AN, II

"Indeed, the first House (of worship) established for men was at Bakka (Makkah), full of blessing and guidance for all men. In it are clear signs, the Station of Abraham. Whoever enters it shall be safe. Pilgrimage thereto is a duty men owe to God, all those who can afford the journey. But if any reject this, God is in no need of any of His creatures."

HOLY QUR'AN, III

Children count for no less than adults in the eyes of Allah, and throughout Islam, children at an early age are able to recite large portions of the Holy Qur'an.

month is very large, and commonly exceeds a million. Organizing such a vast number of people, seeing to their health and other needs, is a formidable task which the Saudi Government performs with great efficiency.

Most foreign pilgrims arrive either by air or by sea through Jiddah, the port of Makkah, and there the Government has a special *hajj* Administration. From Jid-dah they go by bus to Makkah (some fifty miles away), each group of pilgrims being assigned according to their rites (Hanafi, Shafi'i, Maliki, and so on) to a *mutawwif* in Makkah. A *mutawwif* is a special guide and mentor whose duty it is to see that the pilgrims under his wing perform the rites of the pilgrimage correctly, have no difficulties while in the Holy Land and return to their homelands happy and satisfied, having gained the blessing of the pilgrimage properly performed. Each *mutawwif* has under him a number of assistants whose duty it is to accompany groups of pilgrims. Of course, a pilgrim who knows the language and is familiar with Makkah can do without a *mutawwif*, relying on one of the many guides to the *hajj* printed in Arabic or other languages.

Before entering the sacred territory around Makkah – indeed, sometimes from the start of his journey – the pilgrim puts himself in a state of sanctity by ablution, prayer and donning the pilgrim's dress (*Ihram*), which for a man consists of two unsewn towels, one worn wrapped around the lower part of the body, the other thrown over the upper part, and unsewn sandals. There is no special dress for a woman except that her face must remain unveiled, no matter what her local customs may be. The reason for these regulations is to emphasize the equality of all pilgrims, high and low, before God.

On and off during his journey and until he enters Makkah the pilgrim chants a short formula of acceptance of the pilgrimage duties (the *Talbiyah*). This is: "Here I am in answer to thy call, O God, here I am! Here I am! Thou hast no associate! Here I am! All Praise and Favour and Kingship are thine! Thou hast no associate!"

The rites of the *umrah* are *Tawaf* (circumambulation of the Ka'bah), *Sa'y* (running between al-Safa and al-Marwah) and shaving of the head or clipping of the hair. On arrival in Makkah the pilgrim performs *Wudu* (ablution before prayer) and goes straight away to the Sacred Mosque which he enters preferably by the Bab al-Salam (Gate of Peace). Around the Ka'bah is a paved area (the *Mataf*) on which the pilgrim performs his *Tawaf*, beginning at the Black Stone and going around the Ka'bah seven times in an anti-clockwise direction. The pilgrim makes the first three rounds of the Ka'bah at a fast pace and the remainder at walking pace, all the while glorifying God and supplicating His favour and mercy in set phrases generally repeated after his guide. As the pilgrim passes the Black Stone he either kisses it, or touches it or simply makes a motion of his hand towards it. As the throng making *Tawaf* is generally very large, the last is by far the most common. A policeman is posted on either side of the Black Stone to keep the pilgrims on the move. It is a remarkable fact that the *Mataf* is never free from pilgrims, night or day, except at the times of congregational prayer. Muslims in no wise worship the Black Stone. They kiss or touch it because it is known that the Prophet Muhammad did so and thereby they establish a physical link between themselves and the Prophet. And he did so because it was a link

between himself and Abraham. *Tawaf* is the first and last religious act of the pilgrim to Makkah.

After performing his *Tawaf* the pilgrim then proceeds to the Station of Abraham and there performs two cycles of individual prayer. Before going out from the Sacred Mosque to the Mas'a he may drink some water from the Well of Zamzam. This water is slightly brackish but is drunk in large quantities by the pilgrims, who often fill their water bottles with it to take home.

The second rite of the *umrah* is *Sa'y* (running) between al-Safa and al-Marwah. For this the pilgrim leaves the Mosque by the Bab al-Safa (Safa Gate) and mounts the rocky hillock of that name. After a short prayer he proceeds at walking pace towards the second

"Thus We appointed you a midmost nation that you might be witnesses to the people, and that the Messenger might be a witness to you. Turn thy face toward the Holy Mosque; and wherever you are, turn your faces towards it."

HOLY QUR'AN, II

An historic picture of Makkah, dating from the 1950s, shows the prevailing architecture backed by the so-called Black Hills. A minaret of the Great Mosque is seen in the foreground.

"And when We settled for Abraham the place of the House: 'Thou shall not associate with Me anything. And do thou purify My House for those that shall go about it and those that stand, for those that bow and prostrate themselves; and proclaim among men the Pilgrimage, and they shall come unto thee on foot and upon every lean beast, they shall come from every deep ravine that they may witness things profitable to them and mention God's Name on days well-known over such beasts of the flocks as He has provided them: "So eat thereof, and feed the wretched poor." Let them then finish with their self-neglect and let them fulfil their vows, and go about the Ancient House.'"

HOLY QUR'AN, XXII

hillock, al-Marwah, all the while saying prayers and supplications. The second fifth of the distance between the two hillocks, between two marker posts, is covered at a fast pace.

Having performed the *Sa'y* between the two hillocks seven times the pilgrim ends up at al-Marwah where he has his head shaved or, more commonly nowadays, his hair cut, which is the third rite of the *umrah*. With this he has completed the *umrah*, and if he has come before the ninth of the month with the intention of separating his *hajj* from *umrah* (*Tamattu*), he is now free to put off his *Ihram* dress, have a bath and put on his ordinary clothes, entering into the social life of Makkah. If on the other hand, his intention was that his *hajj* and *umrah* should be joined (*Qiran*), then he remains in *Ihram*.

On the eighth of the month of *Dhu'l-Hijjah* the pilgrims prepare for the culmination of the pilgrimage to Makkah. Those who have performed the *umrah* separately bathe and put on their *Ihram* dress again and go to the Mosque to perform *Tawaf*. Then the whole mass of the pilgrims and even inhabitants of Makkah move to Mina, four miles away, arriving for noon prayers. Mina is a remarkable place: for five or six days of the pilgrimage month it is thronged. For the rest of the year it is a ghost town.

Later, on the eighth or early on the ninth of the month, the pilgrims move to the Plain of Arafat, some thirteen miles south-east of Makkah and outside the sacred territory, where the *mutawwifs* have set up their thousands of tents, each with its distinctive flag, arranged in streets. On the morning of the ninth of *Dhu'l-Hijjah* the pilgrims move about freely, talking with other pilgrims and making new friends from many distant lands. Noon and afternoon prayers are combined at mid-day and the Imam gives a short sermon from the pulpit of Namirah Mosque on the Jabal al-Rahmah (Mount of Mercy), a distinguished landmark of Arafat, on which the Prophet gave his Farewell Sermon in which he summarized the duties of a Muslim.

The whole of the afternoon of the ninth is spent in prayer on the Plain of Arafat. This is the *Wuquf* (Standing), which is the culmination and cornerstone of the pilgrimage to Makkah. Whoever misses it cannot be said to have performed the pilgrimage. In *Wuquf* the pilgrim stands bare-headed all the afternoon in the open air glorifying God, reading the Qur'an and crying aloud "*Labbayka 'llahumma Labbayka* (Here I am, O God, here I am!). The infirm may sit or seek shade during their devotions but it is considered more meritorious to remain standing all the time.

As soon as the sun sets the whole immense throng gets on the move, making for Muzdalifah, an open plain about halfway between Arafat and Mina. There the pilgrims say their sunset and night prayers combined. Controlling the movement of over a million human beings, in all forms of transport, is a supreme feat of administration by the Saudi police. The pilgrim spends the night under the stars at Muzdalifah and gathers seventy pebbles, each about the size of a chick-pea. Early the next morning (the tenth) after prayer he proceeds to Mina, where the pilgrimage is concluded.

In Mina are three stone pillars sur-rounded by low walls called *jamrahs*. At the one nearest Makkah (Jamrat al-Aqabah), on the morning of the tenth day, the pilgrim casts seven of his pebbles calling out each time "*Allahu Akbar* (God is most Great)". This is symbolic of man's casting out evil from himself. Then, if necessary, the animals are sacrificed and some of the meat given to the poor. The pilgrims must then return to Mina, for it is there that the pilgrimage ends. With a final shaving of his head or symbolic clipping of his hair the pilgrim emerges from the state of *Ihram* and his pilgrimage is concluded. He bathes, puts on new clothes and looks forward to returning to his home a *hajj* or *hajji*. He must, however, spend the two or three days after the tenth day of Dhu'l-Hijjah in Mina, cast his remaining sixty-three pebbles at all three *jamrahs*, and perform *Tawaf al-Ifadah*.

Having completed his pilgrimage the pilgrim is generally eager to be on his way, but there are many who linger in Makkah for days, weeks or even months, some for the rest of their lives. Delay also arises from the difficulty of arranging transport for such a vast multitude. When the day of his departure is fixed the pilgrim goes to the Sacred Mosque for the last time and performs a final *Tawaf* (*Tawaf al-Wida* or Tawaf of Farewell). He leaves the House of God walking backwards all the time, praising and thanking God and praying that this may not be the last time he enjoys the grace and favour of visiting His Holy House and goes out from the Sacred Mosque by the Bab al-Wida (Gate of Farewell). Then with joyful heart he sets off on his journey home.

On the approach to the final act of worship, the pilgrim passes through the city of Makkah to the proximity of the Great Mosque. Regular prayer, five times daily, proceeds as usual.

Since the photograph below was taken, the floor of the Great Mosque has been paved throughout; the practice of religious observances is otherwise as it has been for centuries.

"God has appointed the Ka'bah, the Holy House, as an establishment for men."

HOLY QU'RAN, V

Islamic dignitaries enter the Ka'bah (far left and below), which contains a spare and unadorned chamber, with no intervention of human artifice needed to add to its unique sanctity. The photograph (middle left) shows King Faisal with Muslim leaders completing the hajj in the mid-1970s. Most pilgrims wish to kiss the Black Stone (bottom left) and to worship at the shrines of the Station of Abraham (left) and the Well of Zamzam.

" 'Take to yourselves Abraham's station for a place of prayer.' " HOLY QU'RAN, II

But since it is vouchsafed to the vast majority of Muslims to make the pilgrimage to Makkah only once in their lifetimes most pilgrims combine their pilgrimage with a visit to al-Madinah, sometimes before, but generally after the pilgrimage. There they visit the Prophet's tomb and those of the early Caliphs in the Sacred Mosque. They usually spend several days in this second city of Islam, the city to which the Prophet Muhammad fled from persecution in his native city, where he established the Islamic State and where he lies buried with so many of his noble companions.

The pilgrimage to Makkah used to be an arduous and often perilous adventure, but today it is done in comparative comfort and perfect safety. Nevertheless, owing to the vast numbers of pilgrims, it is still a challenging enterprise, especially when the pilgrimage season falls in the summer months. Yet, when the *hajji* is safe at home with his family and when the month of the *hajj* comes round again he feels that there is nowhere he would rather be than with countless thousands from all corners of the earth thronging the Sacred Mosque and the streets of Makkah, or standing in prayer on the Plain of Arafat.

Al-Madinah the Radiant

Second only to Makkah in sanctity is the city of al-Madinah, whose night-time profile is dominated by the Great Mosque with its green dome and exquisite interior. It was to al-Madinah that the Prophet fled (in 622 CE) when his teachings were resisted by his fellow citizens in Makkah. Al-Madinah, whose ancient name was Yathrib, lay on a principal north-south caravan route. Its essentially Arabian character largely survives today.

Islam in Today's World

"SURELY in the creation of the heavens and earth and in the alternation of night and day there are signs for men possessed of minds who remember God, standing and sitting and on their sides, and reflect upon the creation of the heavens and the earth: 'Our Lord, Thou has not created this for vanity. Glory be to Thee! Guard us against the chastisement of the Fire.' "
Qur'an III, 187

Islam and Knowledge

"Hast thou not seen how that God sends down out of heaven water, and therewith We bring forth fruits of diverse hues? And in the mountains are streaks white and red, of diverse hues, and pitchy black; men too, and beasts and cattle – diverse are their hues. Even so only those of His servants fear God who have knowledge."
Qur'an XXXV, 26

"Say: 'Are they equal – those who know and those who know not?' Only men possessed of minds remember."
Qur'an XXXIX, 12

". . . God will raise up in rank those of you who believe and have been given knowledge."
Qur'an LVIII, 12

These verses are but a small sample of the many in the Holy Book of Islam, the Qur'an, where knowledge and men of knowledge are given such a high place. From them we can see that Islam looks at knowledge – including science – not just as a friend of faith and of God-fearing men, but, more imortant, as the right way to piety; hence the special position of the 'men of knowledge'. Islam not only encourages people "to seek knowledge from the cradle to the grave" (as the Prophet Muhammad has instructed his followers), but considers fact-finding and scientific discovery as a form of worship, provided no evil is intended. In fact, the

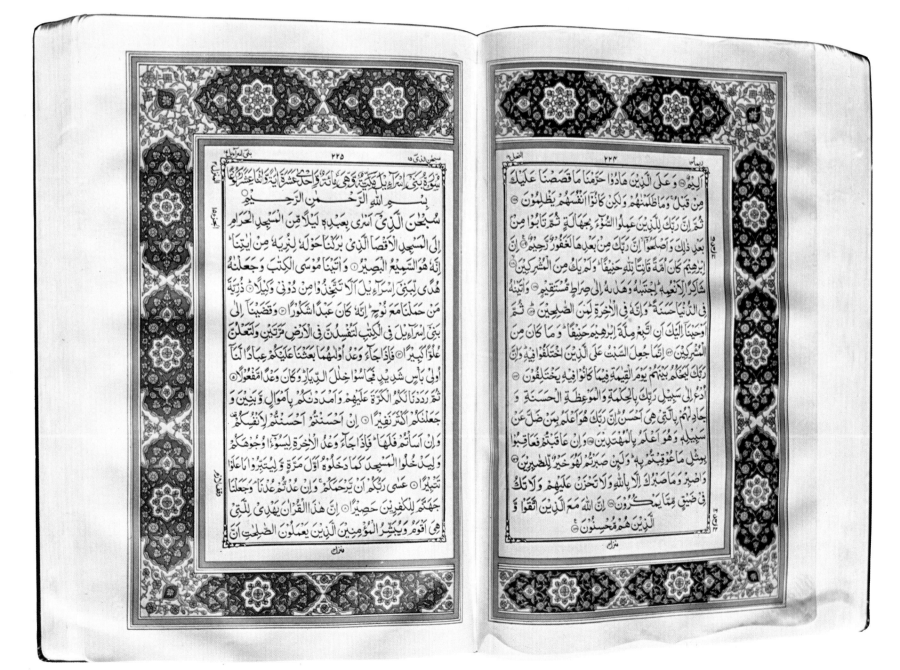

Prophet Muhammad is reported to have said, "To seek knowledge is obligatory on every Muslim, male and female." He also said, "Whoever takes a road in search of knowledge God will ease for him a way to Paradise." The first verses revealed by Almighty God to the prophet Muhammad were directly related to the question of knowledge and the search for it. The revelation of the Holy Qur'an began with the words "Recite: In the Name of thy Lord who created, created Man of a blood-clot. Recite: And thy Lord is the Most Generous, who taught by the Pen, taught Man, that he knew not" (XCVI, 1-5). Reading and the pen – the basic tools in the search for, and dissemination of, knowledge!

The road to knowledge which leads to paradise has many landmarks, and the Qur'an has much to say about them.

On the liberation of the mind from the shackles of convention, tradition and every sort of prejudice that may affect one's judgement, we read in the Qur'an: "And when it is said to them, 'Follow what God has sent down,' they say, 'No; but we will follow such things as we found our fathers doing.' What? And if their fathers had no understanding of anything, and if they were not guided?"

The words of the Qur'an, the Holy Book of Islam, are believed by Muslims to have originated from God himself, who revealed them to the Prophet Muhammad. It has become perhaps the world's most influential book. It is recited frequently by believers and is constantly under study, as in a library of al-Madinah (above).

In another part we read: "And when it is said to them, 'Come now to what God has sent down, and the Messenger', they say, 'Enough for us is what we found our fathers doing.' What, even if their fathers had knowledge of naught and were not guided?" (V, 104). These and other verses express the Qur'an's strong condemnation of blind imitation and the mere acceptance of traditions inherited from others, even from one's own father. The Qur'an actually gives mention to "thinking", the "mind" and synonymous expressions in no less than three hundred places.

Contemplation and observation are of equal importance: the Qur'an has instructed Muslims to take advantage of the gifts of mind and time provided to them by their Bounteous Lord. They are encouraged to go through the land and observe the marvellous and intricate systems in the skies as well as on earth, animate and inanimate. "Surely in the creation of the heavens and earth and in the alternation of night and day there are *signs for men possessed of minds*" (III, 195). "What, do they not consider how the camel was created, how heaven was lifted up, how the mountains were

hoisted, how the earth was out-stretched?" (LXXXVIII, 17-20). "*Hast thou not regarded* thy Lord, how He has stretched out the shadow? Had he willed, He would have made it still. Then We appointed the sun, to be a guide to it . . . It is He who appointed the night for you to be a garment and sleep for a rest, and day He appointed for a rising. And it is He who has loosed the winds, bearing good tidings before his Mercy; and We send down from heaven pure water so that We might revive a dead land, and give to drink of it . . ." (XXV, 46-50). "What, have they not *beheld* heaven above them, how We have built it, and decked it out fair, and it has no cracks? And the earth – We stretched it forth, and cast on it firm mountains, and We caused to grow therein of every joyous kind for *an insight and a reminder* to every penitent servant" (L, 6-8). There are many more examples; out of more than six thousand verses in the Qur'an no less than seven hundred deal with natural phenomena.

One of the necessary steps in the search for facts is the process of comparing and contrasting the evidence. Scores of Qur'anic verses teach us to do just that. "Not equal are the two seas; this is sweet grateful to taste, delicious to drink, and that is salt, bitter to the tongue" (XXXV, 13). "It is He who sent down out of heaven water, and thereby We have brought forth the shoot of every plant, and then We have brought forth the green leaf of it, bringing forth from it close-compounded grain, and out of the palm-tree, from the spathe of it, dates thick-clustered, ready to the hand, and gardens of vines, olives, pomegranates, like each to each, and each unlike to each. Look upon their fruits when they fructify and ripen! Surely, in all this are signs for a people who do believe" (VI, 98).

The Qur'an teaches man to be careful and enlightened in his judgements, and to base these judgements on a foundation of knowledge, rather than mere guess-work. It teaches: "And pursue not that thou hast no knowledge of; the hearing, the sight, the heart – all of those shall be questioned of" (XVII, 38).

Humility also is a key feature of Qur'anic teaching. In order that we may

The essential simplicity of the faith is upheld by Saudi Arabia – in its village mosques (right), and in the adherence to the rules of regular prayer (far right).

not think that we know everything (and become arrogant or ignorant), the Qur'an tells the Prophet: "They will question thee concerning the Spirit. Say: 'The Spirit is of the bidding of my Lord. *You have been given of knowledge nothing except a little*'" (XVII, 87). "He knows what lies before them and what is after them, and *they comprehend not anything of His knowledge save such as He wills*" (II, 257).

The Views of Islamic Scholarship
Though the reaction of the Muslim masses to the scientific and technological achievements of the present age is a mixed one, ranging from the dazzled and bewitched to the sceptic or nonchalant, it seems that the scholars of Islam agree on the following points.

Science and technology are not the property of any one person or nation, and they are not the products of any specific religion or ideology. So there is nothing wrong in accepting and contributing to them. In fact, whatever is beneficial to man in science and technology is recommended for a Muslim. For the Prophet of Islam said: "Wisdom is the believer's lost camel, wherever he finds it he has the greatest right to it." The Holy Book of Islam tells us that scientific investigation leads to the discovery of the marvellous works of our Creator; therefore, it should be appreciated and encouraged. This explains the great contributions made by Muslim scholars who bore the torch of knowledge during the Middle Ages when science and scientific investigation were regarded with great

suspicion elsewhere, particularly in the West.

Science and technology are a means of discovery. Neither they nor man are creators or substitutes for the Creator, because science only unveils what is already present in the universe. Therefore, scientific achievements, however marvellous, should not lead us to atheism; the two things are unrelated.

The Qur'an tells us that whatever is in the skies and whatever is on earth were made serviceable to man by his Lord and Master, Almighty God. "Have you not seen how that God has subjected to you whatsoever is in the heavens and the earth, and He has lavished on you His blessings, outward and inward?" (XXXI, 19). We are also told that man was created to be "On the earth a viceroy (of

"From whatsoever place thou issuest, turn my face towards the Holy Mosque."

God)" (II, 28), and that man has been honoured by God and given preference above many of God's creation (XVII, 70). Accordingly, we must not be slaves to things material, and we should be above the pursuit of sheer animal satisfaction. Man should take his responsibility seriously, remembering his proper place in the universal scheme.

Since science and technology are amoral, they can be used both to the advantage of man and to his disadvantage and destruction. The only way we can guard against the evil misuse of the scientific achievements of this age is by reviving religious consciousness and by adhering

to the moral values of Islam, values which preach man's responsibility to God, on the Day of Judgement, for the security and peace of his fellow men.

Science and technology can help man only in matters material. Faith alone can help him achieve spiritual satisfaction and psychological well-being. As the Qur'an puts it, "It is in the remembrance of Allah that hearts may find serenity and peace." (XIII, 28).

Renderings of the Qur'an from *The Koran Interpreted* by Arthur J. Arberry, published by Oxford University Press.

6 The Cultural Heritage

What men recite and sing, what they forge and fashion, have been determined above all by the genius of holy scripture and the demands and joys of life in the desert and oasis. But the cities have seldom lacked an infusion of ideas and skills from the wider world.

The dagger is of typical formalistic Arabian design, avoiding direct representation.

The superb craftsmanship of the Makkan veil (left and far left) *in gold and pearls dates from the last century.*

THE truest culture of Arabia rests not in things but in words, in the language. This is not only because in the nomadic life a man can possess no more than he and his camel can carry, but because the Holy Book, the Qur'an, is the fount of his culture as it is of his faith, and the verbal richness of the Qur'an is without parallel.

As Islam became established throughout Arabia, the followers of the Prophet drew on the heritage of Arab tribal thought. Adherence to the Holy Law constituted the primary act of faith. The absence of a priesthood meant that no clear distinction arose between the religious and the secular. No part of a man's daily life, or his thought, or his culture, lay outside his religion.

The religious scholars who chronicled the early centuries of Islam incorporated in their works the sagas and genealogies of tribal life as well as the career of the Prophet and the Community of the Faithful. The traditions they recorded became precedents for the legal and social fabric of Islam. This body of writing emphasizes the significance of human lives and human acts. It contributed to the forming of a self-aware Islamic culture in the Land of the Prophet.

For its part, the Holy Qur'an itself, in its style, not only took into consideration the poetic traditions of the Beduin, but also challenged their literary talent. Before the appearance of the Holy Book, the Beduin had no written code of law,

and only the custom of the blood vendetta ensured the protection of a man's life. Leaders had to rely on their own merits for their authority: it was necessary for such men to demonstrate the qualities which entitled them to their position. The spare nomadic life of the Beduin offered little chance for the development of the material arts. Only those forms which could survive the harsh demands of their existence were cultivated.

The nomad jealously nurtured his language as his single unalienable good. By nature he was, and is, a rhetorician. The poet, the man of eloquence, was prized almost above all others in the community. His gifts and powers, believed to have been inspired by spirits, had already evolved a complex art form.

Weaponry

Brass, wood and leather are the traditional materials for decorated shields. The leather is of camel hide, and the wood is often tamarisk.

Powder horns (above) *take their design with surprising literalness from the shape of ram's horns. The silversmith's craft in Arabia has for centuries been lavished on the hilts of swords* (left) *and daggers, and their sheaths.*

Although skilled smiths plied their trade in every permanent settlement, the development of intricate workmanship in precious metals was largely confined to major centres such as Makkah, Jiddah and the Gulf ports. Metal work was often imported from Oman and Yemen. Distinctive designs evolved in central Arabia and regional styles emerged in, for example, Qasim and Sudayr. Until the second quarter of this century, it was customary for every male to regard himself as properly dressed only when he was armed – with dagger or rifle or both – for ceremonial rather than defensive purposes.

Poets sang of their lives, loves and land, but they also served as promulgators of the virtues and merits of their own tribes. The obligations of social values such as hospitality, generosity and courage were a matter of honour. Failure to uphold this unwritten code resulted in insult, and it was in this respect that poetic panegyrics possessed an enormous moral force for the Beduin, and had a regulatory effect within the community. The Prophet himself had to contend, through Muslim poets, with opponents who used the gift of poetry against him in al-Madinah.

The first revelations to Muhammad were spoken in rhymed prose consisting of short phrases. These were taken down during his lifetime and were grouped into chapters which became collectively known as the Recitation, or Qur'an.

There is no trace of Arabic prose before Islam, and although examples in the same form may have existed before, they were never written down. It was only the special nature of Muhammad's messages which caused them to be recorded. The Holy Book's concern was not to produce a literary work, but to communicate the meaning which formed itself in it. To do this, the Qur'an initially employed a forceful, rhythmic and rhyming prose, for example:

"We have taught Muhammad no poetry, nor does it beseem him to be a poet. This is but a warning, an eloquent Qur'an to admonish the living and to pass judgement on the unbelievers." *Qur'an* XXXVI, 69.

Islam gathered in not only the poetic traditions but the practice of pilgrimage. Makkah's sanctity, reaffirmed and redefined by Muhammad, had attracted pilgrims from very ancient times. The last stopping place on the route from the south, lying somewhere between Taif and Makkah, was the fabled town of Ukaz. Here, during the four-month season of the "holy truce", travellers gathered to meet their fellows, to trade, to recuperate for the last leg of their journey, and to recite.

Poems were composed in honour of the powerful and were paid for in gold and silver. Swift fame was guaranteed to the

Embossing

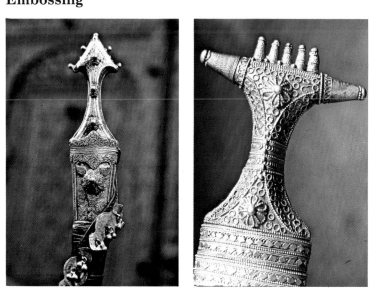

Influences from Oman and Turkey have mingled with traditional Arabian techniques to produce a variety of designs for dagger-hilts and sheaths (shown here).

With the introduction of firearms in the late eighteenth century, metal-smiths turned their skills to the decoration of rifles.

successful poet. Here first developed the *Qasidah*, the ode in celebration of desert heroes – "appearing with Homeric suddenness", as Philip Hitti, the historian has written, "and surpassing the Iliad and Odyssey in metrical complexity and elaboration."

Unquestionably, the poetic rhythms have been influenced by the gait of the camel. First to emerge was the rhythmic prose of the sages and travelling poets. From such prose grew the *Rajaz*, the four or six beat metre, rhymed prose for the father and song for the mother, spoken or sung to the lilt of travel by camelback.

And so eloquence was, and has been ever since, allowed its place in Arabian culture. The flow of poetry and well-turned precepts has continued down the centuries, sagas of battles, journeys, loves and loyalties, moral tales and aphorisms as guides to the conduct of life, passed by word of mouth, from generation to generation, sometimes sung or chanted, sometimes accompanied by the stringed *rababa*.

The pure doctrine discouraged dancing and licence, and any extravagance of display or decoration. Yet no group in Saudi Arabia are without their traditions of communal rejoicing. And the sense of elegant design and craftsmanship is evident from the meanest artefact or utensil of daily life to the finest and most intricately wrought of garments or weapons.

The nomadic life of the desert has always existed in interdependence with the settled life of the oasis, or well-watered south-west, or the cities and ports. No Saudi Arabian settlement was without its craftsmen of ancient tradition bronze-smiths, brass-smiths, gun-smiths and swordsmiths, potters and weavers and dyers, makers of incense burners and coffee mortars, makers – and players – of musical instruments.

In the earlier past would have been found fletchers and bowmakers, and specialists in the manufacture of intricate bird traps. And in the ancient past – revealed today in the Riyadh Museum of Archaeology and Ethnography – elegant stone tools were worked by the Neolithic inhabitants of the Rub al-Khali and Eastern Province.

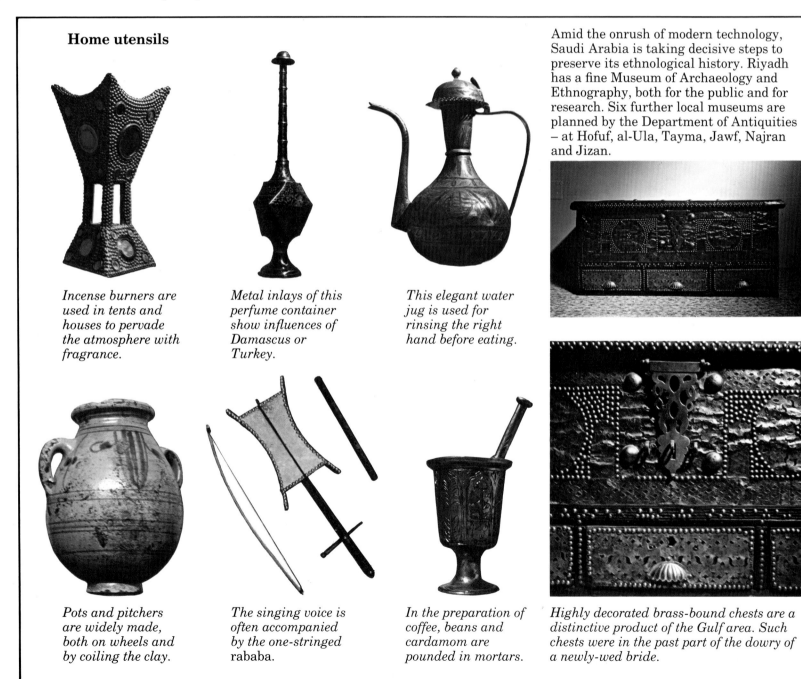

Home utensils

Incense burners are used in tents and houses to pervade the atmosphere with fragrance.

Metal inlays of this perfume container show influences of Damascus or Turkey.

This elegant water jug is used for rinsing the right hand before eating.

Amid the onrush of modern technology, Saudi Arabia is taking decisive steps to preserve its ethnological history. Riyadh has a fine Museum of Archaeology and Ethnography, both for the public and for research. Six further local museums are planned by the Department of Antiquities – at Hofuf, al-Ula, Tayma, Jawf, Najran and Jizan.

Pots and pitchers are widely made, both on wheels and by coiling the clay.

The singing voice is often accompanied by the one-stringed rababa.

In the preparation of coffee, beans and cardamom are pounded in mortars.

Highly decorated brass-bound chests are a distinctive product of the Gulf area. Such chests were in the past part of the dowry of a newly-wed bride.

The main centres, above all Makkah, would attract those with the finer skills: calligraphers and illuminators of holy manuscripts, ceramicists and workers in gold and silver thread, fine leatherworkers, cabinet-makers and chest-makers (this was a speciality of the Gulf, with its seafaring tradition), and those skilled in embossing and engraving, especially of guns.

Many of these crafts were carried on in the tribes. Today they have largely been supplanted by imported, mass-produced goods. But the day of the Saudi craftsman is not done, for the discerning prize quality "Arabian" handiwork.

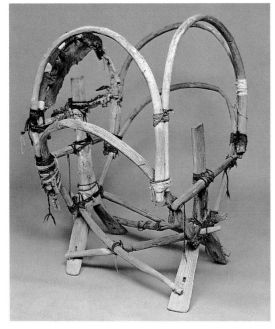

The maksar, *or woman's riding litter, is constructed from a saddle frame of bent wood with elongated horns* (above), *and is covered with a blanket for use* (top).

A classic camel pack (above) *is made from a continuous panel of sheep's wool woven with cotton and stitched at the sides to form a double bag on the* camel's sides; tassles provide rich ornamentation.

Jewellery

In the self-sufficient life demanded by the desert, traditional crafts retain their importance. Each settlement will have amongst its numbers weavers, leatherworkers, coppersmiths and silversmiths and, until recently, gunsmiths.

Metalworking is a fine skill much prized by townsfolk, villagers and Beduin alike, and for centuries jewellery has formed an integral part of female attire in Arabia. The jewellery is both capital and a celebration of matrimony and the approach of motherhood. A portion of a woman's bridal settlement is paid in jewellery; thereafter this becomes part of her personal wealth to keep or dispose of as she will. It is also the usual custom to present a woman with new pieces of jewellery whenever she bears a son. A Beduin bride's dowry will still largely comprise a rich mass of silver jewellery, and at her wedding she may be heavily caparisoned with headpieces and collars, earrings and necklaces, bangles and bracelets, besides amulets and belts. Since red, blue and green are regarded as protective, the silverware is often studded with amber, coral, lapis lazuli, garnets, agate, carnelian or turquoise. The individual pieces are wrought anew for each bride, and as a rule all are melted down at her death. Yet the designs (so widely admired today throughout the world) have remained extraordinarily constant for hundreds, indeed thousands, of years, as pre-Islamic grave relics demonstrate.

Necklaces, frequently adorned with such ancient motifs as hand charms and crescents, have long stood as a symbol for love in romantic poetry. Many other jewellery forms are decorated with relief work which may include granulation, filigree, repoussé or niello details. Chain links and complex wire work based on the figure eight are also common, as are bells and coinage of all sorts.

Pictorial symbols and their stylized geometric equivalents, such as hands, crescents and triangles, are frequently found in Saudi jewellery and, as in much other Islamic art, provide protection from evil (the crescent's power in this respect is mentioned in Isaiah 3:8). The sign of the hand (the so-called hand of Fatima, daughter of the Prophet Muhammad) is closely associated with the number five representing the five tenets of Islam; a combination of related pieces worn together often offers an allusion to this.

Extracted from: (left) H. C. Ross, *Bedouin Jewellery in Saudi Arabia; (right)* John Topham, *Traditional Crafts of Saudi Arabia.*

Heavy silver coinage decorates the fringe of a Beduin headpiece (opposite top), *while a forehead pendant* (opposite middle) *is formed from turquoise ornamented with pearls. Bracelets from central Arabia are characterized by geometric chasing* (top left), *and soldered ornamentation* (top middle); *the ring* (top right) *is worn on the fourth finger. The leather, stamped-silver strap-and-buckle bracelet* (middle) *comes from the Asir. The general term for necklace is* qiladah; *a necklace with five amber beads* (bottom left) *is called a* qiladat anbar, *while a neckpiece* (bottom right) *is a* kirdalah.

The Government of Saudi Arabia

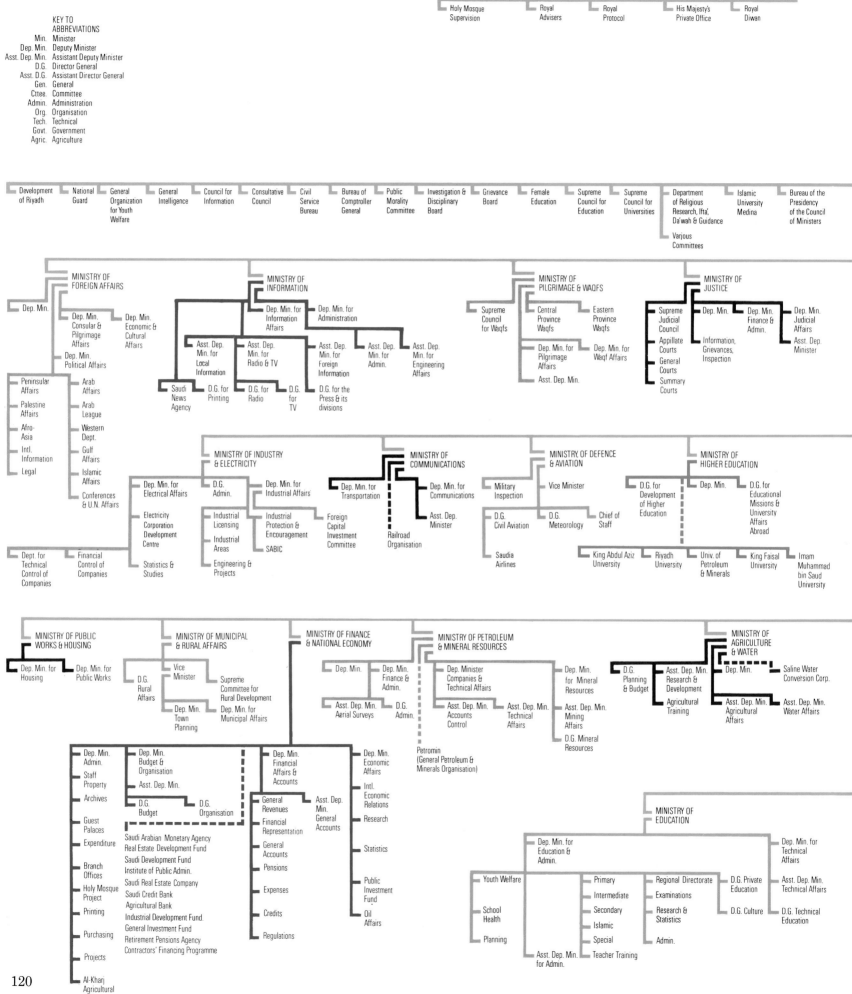

120

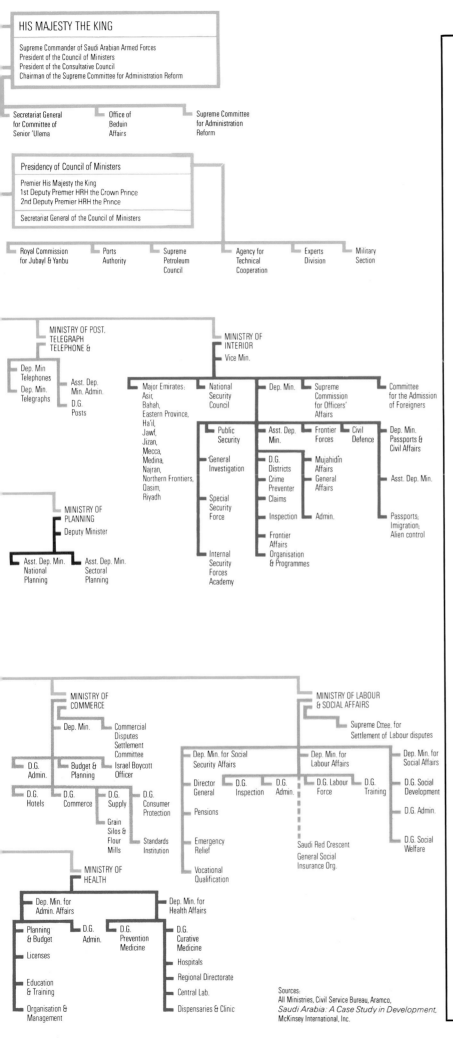

7
Government

A monarchy built upon consultation and consent has proved flexible enough to sustain benevolent and enlightened rule in a period of unprecedented change. The Qur'anic foundation has held firm, supporting the complex structures required to govern a modern state.

Sources:
All Ministries, Civil Service Bureau, Aramco,
Saudi Arabia: A Case Study in Development,
McKinsey International, Inc.

The lines of authority and rule, evolved from the days of King Abdul Aziz, but formalized under the late King Faisal, give to Saudi Arabia a coherent and effective Government structure; the diagram opposite should be reviewed in the light of latest developments.

Monarchy

MORE than any other country in the modern world, Saudi Arabia is identified with her monarch. The King represents his people in a unique and individual way; he is their champion and they trust him. He speaks to them directly on all major matters which affect the welfare, honour and interests of the nation.

Kingship in the Arab lands has always been based on identity with the teaching of the Prophet and on prowess in war and peace. In addition, the people have expected their king to acquire wisdom, experience and the art of diplomacy.

Although the monarchy of Saudi Arabia is often described abroad as 'absolute', this is not accurate in the sense that Far Eastern monarchies were at one time absolute. No divinity has ever attached to Islamic kings. They are as their subjects are. Allah, alone, is God and under him all men are equal. It is not done to bow to an Arabian monarch.

The King's role is to lead his nation and keep in constant touch with the people. The legislative and executive power in Saudi Arabia is exercised by the Council of Ministers. When they draft a decree, they submit it to the King for signature. He may return it for further consideration, but the whole active operation of the government machine is carried out by the Council.

The King either is or appoints the Prime Minister who chooses his colleagues. Their names are also submitted to the King who has a close working relationship with his Council. The Prime Minister has wide powers of supervision and control over the Ministries and departments, and he is responsible for directing the policy of the State. He also gets reports from the audit council and from the Grievance Bureau, essentially the Saudi Arabian version of the Ombudsman.

The proof of the efficacy of any given form of government is the success it achieves. Saudi Arabia has greatly strengthened her international Arab and Islamic power and prestige. Beneficial agreements have been tenaciously negotiated with the foreign oil companies as the Saudi Government has sought a modern oil industry, maximising indigenous control and exploitation. The standard of living of Saudi Arabia's people has been improved at a rate which no-one could have foreseen, and at the same time friendly relations with other powers in the West and in the East have been preserved and promoted. It is undeniably a success story.

Saudi Arabia has no intention of introducing Western-type parliamentary democracy. In this unique country the Qur'an appears a firmer basis for law, order and progress than the ballot box. Moreover there must be a wide degree of real democracy in a nation where the individual dignity of all men is recognized. The Head of State is available to anybody with a petition to present or a complaint to make, and this right is constantly exercised; the King is referred to by his given name. Ordinary citizens can and do have direct access to him on fixed days of the week. The King personally initiates the appropriate action or enquiry. However, proposals have been made over the years to broaden the base of government decision-making and, in 1980, constitutional provision was made for a consultative assembly of leading citizens, the Majlis al-Shura, to be instituted.

The monarchy of Saudi Arabia is refined by the Islamic concept of government which considers that "every shepherd is responsible for his flock" (as the Prophet said), and "were a sheep to fall from the bank of the Euphrates (the governor) will be responsible on the Day of Judgement for having failed to make a safe path for it." It reflects the tribal notion of administration exemplified by the proverb, "The master of the people is their servant."

The House of Saud – the Royal Family of Saudi Arabia

When the late King Abdul Aziz ibn Saud by royal decree in September 1932 changed the name of his realm from "Hijaz and Najd and its Dependencies" to "The Kingdom of Saudi Arabia", not only did the new style express the unity of a greater part of the Arabian peninsula than at any time since the Prophet Muhammad but also forever identified the new country with the family of its founder – the House of Saud.

Today, His Majesty King Fahd ibn Abdul Aziz ibn Abd al-Rahman Al Faisal Al Saud, eighth son of the late King Abdul Aziz and fourth to succeed him, is ruler of the modern Islamic state of Saudi Arabia, in the government and administration of which other members of the large Royal Family also play an active and leading role.

Major posts, however, are often filled by Saudi citizens who are not connected to the Royal Family.

Administration

SAUDI ARABIA IS an Islamic monarchy which has been developing from monarchical to ministerial rule. The duties of the King-Imam are defined in the Shari'ah law (religious Islamic law as recorded in the Qur'an and interpreted in the Hadith, the Prophet's sayings) which recognizes the Imam not as an absolute hereditary monarch but as one who reigns in order to rule for the public good.

The modern history of Saudi Arabia begins with the recapture of Riyadh by King Abdul Aziz ibn Abd al-Rahman Al Faisal Al Saud in 1902. Other conquests followed and the Kingdom's international position was confirmed by a series of treaties, the most important of which was the Treaty of Jiddah signed in 1927, when Britain recognized the complete independence of the state in return for a pledge by King Abdul Aziz to abstain from attacking the Gulf Sheikhdoms. In 1932 the name Saudi Arabia was adopted.

The Royal Decrees, proclaimed in 1953 and 1958, which provided for a Council of Ministers and laid down its functions, may be regarded as the beginning of the "constitutional regime".

At the present time King Fahd heads the Government as Prime Minister; the First Deputy Prime Minister is Crown Prince Abdullah ibn Abdul Aziz, who also has charge of the National Guard, and the Second Deputy Prime Minister is Prince Sultan ibn Abdul Aziz, also Defence Minister. The other members of the Council of Ministers – some of whom belong to the Royal Family – include the Ministers of Defence and Aviation, the Interior, Finance and National Economy, Foreign Affairs, Petroleum and Mineral Resources, Justice, Industry and Electricity, Planning, Agriculture and Water, Transport, Communications, Commerce, Higher Education, Education, Information, Health, Labour

Administrative headquarters

The Administration Centre for the industrial city of Jubayl with its efficient offices grouped around a refreshing, landscaped court in the middle of the building (top). *The Ministry of Interior with its innovative cantilevered construction is a new landmark in Riyadh's Olaya district* (middle). *Samarec's Jeddah headquarters uses motifs from both traditional and modern influences* bottom left). *The Ministry of Post, Telegraph and Telephone* (bottom right) *combines a hexagonal structure with traditional colonnades and screening.*

and Social Affairs, Pilgrimage and Waqfs, Public Works and Housing, and Municipal and Rural Affairs.

Ministers are responsible to the King. Almost all the apparatus of modern government – ministries, civil service, budgeting systems and so on – has been set up since 1955; in the early 1950s the Ministry of Finance was the only executive department of government. An independent judiciary and a modern judicial system were part of a reform programme begun in 1962, but the first Minister of Justice was not appointed until 1970.

Although there are no elections and no political parties, Saudi Arabia has its own form of Islamic democracy. All men are regarded as equal, and differences are minimized between the rich and the poor, the governors and the governed. Ministers and officials keep their doors open so that anyone with any business can call in, without prior appointment, and be offered refreshment in accordance with Arab customs. A morning visitor to a senior official may find himself waiting with a large number of other callers; and since most of the official's morning may be spent receiving visitors in this way, he often needs to return to his office in the evening to do uninterrupted work when the office is closed.

An element of decentralization was introduced in 1963 when the country was divided into four provinces: Western (Hijaz), Central (Najd), South Western (Asir) and Eastern Province (Hasa), each with an appointed governor, or Emir, who is charged with local administration, maintenance of order and implementation of Shari'ah judgements.

Today the country is divided into 14 Administrative Divisions: Riyadh, Makkah, al-Madinah, the Eastern Province, Asir, Najran, Jizan, Bahah, Qasim, Hail, Tabuk, Qurayyat, Jawf, and the Northern Frontier. Various ministries have field offices, and the Ministry of the Interior is responsible for appointing the Emirs, but Saudi Arabia has no effective local government as the term is understood in Western democracies.

The municipalities are completely dependent on central Government for funds. The people expect the Government to provide whatever utilities and services are necessary, and the Government accepts an obligation to do so. The only form of local election is for council members, called al-Majlis al-Baladi, who have a purely advisory function, their advice being directed to the chief municipal executive. A "direct system" of local administration was approved in principle by Royal Decree in 1963.

Oil provides nearly all the Government's revenue, which in turn through contracts, salaries, loans and subsidies and gifts is the prime source of wealth in the economy. There is no income tax. Because of the heavy dependence on oil products, many of the Government's plans are aimed at diversification: by increasing farming and stimulating industry and mining.

The Civil Service Commission is responsible for staffing policies throughout the public service. Considerable efforts are being made in the direction of administrative innovation and reform, and impressive training schemes are being introduced to improve the structure and processes of public administration. The Institute of Public Administration, which was established in Riyadh by Royal Decree in 1961 as a semi-independent public agency, provides training and further education for civil servants, undertakes research, and assists government departments in reorganization and reform. It is probably the biggest and best equipped institute of its kind in the Middle East.

The Government's general objectives are to provide for national security and economic and social stability, and to raise the living standards of the people, while maintaining the religious and moral values for which the Kingdom, as the original homeland of Islam, is so well known.

The most difficult administrative problem is the shortage of manpower. Although increased effort is remedying this through the process of "Saudization" – including study of a possible wider working role for women beyond education and social services – it is unlikely that the Government will achieve its social and economic objectives without considerable short-term help from non-Saudis. Their numerical presence is being tightly controlled and it will be a matter of great interest to see how Saudi Arabia continues to develop towards objectives which anywhere else would be considered virtually irreconcilable.

Statistical sources: Ministry of Education and Ministry of Planning.

The Basis of Law

IN SAUDI ARABIA - uniquely in the modern world – Islamic law, in its Hanbali interpretation, still reigns virtually supreme. Article six in the Fundamental Law of the Hijaz, 1926, unequivocally declares that "The law in the Kingdom of the Hijaz shall always conform to the Book of God, the Sunnah of the Prophet and the conduct of the Companions of the Prophet and of their Pious Followers." A year later King Abdul Aziz proposed that a code of Islamic law should be drawn up based not only on the doctrine of the Hanbali school but on that of whichever school seemed closest to the Qur'an and Sunnah (or practice of the Prophet) on the particular point concerned. The Hanbali *ulama* (scholars learned in the school of law named after the great jurist-theologian Ahmad ibn Hanbal, who died in 855) persuaded him to abandon this project, and regulations issued in 1928 and 1930 made it obligatory on the *qadis*, or judges, to follow the recognised Hanbali texts. But in 1934 he affirmed his own policy, when he said: "We are seekers of the truth. We will accept what is sound in any school of thought or from any *alim* (learned Muslim scholar) . . . We obey neither Ibn Abd al-Wahhab (the founder of the Wahhabi school of thought) nor any other person unless what they said was clearly endorsed by the Book of God and the Sunnah of the Prophet. God made us – me, my fathers and ancestors – preachers and teachers according to the Qur'an and the Sunnah. So, whenever we find strong proof in any of the four schools, we will refer to it and be bound by it. Should we fail to find the evidence there, then we would resort to the teachings of Imam Ahmad ibn Hanbal."

Until about the middle of the last century, Islamic law (the Shari'ah or "path to a watering place") was dominant throughout the whole Muslim world. It was regarded as being firmly based on divine revelation, the only way in which man could distinguish between virtue and vice.

How was the divine will to be ascertained? First, from the Qur'an or "Book of God", which is regarded by orthodox

Muslims as having been written from eternity in Arabic in heaven and revealed to Muhammad, as occasion demanded, by the archangel Gabriel. But there is comparatively little in the Qur'an which is of direct legal significance; so the second of the *usul al-fiqh* (or sources of the divine law as put together and systematized by the jurist-theologians of Islam) was the Sunnah or practice of Muhammad, equally inspired in content although not in form, and derived from a mass of Traditions (*hadith*) as to what he had said, done or allowed to be done. Even this, however, was not enough. In very early days a judge or jurist would, where necessary, fall back on his own opinion (*ra'y*) of what was consonant with the spirit of the faith. But the view soon gained ground that this was far too fallible and subjective a source for a divine law: too fallible, so *ijma* or the consensus of the Muslim community (in practice, that of its jurists) came to be accepted as another reliable indication of the divine will; too subjective, so the "opinion" of an individual judge or jurist was replaced by *qiyas*, or the science of analogical deductions from one of the primary sources.

In early days, any qualified jurist was regarded as entitled to exercise *ijtihad*: that is, to go back to the authoritative sources of the law and deduce from them the solution to a particular problem. But soon the jurist-theologians began to draw together in schools, based in some cases primarily on a geographical area, and in others on their allegiance to some outstanding lawyer or theologian. With the crystallization of these schools, most Muslims came to regard the "door of *ijtihad*" as having been virtually closed, and all future lawyers as mere *muqallids* (men bound to accept as authoritative the views of the great scholars of the past). With the passage of time, moreover, the number of law schools in orthodox or Sunni Islam became limited to four; the Hanafis, Malikis, Shafi'is and Hanbalis. The Hanbali school relied on traditional rather than "speculative" material.

There were, however, a very limited number of Muslim jurists who not only proclaimed that the "door of *ijtihad*" had never been closed, but that they were themselves *mujtahids*, or men who had the right to exercise the faculty of *ijtihad*. Hence the suggestion made by King Abdul Aziz about following the doctrine of whichever school seemed closest to the Qur'an and Sunnah on any particular point. The opposition of the Hanbali *ulama* was not only to such freedom of choice but to the very idea of any official compilation of the divine law. As a result, the law in Saudi Arabia is still derived principally from some six Hanbali texts, although some *qadis* exercise a certain amount of discretion.

The degree of legal orthodoxy which still prevails in Saudi Arabia contrasts with the course of development, since the middle of the last century, in the greater part of the Muslim world, where the Shari'ah has been progressively displaced by codes of commercial, criminal and even civil law which are largely of Western inspiration, and the Shari'ah, as such, has been chiefly confined to the law of personal status (marriage, divorce, succession, etc). Even in this sphere, moreover, the Islamic law has often been reduced to a codified form, during the last half century, by legislation based on a process of selection and reinterpretation. As a result, Saudi Arabia is virtually the only country today in which the criminal law of Islam is still in full force – characterized first by the treatment of homicide and wounding primarily as civil wrongs which involve blood-money or some other form of compensation; then by the imposition of certain very severe penalties for a few precisely defined crimes such as theft, brigandage, illicit sex relations and the consumption of alcohol (provided the offence can be proved by the oral testimony of the requisite number of unimpeachable, adult, male witnesses); and by discretionary punishments in all other cases. This is why one sometimes still hears of an adulterer being stoned to death, or a thief having his right hand amputated.

Throughout the Muslim world, however, a number of other courts, such as those of the local governor, the police and the inspector of markets, have always exercised jurisdiction alongside that of the *qadis*, together with a Court of Complaints presided over by the Caliph himself or some powerful official appointed by him, which acted, *inter alia*, as an unofficial court of appeal. And none of these other courts were, in practice, as strictly bound by the Shari'ah as were those of the *qadis*.

It was inherent in the theory of Islamic jurisprudence that there was exceedingly little scope for State legislation. According to a commonly accepted classification, all human actions were subsumed under one of five categories: what God had positively commanded, had recommended, had left legally indifferent, had reprobated or had actually forbidden. So it was only in the middle category (things left legally indifferent) that there was, in theory, any scope for human legislation. For the rest, the Shari'ah was regarded as a divinely given blue-print by which all Muslims should abide.

In Saudi Arabia much of this concept still survives – although, in concession to the exigencies of modern life, an increasing number of administrative regulations promulgated by the Government stand beside the Shari'ah. These have the force of law; but they are normally termed either *nizam* (regulation) or *marsum* (royal decree) rather than *qanun* (which is the normal term for legislation throughout the Middle East). Such royal decrees have provided for a hierarchy of courts – Summary Courts, High Courts and a "Commission of Judicial Supervision". Summary Courts are of two types, one of which deals with Beduin affairs and the other with minor criminal and financial cases in urban areas. High Courts consist of three or four judges and try the more serious criminal and financial cases, together with matters of personal status or family law. In the more remote districts, local governors, sometimes assisted by a *qadi*, deal with crimes, civil litigation, tribal customs and mediation. The Office of the Chief *Qadi* and the Commission of Judicial Supervision have now been replaced by a Minister of Justice and a Supreme Judicial Council. The Supreme Judicial Council, which consists of twenty members chosen from the leading jurists and *ulama*, has the function, *inter alia*, of issuing *fatawa* or opinions on points of law and religion, and thus of adapting the law as traditionally accepted to the changing needs of contemporary life. But the ultimate responsibility for promulgating and implementing legislation remains with the Council of Ministers and with the King himself whose decrees have the force of law, who endorses the regulations formulated by the Council of Ministers and by whom sentences of execution or amputation must normally be confirmed.

One of the major functions of the Judicial Council is to resolve any conflict between the Qur'an and Sunnah on the one hand and the demands of modernization on the other.

125

Defending the Country

Saudi Arabia's vast size and scattered centres require formidable defence. Since 1965, under the leadership of H.R.H. Prince Sultan ibn Abdul Aziz, the Minister of Defence and Aviation, enormous efforts have been made to build up a sizeable army, an air force with about one-third the army's manpower, and a navy, all equipped with the latest in modern hardware.

In recent years the Kingdom has sought to diversify its sources of equipment to avoid creating an over-dependence on any single supplier. This policy is reflected in major procurement programmes with the U.S., Britain and France, and other deals with West Germany, the

Royal Saudi Air Force Tornados (above) *flying low over the desert during the Gulf conflict.*

At sea, ships from the Royal Saudi Navy protect the Kingdom's coast (opposite bottom) *alongside allied forces.*

The Royal Guard (opposite top) *is responsible for the security of the Royal family and palaces, and is present on all State occasions.*

Source: Royal Embassy of Saudi Arabia – Information Office

Netherlands, Italy and China.

The Royal Saudi Air Force is among the most formidable in the Middle East. Under the Peace Shield agreement with the U.S. F-15 and F-5 fighters can deliver an impressive combat punch, along with British Lightnings. AWACs early warning systems give an umbrella of protection. Under the Yamamah Offset Programme with Britain the R.S.A.F. will procure Tornado combat jets and light bombers as well as Hawk fighters, PC-9 aircraft and Maverick air-to-ground missiles. Other missile systems include Hawk, Crotal, Shahin and SAM missiles.

The large army includes mechanised armoured infantry, airborne brigades, and artillery battalions along with surface-to-air missile batteries. The Royal Guard Brigade is part of the Saudi combat units. The highly trained and well equipped National Guard has a separate command structure under the leadership of Prince Abdullah ibn Abdul Aziz.

The Royal Saudi Navy has over the years been transformed from a token force of patrol boats into two modern fleets which include missile boats, frigates, minesweepers, torpedo boats and supply ships, as well as command and communications equipment covering

the entire Gulf and Red Sea coastlines of the Kingdom.

Training for the armed forces is carried out in four giant Military Colleges and three large Military Cities, such as the one at Hafr al-Batn in northern Najd. Here soldiers are given a rounded education to fit them for their combat duties as well as service to the community: the armed forces pride themselves on the various civil defence tasks which they undertake in rural areas, in agriculture, construction, teaching, fire-fighting, emergency aid and medical assistance.

Saudi Arabia's commitment to the development of a mutual defence structure with the other GCC states was tried and tested during the invasion of Kuwait by Iraq. Pilots from the Royal Saudi Air Force flew cover for allied bombers in F-15 jets and also conducted low-level bombing runs in their Tornados. By the third week of the military operation, Saudi pilots had flown 4,400 of the total 67,000 air sorties against Iraqi targets.

On land, Saudi forces took part in the fierce battle to expel Iraqi forces from Al-Khafji, a Saudi town close to the Kuwaiti border. Within 48 hours they re-captured the town, taking over 400 prisoners and destroying nearly 100 Iraqi tanks.

At sea, the Royal Saudi Navy also played a major role: the guided-missile patrol craft HMS Faisal detected an Iraqi ship laying mines in Saudi territorial waters. Launching a single Harpoon anti-shipping missile from a distance of 22 sea miles, HMS Faisal sank the Iraqi vessel.

The Kingdom's efficient coordination with the GCC forces and those of other countries was crucial in the rapid resolution of this conflict.

World Affairs

THE 1990s HAVE SEEN Saudi Arabia's influence in regional and world affairs expanding.

Wealthiest of Middle Eastern countries, the world's biggest oil producer, heartland of Islam and protector of Islam's holy places, Saudi Arabia's significance is inescapable. In the climate of peace following the convulsion caused by one neighbour's invasion of and expulsion from another, Saudi Arabia's role has emerged as of central importance.

Iraq's invasion of Kuwait in 1990, and its expulsion in 1991, put Saudi Arabia to the test. Under King Fahd's leadership the country responded robustly and decisively. The principles on which its policies have rested for the past several decades were upheld and served it well.

These principles are the integrity of Islam, the brotherhood of Arab nations, political level-headedness and restraint of rhetoric, economic stability and support for the rights of the Palestinian people. In addition a pragmatic, if circumspect, alliance with other major powers throughout the world ready to work alongside Saudi Arabia in its development and defence without exercising undue influence within the country.

The management of the alliance of Arab states plus the US, Britain, and other Western powers operating from Saudi Arabia and some of its Gulf neighbours, which reversed Iraq's assault on Kuwait, proved the effectiveness of Saudi Arabia's policies and of its leadership. A revived security in the region subsequently prevailed, with a minimum sense of excessive foreign, non-Arab intrusion. After an alienation from Iran, across the Gulf, that had persisted since the late 1970s, a workable relationship was restored between the two countries.

The alliance in support of the rule of law revived – under Saudi and Egyptian leadership – the functioning of the Arab League. The influence of the quasi-revolutionary ideologies of the region diminished. It brought states as disparate as Egypt and Syria into an unprecedented

closeness with the Gulf Cooperation Council (GCC), resulting in the Damascus Declaration of March 1991.

A typical moderation characterized Saudi Arabia's attitude towards its defeated opponent, Iraq, and its then leader's misguided supporters elsewhere in the Arab community. The trustworthiness of Saudi Arabia's traditional friends in the West was confirmed. Confidence was established in the effectiveness of its armed forces, both as a fighting force and as partners in a complex alliance. A more profoundly self-reliant and assured Saudi Arabia emerged, with its role enhanced, and its identity and uniqueness reasserted internationally.

The handling of its oil wealth remains crucial to the Kingdom's role. The post-conflict period saw Saudi Arabia emerge once again as the dominant figure in OPEC, capable of meeting the shortfall in world petroleum supply caused not only by rising demand but the temporary extinction of Kuwait and Iraq as world suppliers. Saudi Arabia has long remained a dependable influence in the stabilizing of petroleum prices, sensitive to the distorting force of volatile prices in a world easily subject to recession and economic instability. International economic prosperity is not only good for petroleum sales but for the home based export-producing manufacturing indus-

try and the international business worldwide in which Saudi Arabia has invested much of its oil-generated wealth.

The Kingdom participates, inevitably, in the big league in the world economic community. In the field of aid, Saudi Arabia has benefited 97 countries, with massive assistance going to Islamic and Third World countries (particularly Africa) in the form of development grants and loans, and for famine and disaster relief and prevention. It is a major contributor to the International Monetary Fund, the Arab Monetary Fund, the World Bank, and the Jeddah-based Islamic Development Bank. It is the largest donor of aid in the world in relation to GNP (at 6 per cent). Emphasis is given to the needs of, first, the Islamic world, then the Arab world, and finally the rest of the world.

Inescapably, Saudi attitudes are central to the formation of the policies adopted by its fellow members of the Gulf Cooperation Council (GCC), founded in 1981 between Saudi Arabia and its neighbours Kuwait, Oman, Bahrain, Qatar and the United Arab Emirates, and today headquartered in Riyadh. The GCC embraces not only defence, but economics and international diplomacy beyond its members boundaries.

It was Saudi Arabia who initiated and has repeatedly hosted the 38-nation

HRH Crown Prince Fahd (as he was at that time) presides at a session of the Third Islamic Summit Conference (the "Makkah Summit"), held at the Conference Centre in Taif (left) under the flags of the thirty-eight participating nations.

Since the Summit Meeting of 1982 (above), King Fahd has played a leading role at the meetings of the Gulf Cooperation Council.

Organisation of Islamic Conference, which has had its headquarters in Jeddah since its instigation in the early 1970s by the late King Faisal. Through the OIC, convening in Taif, Saudi Arabia had secured Islamic consensus on major issues such as Afghanistan during the period of Soviet occupation, on Lebanon, in which King Fahd played a major personal role in the restoration of peace, and particularly in support of the rights of the Palestinian people.

Above all, Saudi Arabia works for a *concerted* policy on the major unresolved issue in its principal theatre of influence. While in common with most Arab states it broke with Egypt on the unilateral accord it signed with Israel at Camp David in 1978, Saudi Arabia was among the first to welcome Egypt back to the Arab League; King Fahd cemented ties between the two countries by his visit of 1989. With the ending of the Cold War in the early 1990s, Saudi policy hastened the marginalizing of extremist groups and attitudes on the Palestine issue, and helped to bring about a fresh recognition of Palestinian realities during the Bush administration. The flow of Heads-of-State through Riyadh speaks of Saudi Arabia's pre-eminence in the region.

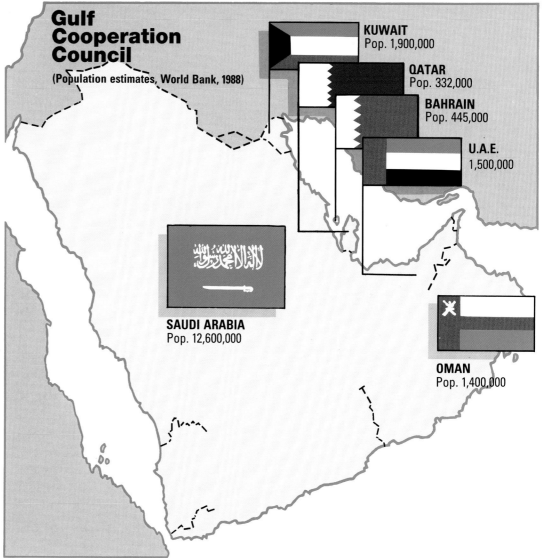

Gulf Cooperation Council

(Population estimates, World Bank, 1988)

KUWAIT
Pop. 1,900,000

QATAR
Pop. 332,000

BAHRAIN
Pop. 445,000

U.A.E.
1,500,000

SAUDI ARABIA
Pop. 12,600,000

OMAN
Pop. 1,400,000

8
Industry and Development

Saudi Arabia came to riches through the long, hard school of poverty. There was to be no place for profligacy. Rather, the bounty of oil and mineral resource was to be made to provide, for generations to come, the infrastructure of modern statehood; and to fund a free economic system where human enterprise, working within a total plan, would ensure self-generating growth.

The boom of the world's most plentiful capital of mineral energy in the form of oil has turned Saudi Arabia from one of the poorest countries in the world to the richest of all, in terms of reserves, in scarcely more than a single generation. Some oil is obtained offshore (left).

Introduction

THE ECONOMIC SITUATION of Saudi Arabia during the last quarter of the twentieth century is unprecedented in the history of the world. This is a country whose sparse population had been subjected to a harsh, if ennobling poverty, that came into undreamt of riches.

The Kingdom indeed proved to be blessed with the largest oil reserves of any country in the world, and it can certainly be credited with their skilful exploitation. By 1977 Saudi Arabia was already second only to West Germany in monetary reserves. It was able until the oil price crash of 1986, to balance its budget despite the enormous expenditure under its 5-Year Plans and it was remarkable for its avoidance of a foreign deficit.

The boom years until 1986 did not in fact represent, as might be thought, an economic paradise; indeed, they presented responsibilities and challenges which, in their way, were only a little less frustrating than poverty. The persistent danger has been that of disrupting the balance of traditional Saudi life by the sudden changes that the rush of new wealth and spending can bring.

Since the reign of the late King Faisal, Saudi policy has largely separated oil from politics, except in the context of the Palestinian situation in the early 1970s. The oil industry has been allowed to form its own markets and decisions on economic grounds. The government, realising the fundamental interdependence of the industrial economies and the oil producers, concentrated on trying responsibly to maintain a steady world supply at a stable price. For as long as was feasible in the 1980s Saudi Arabia absorbed much of the cost of world overproduction of oil by voluntarily curbing its own production and export in line with the long-term interest of the international community. When the price fell dramatically in 1986 the Kingdom again bore the brunt of production cutbacks.

In the late 1980s and the first half of 1990, production was fairly stable between 5.5 and 6 million barrels per day (mbd). The Iraqi invasion of Kuwait in August 1990 effectively cut off the output of both countries and Saudi Arabia had to respond rapidly in order to prevent panic on the international markets. Production was lifted to 8 mbd before the end of that year and capacity later increased to 10 mbd, matching the high point of the early 1980s.

In the initial stages of its development in the 1970s and early 1980s, the Kingdom openly accepted its dependence on the skills and products that the Western and Far Eastern economies could offer – there was no other way in which its ambition to develop the infrastructure of the entire country in a short space of time could be fulfilled. By 1985 and the end of the Third 5-Year Plan with its massive expenditure on every conceivable type of project – roads, ports, airports, communications, water, power generation, industrial facilities, food production, health, housing and education – the infrastructure of the economy had been largely completed.

Since then the emphasis in the economy has changed, with government encouragement, to production of goods and services within the private sector, with the aim both of satisfying the domestic market and opening up export opportunities.

Before 1985 development was carried out largely through government participation in joint ventures with foreign companies: the classic example was, of course, ARAMCO, which was progressively "Saudized" in terms of both ownership and workforce. Today the company is entirely Saudi owned, with a new name – Saudi Aramco – and the thrust is towards privatising state-owned enterprises in general. The Saudi Arabian Basic Industries Corporation (SABIC), which is 70 per cent owned by the Saudi Arabian Government and 30 per cent by Gulf investors, was responsible for hydrocarbon-based raw materials production in a series of joint ventures with foreign firms. Now private Saudi capital is being invited into its enterprises, and it is envisaged that ultimately 100 per cent of SABIC's businesses will be offered to the public.

The creation of a Saudi stock market is intended to stimulate the injection of private capital into what hitherto has been a state-led process of industrial development. The fledgling stock market boomed in 1988, reflecting investor confidence with the ending of the Gulf War.

At the same time, now that the infrastructure is in place, the private business and industrial sector is being encouraged to become the work-horse of the economy. Both the state and private sectors are being encouraged to diversify away from oil and raw material production into value-added down-line products for the domestic, Gulf and overseas markets. Former SABIC enterprises, particularly Petrokemya, are finding successful markets for their products. The training of Saudis in high-technology skills is a priority, to make local manpower available on the job market.

Raw materials, energy, industrial infrastructure and government assistance through the Saudi Industrial Development Fund, are all abundantly available, particularly at the gleaming new industrial cities of Yanbu and Jubayl, and six more industrial cities are planned at al-Madinah, Hail, Tabuk, Ar'ar and in Asir and al-Jawf. Foreign participation, now with the private sector, continues to be the key to progress, to ensure technology transfer, sound management and efficient export marketing. This is the aim underlying the multi-billion dollar economic off-set programmes linked to the recent major arms deals with the U.S. and Britain – the Peace Shield and al-Yamamah programmes respectively.

The effects of this policy of import substitution and export development are already being felt. The contribution of the industrial sector to GNP stood at 5 per cent in 1990, and is expected to rise to 8 per cent by the end of the Fifth Five Year Plan. Productivity from a labour force well in excess of 500,000 is expected to increase at a rate of 5 per cent annually. In addition to ventures primed by SABIC in the field of petrochemicals, fertilisers, metals and plastics, there are already over 2,250 manufacturing companies producing such goods as cement, building supplies, cables, steel pipes, food products, paint, paper products, hides and plastic products. The "Made in Saudi Arabia" logo is now a commonplace sight. The private sector's share of non-oil GNP had increased to 50 per cent by 1991.

By such means the Kingdom is striving to ensure its future. But the future will stretch indefinitely beyond the period of history in which petroleum and petroleum products are likely to be on stream. Over the years the Kingdom has prepared for this prospect by investing some of its income abroad, especially

Joint Commission Central Press Headquarters in Yanbu.

during the years of surplus in the early 1980s. During that period, the Saudi Arabian Monetary Agency (SAMA), with its team of international banking advisers, sought to invest the Kingdom's income in a variety of areas, much of it in the United States where American dollars allowed for a high level of liquidity. Substantial amounts were also channelled into the international banks who were lending vast sums to the Third World, thus storing up debt problems for the future. Other investment was made in the economies of strong industrial countries like West Germany and Japan. Although SAMA proceeded cautiously when directing money into foreign corporate ventures, for fear of arousing hostility from abroad.

Unlike Kuwait, the Kingdom's surplus investment philosophy intended the money to be used before long for development at home, not as a profit-making "pension fund" for future work-free generations.

The problem of investing a surplus did not remain a difficulty for long. As oil revenue dropped but investment in the infrastructure continued, a regular annual deficit has been incurred. In 1989 this reached $9,228 million, but partly as a result of a dramatic improvement in the balance of trade, this deficit was halved by the early 1990s.

Private fortunes too have been inevitably made in Saudi Arabia today. Some

of this wealth is being invested at home; the rest, both of necessity and the desire for breadth of security, finds its way abroad.

In the month following Iraq's invasion of Kuwait, the Kingdom's commercial banks lost 11 per cent of their total deposits. Yet the maturity of the banking sector was more than evident during the crisis as the value of the Saudi riyal against the US dollar remained stable and all banking operations continued as normal. Cash from increased government oil revenue soon flowed back into the system and a mini-boom fuelled by the influx of over half a million foreign troops more than compensated. The banks reported increased profits as well as an encouraging trend for Arab investors to transfer their capital back to Saudi Arabia, where it can be used to fund the rapid expansion of the private sector.

Internationally, Saudi Arabia has grown, with its wealth, to play a major role in financial affairs; it is actively engaged through such institutions as the International Monetary Fund in discussions and moves on the future of the world economy and its monetary system.

Development aid continues to be a major outlet for Saudi wealth, between 1976 and 1989 this averaged 6 per cent of

the GNP although it has since dropped. The Kingdom has its own Saudi fund for Development and is also active in international organisations like OPEC and the UN, as well as Arab agencies such as the Islamic Relief Organisation and the Arab Fund for Economic and Social Development.

It was at home, however, that the new wealth was concentrated – with the Saudi people themselves. In a decade and a half their country and their living standards have changed as never elsewhere before. With the infrastructure came a rush of consumer imports from cars to canned foods in new modern supermarkets. For the government spending passed through the economy to private Saudi hands, as workers, businessmen, and civil servants became the beneficiaries of new kinds of cheap loans and welfare. But with the wealth has come responsibility too: the responsibility of productive Saudi citizenship, of learning new skills and applying them with the tools of modern life that the Government provides. As a leading Government spokesman stated, "We are making it clear from the very beginning that being a Saudi only entitles you to prove yourself. It does not entitle you to become the boss, or to run things, or to assume positions for which you are not qualified."

As the Kingdom moves towards the end of the century, the Plans for the 1990s continue to stress the importance of diversification, particularly in the private sector. Alongside this there is a continuing emphasis on manpower and training so that every Saudi citizen can play a fulfilling role in the future of their country.

(*See* Section 11)

Development

UNTIL 1986, the country's immense oil revenues made it possible, in a way which is perhaps historically unique, for the Government to plan virtually any developments, including a total transformation of the economic and industrial base, without financial constraint. In theory, everything could be done at once.

In practice, pumping huge sums of money into a relatively undeveloped economy causes inflation, social upheaval and innumerable bottlenecks. Opposing political pressures quickly arise, as they did in Saudi Arabia.

On the one hand there were impatient young Saudis who complained that the Government was moving too slowly. On the other hand, older and more cautious voices were asking for a system of priorities and for greater care in protecting a social structure which is inevitably being shaken by the speed of change. Since 1986, with the fall in the oil price, the economic slowdown, and the completion of the infrastructure, development plans have taken a new direction: the Government has laid the foundations for a mature economy to evolve, in which its priority is to provide the trained manpower, low-cost energy and raw materials, and favourable financial climate for the private sector to diversify rapidly and become the engine of the economy.

Sustained development continues to be the Government's declared aim, despite the climate of financial stringency and deficit budgeting. The early 5-Year Plans had no such constraints: the Second Plan's (1975-80) appropriations were nine times larger than the First's, and those of the Third (1980-85) were half as much again. The 1981-2 budget saw the second biggest allocation of state funds: SR298 billion. Yet, despite its size, revenue still exceeded expenditure by SR42 billion. The following year saw the largest planned expenditure at SR313.4 billion, with the budget breaking even. Since then the Kingdom has had to face the fact that its development process can be sustained only by deficit budgeting. The first annual deficit budget occurred in 1983-4. Since then annual shortfalls in the region of SR25 billion have been financed by the issue of treasury bonds. The 1992 deficit is to be of SR30 billion.

Of course, oil revenue provides the basic state revenue. Increasingly foreign investment and taxes on foreign activity within the Saudi economy help to make up the deficit. Although tax holidays of up to ten years are extended to companies bringing in foreign expertise.

In the early years of the 1975-80 (Second) Plan it soon became apparent that the Government could not immediately disburse as much money as had been hoped; Ministries were congratulated for spending as much as possible and creating the capacity to project, design, monitor and assess new work. And as the money passed through the economy it fuelled bottlenecks at the Ministries, the ports, the hotels and for houses. Inflation soared rapidly as the new money chased goods and services which the economy could not supply, or even import and distribute quickly enough to meet the demand.

By 1978, however, the frustrated queues of ships waiting outside the ports of Jiddah and Dammam had disappeared as great efforts created new berths and more than adequate capacity. Inflation levelled out as the Ministry of Finance and National Economy sharply but effectively applied the monetary brakes;

Pipelines now run 750 miles across Arabia from the Gulf to the Red Sea.

contractors waited for payment as spending Ministries found their money delayed; delayed too were compensation payments for land expropriated by the Government for development work; the doors of the Real Estate Development Fund closed for nine months to citizens seeking to take its soft loans and fulfil its motto of "a new home for every Saudi". Thenceforth control of the vicious inflation became the paramount fiscal aim of the Minister of Finance. But the Government also shielded its people from the inflation as well as unnecessary poverty with controls on prices and rents, subsidies on basic foodstuffs, increased consumer protection with quality standards, inceased wages, and capital assistance for homes, businesses and industry. By standard statistical measures of per capita economic growth, total GDP per capita rose almost five per cent per annum during the Second Plan.

With recession and economic slowdown throughout in the West, Saudi Arabia increasingly became a focal point for international exporters of goods and services. It continued to be one of the largest centres of new design and building. Demand for new equipment, construction materials, electrical generators, factory plant, or arms, made it a key international market from suppliers all over the world. Similarly with consumer goods, whether for cameras or cakes, the Kingdom could choose from the best in an atmosphere of intense competition, which forced generous prices on the suppliers. Beforehand there had been suspicions in the Government that many more unscrupulous foreign contractors and suppliers had not been giving of their best, or at least not without considerable profiteering. That changed under the stimulus of competition and as Saudi skills at negotiating improved. On several occasions construction bids were simply cancelled on major jobs and new ones called in search of a fairer price.

With the Third and Fourth Five Year Plans of 1980 and 1985 the thrust of Saudi development shifted from basic infrastructural development of the cities, roads, ports and telephones towards the longer term development of its productive and human resources. The planners well realized the difficulty of the task and made considerable allowance for

changes based on closer monitoring of performance. For while foreign designers and labourers can be temporarily imported to build highways, with the consequent social stresses of a massively increased foreign population, it is much harder to create a productive economy based on a Saudi workforce. Whereas in the Second Plan, supply bottlenecks, principally under-capacity at the ports, had been the major problem, manpower has since become an important area of concern. The Fourth and Fifth Five Year Plans aimed for a reduction in requirements for foreign labour. Saudi employment grew by an average of 7 per cent, and in 1990 alone 46,000 more jobs were

created for Saudi citizens. Capital-intensive agricultural and industrial technology should save labour, and those released from the declining construction and rural sectors, together with women, who are expected to work more widely, will help supply demand in the burgeoning private sector.

The shortage of water has in the recent past been a limiting factor. Irrigation has consumed, in recent years, about seventy-five per cent of the available water supply. The growing demands of industry and the cities could not be met from local sources.

Even in the Eastern Province, where water had not hitherto been a problem,

Saudi Aramco's LPG refinery at Yanbu, the new industrial city on the Red Sea.

Future growth depends on an increasingly Saudi labour-force.

shortages could have been felt, because this is also the region in which most of the country's oil and gas is situated, which means that industrial demand is growing very fast. The Kingdom's desalinated water programme has eased this, a National Water Policy was also forged to help harness the vast supplies of ancient water in aquifers under the Kingdom's eastern half.

Industrial development requires large and continuous amounts of energy. During the foreseeable future, oil and natural gas will provide most of this energy, and Saudi Arabia, is of course, uniquely well endowed. The reserves should last for many decades. But alternative sources of energy are being actively explored. For example, joint venture research and development work in solar energy and an assessment of nuclear power.

The lack of trained manpower, however, proved to be the most acute and frustrating shortage of the Kingdom's industrial development. The problem was most severe at managerial level where demand continues to exceed supply. Every trainable Saudi Arabian could be absorbed and still the need would not be met. Successive Five Year Plans have made provision for these requirements and further expanded the already large educational and training programmes. Money alone cannot provide teachers and train officers as rapidly as it can supply equipment. The emphasis is on the production of educational excellence, especially in the training of teachers and civil servants.

At the same time, the demand for production and service workers, and for labourers both skilled and unskilled remains huge. The established vocational and craft training centres are beginning to meet the need of the domestic labour market, and the gradual Saudization of

the workforce is being accomplished as planned, with a steady decrease in the number of residence permits being granted to foreigners, particularly Europeans.

This influx of manpower created its own requirements and challenges. For instance, they were in need of housing and over 30 new towns and some 75 new municipalities were created. The volume of construction grew for years at an average annual rate of 60 per cent – on top of a very high existing base-level. Vast amounts of government money were involved, but again money alone was not enough. Sufficient materials and specialized equipment – not only for houses, but also for hospitals, schools, power stations, airports and so on – were sometimes not available within the time envisaged. But most targets set in the recent plans have been met.

Although the Saudi Arabian Government, despite the deficits, is hardly short of revenue, foreign investment in most of these development projects is welcomed. Partnership between Saudi businessmen and foreign or international companies is considered more advantageous than if Saudi Arabia just bought the machinery, the patents and the personnel required.

Partnership guarantees a continuing interest, through which not only supplies of capital but supplies of experienced and talented people are most likely to be found.

Amid all this expansion, the social and religious values of Islam remain the permanent guideline: and these, in turn, have economic implications. For a Muslim, it is a duty to give alms, and not demeaning to ask for, and to receive, them. This principle, rather than socialist philosophy, is the foundation of Saudi Arabia's welfare state. Free education and free medical services, pensions and social insurance of every kind, have been provided, and are expanded, as fast as the problems of construction and personnel allow. In addition, a wide range of subsidies has been built into the economy – subsidies for farmers, subsidies against the rising cost of materials, subsidies on imported food, subsidies for housing. The Government, however, strongly believes that while the poor should be protected and basic opportunities provided, subsidies should not be allowed to get out of hand. Great importance is attached now to creating a climate in which natural Saudi enterprise can flourish.

Heavy and hydrocarbons industries of world importance are based at Jubayl, which has risen under the control of a Royal Commission from a tiny fishing village to become a mainstay of the Kingdom's industrial future.

Gross Domestic Product by Economic Activity

Economic activity of the principal sectors of the economy as a percentage of GDP (excluding producers of government services).

Figures based upon SAMA Statistics for 1989 (1409/1410)

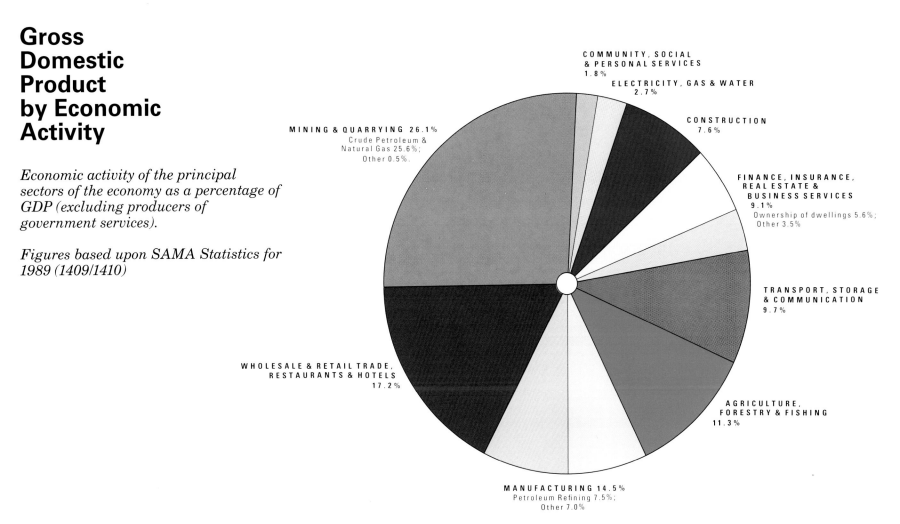

COMMUNITY, SOCIAL & PERSONAL SERVICES 1.8%

ELECTRICITY, GAS & WATER 2.7%

CONSTRUCTION 7.6%

MINING & QUARRYING 26.1%
Crude Petroleum & Natural Gas 25.6%;
Other 0.5%.

FINANCE, INSURANCE, REAL ESTATE & BUSINESS SERVICES 9.1%
Ownership of dwellings 5.6%;
Other 3.5%

TRANSPORT, STORAGE & COMMUNICATION 9.7%

WHOLESALE & RETAIL TRADE, RESTAURANTS & HOTELS 17.2%

AGRICULTURE, FORESTRY & FISHING 11.3%

MANUFACTURING 14.5%
Petroleum Refining 7.5%;
Other 7.0%

The Money Story

After the Second World War, Saudi Arabia survived on a subsistence economy with almost no infrastructure. The oil income started from $10 million in 1365/66 AH (1946 CE). It reached the level of SR790 ($212) million in 1952. The Government Budget for the last fiscal year of King Abdul Aziz's reign 1371/72 (1952/53 CE) allowed for expenditure of SR758 ($205) million. The country's GDP is roughly estimated to have been around SR4,000 million in 1372 (1953 CE) and imports amounted to SR435 million in that year. That was the year of SAMA's start. Its first six-monthly balance sheet for the period ending 30 Jumada al-Thani 1372 (16 March 1953) listed total assets and liabilities of SR47.5 ($12.67) million.

In those days, Saudi Arabia had a coin-operated silver standard. The country's monetary system consisted of Saudi silver Riyals and cupro-nickel coins. A number of foreign currencies circulated alongside these, particularly the British gold sovereign. The Saudi silver Riyal was, however, the most popular coin and constituted the backbone of the country's currency system. The country had no paper currency of its own. However, some paper notes of foreign origin circulated during the pilgrimage season. The banking system was in its infancy; the volume of deposits was very small and the role of cheques was negligible.

One of SAMA's first tasks was to complete the country's own monetary system. In 1953 SAMA issued Saudi Arabia's first gold coin to replace the British sovereign. This was followed in 1957 by a new gold sovereign of the same size and weight but of different design. Next it introduced decimal coinage in December 1959 when the Riyal was stipulated to be equal to 20 qirshes instead of 22 qirshes and each qirsh was made equal to 5 halalahs. The 1, 2 and 4 qirsh coins were replaced in 1392 AH (1972 CE) by new cupro-nickel coins of the denominations of 5, 10, 25 and 50 halalahs. This completed the decimal coinage system.

An experiment with paper currency was made with the issuance of Pilgrim Receipts on 18 Dhu al-Qa'dah 1372 (July 23, 1953). These Pilgrim Receipts started with the 10-Riyal denominations but were followed by five and one Riyal denominations. The Pilgrim Receipts became generally accepted throughout the

Kingdom and virtually enjoyed the status of paper currency thus paving the way for the issue of official paper currency in Muharram 1381 (June 1961) after the 1377 Charter had removed the constraint against issue of paper currency imposed on SAMA by the 1371 Charter. With the issue of paper currency the gold and silver coins were demonetized by Royal Decree No.6 dated 1 Rajab 1379 (31 December 1959).

In the mid-1950s, a few years after the establishment of SAMA, the country passed through financial difficulties which brought about depreciation in the free market rate of the Riyal, depletion in the country's foreign exchange reserves to the extremely low level of RLs 10.21 ($2.72) million in January 1958 and imposition of exchange controls. But the Government's determined implementation of the Stabilization Programme improved the country's financial and economic position and led to an increase in SAMA's foreign exchange reserves and strengthening of the Riyal. This enabled the Government to abolish all exchange controls and to stabilize the exchange rate of the Riyal.

The new Charter (Rajab 1379/1959 CE) made SAMA responsible for all the normal functions of a central bank including issue of currency, stabilization of the internal and external value of the Saudi

Below: *Special bank branches allow women to engage in business.* Far right: *Banking facilities include automatic teller machines.*

IMF

Saudi Arabia joined the International Monetary Fund in 1957. Its small annual quota was increased rapidly through successive quota reviews from SDR 10 million at first to SDR 1,040 million after the seventh general review in 1980. But 1981 was the year when its estimated general reserves of $110 billion truly made their mark in the fund. (SDR – Special Drawing Right – is a unit of currency unique to the IMF).

In that year the Fund's board approved a special increase in the Kingdom's quota which almost doubled again to SDR 2,100 million with its share of the total rising from 1.74 per cent to 3.5 per cent. This increase in percentage quota with attendant voting rights put the Kingdom among the top handful of Fund members and well ahead of several Western industrial states. At the same time an agreement was made whereby the Kingdom would make available SDR 8,000 million (or just under $10,000 million) to the Fund for its vital programme of lending to troubled member economies, especially those of the developing world. The agreement called for money to become available to the IMF in equal tranches over the next two years; half as much again was also to be made available in the third year, subject to the Kingdom's balance of payments and reserve position. Such sums as were drawn down by the IMF would be paid back in four equal instalments beginning

at the end of the fourth year and ending by the seventh, thereby giving the loans an average life of five and a half years. Interest was to be paid on the basis of the weighted average of returns on government securities in the five currencies making up the IMF's SDR which, since the 1980 agreement reducing the number of currencies involved, comprised the US dollar (by far the heaviest in the basket) the West German mark, the Japanese yen, the British pound and the French franc.

The agreements were seen in international financial circles as tremendously important in supplying the Fund with much needed liquidity for its important work. At the same time, the Kingdom diversified its foreign reserves at good rates of return, with security – and also assisted in "recycling" its petrodollars especially to those developing countries most hurt by oil price increases and then most in need of immediate cash. On its own, the Kingdom would have had difficulty in building the new structures to channel the money itself.

Now, with the deputing of Saudi Arabian Monetary Agency personnel to participate in courses organized by the IMF, three decades after it first joined the Fund, ties between the Kingdom and the IMF continue to strengthen. Saudi Arabia contributed to the financing of some 25 per cent of IMF loans in 1988, and is represented on the IMF's board of directors.

Riyal, management of the country's monetary reserves, handling of Government receipts and payments, and regulation of commercial banks.

Saudi Arabia considered it necessary to sever the link between the Riyal and the Dollar as of 15 March 1975. Since then the policy has been to stabilize the exchange rate of the Riyal with respect to the SDR basket of currencies with a band of 7.25 per cent on either side of the SDR/Riyal parity of Rls 4.28255 per SDR. The exchange rate of the Riyal has changed periodically since then; as the SDR basket has itself weakened, the Riyal has appreciated against it: at the end of 1985 the rate of the Riyal against the SDR was 4.0037. Saudi Arabia's exchange reserves have continually strengthened the external position of the Riyal to make it one of the world's strongest currencies.

The phenomenal growth in the role of SAMA as Government's fiscal agent may be seen from the rise in the Government's expenditure budget from SR758

million in 1371/2 (1951-2) to SR260 billion in 1404/5 (1984-5), a near three and a half hundredfold growth over 33 years.

Government-Related and other Public Service Organizations*

DEVELOPMENT AND INDUSTRY

Royal Commission for Jubayl and Yanbu
Controls the planning and development of the two major new industrial cities.

Saudi Basic Industries Corporation (SABIC)
Supervises and develops the basic industries deriving from the country's oil and mineral resources, covering petrochemicals, iron and steel, fertilisers, methanol, natural gas, aluminium etc.

Saudi Industrial Development Fund (SIDF)
Provides interest-free loans to non-oil private manufacturers.

Saline Water Conversion Corporation
Develops desalination and pipeline systems.

Council of Saudi Arabian Chambers of Commerce
Joint organization for all regional chambers of commerce throughout the country.

Saudi Fund for Development (SFD)
Helps finance projects in the developing world outside Saudi Arabia.

Saudi Consulting House (SCH)
Prepares engineering designs and specifications and supervises architectural or civil and other engineering activities.

Real Estate Development Fund
Provides loans for construction to individuals and organizations for either private or commercial purposes.

FINANCE AND BANKING

Saudi Arabian Monetary Agency (SAMA)
The administrative structure which acts as the central bank. It receives all Government revenues and disburses all Government expenditure, controls the money supply, implements the Government's monetary policy and advises the Government on domestic and international financial matters.

Saudi Credit Bank
Provides interest-free loans to Saudi citizens in special need of assistance in domestic and medical emergencies, and to graduates of craft vocational training centres wishing to establish their own workshops.

Saudi Arabian Agricultural Bank (SAAB)
Provides interest-free loans to finance agricultural and fishing activities, and to sponsor Government agricultural enterprises.

Islamic Development Bank
Established jointly with other Arab governments to finance aid programmes and technical assistance among its 40 Islamic member states.

General Investment Fund (or Public Investment Fund)
Supplies finance to Saudia and Petromin for medium and long term development.

Credit Fund for Contractors
Provides initial funding for Saudi contractors.

ENERGY

Petromin (General Petroleum and Mineral Organization)/Samarec
Responsible for developing the petroleum, petrochemical, mineral and related industries. Samarec – the Saudi Arabian Marketing and Refining Company is a wholly owned subsidiary of Petromin charged with the efficient control of all downstream oil operations, including international distribution.

Saudi Aramco
Wholly owned by the Government, and based at Dhahran, Saudi Aramco accounts for 97 per cent of the Kingdom's oil and natural gas production, with operating and marketing contracts with a consortium of international oil companies.

Electrico (The Electricity Corporation)
Directly responsible to the Ministry of Industry and Electricity for the establishment and maintenance of the Kingdom's electricity supply.

TRANSPORT

King Khalid International Airport (KKIA)
The international terminal for Riyadh.

King Abdul Aziz International Airport (KAAIA)
The international terminal for Jiddah.

King Fahd International Airport (KFIA)
The international terminal for the Eastern region.

Ports Authority
Responsible for the development, operation and management of all the ports in the Kingdom.

Presidency of Civil Aviation
Working under the aegis of the Ministry of Defence, the PCA is responsible for the safe and efficient flow of commercial air traffic within the Kingdom, and to provide passenger and freight airport facilities.

Saudia (Saudi Arabian Airlines)
The national airline, covering services within the country and comprehensive international services worldwide.

Saudi Public Transport Company (SAPTCO)
Runs the comprehensive national bus and inter-city coach service.

National Shipping Company of Saudi Arabia
Runs a fleet of cargo vessels for worldwide trade to and from the Kingdom.

Saudi Rails
Responsible for the Kingdom's railway, linking Dammam, Hofuf, Haradh, and Riyadh.

COMMUNICATIONS

Directorate General of Posts
Handles the day-to-day administration of postal services.

ARABSAT (Arab Satellite Communication Organisation)
Operates for 21 members of the Arab League the axis-stabilised communication satellites for broadcasting purposes throughout the Arab world.

Saudi Press Agency
National news agency responsible for gathering and distributing new items within the Kingdom and abroad, covering the affairs of the Kingdom.

STANDARDS

Saudi Arabian Standards Organization (SASO)
Responsible for establishing standards and measurements for all commodities, products, aspects of safety, meteorological reports and calculations, and for conformity rules for the region.

AGRICULTURE

NADCO (National Agricultural Development Company)
Principal agency for promoting agricultural development, land reclamation, animal husbandry, and marketing.

Saudi Arabian Agriculture and Dairy Company (SAADCO)
Based on Al Kharj, the largest centre of dairy operations in the Kingdom.

Saudi Fisheries Company
Based in Dammam, it promotes the development of the Saudi fishing industry.

Grain Silos and Flour Mills Organization
Responsible to the Ministry of Commerce, with a Government majority of stock, it provides flour and animal feeds for domestic consumption.

*Neither the list of organizations presented here, nor the descriptions given, are intended to be definitive.

Agriculture, Irrigation & Water

THE HIGHWAY EAST out of al-Kharj used to run into the typically barren Najdi landscape of sandy, parched soil relieved by a few dull-green shrubs. In the early 1970s an occasional small roadside plot of wheat or tomatoes, carefully tended by groups of small-scale farmers, barely hinted at the agriculturalists' promise that, once given water, their skills would make the aridity grow green.

Flying into Riyadh airport today proves that the shimmering promise of the past has become a verdant fact in the present. Modern pivot-based irrigation methods have produced the large, distinctive circular wheat fields of the Qasim area and al-Kharj that are so spectacular from the air. The largest fields are a kilometre in diameter and yield large quantities of high-grade grain. The pivot-centred system of irrigation has proved most successful for large-scale commercial farming; more than 15,000 of the units are now in use.

Saudi Arabia is characterized by the vastness of its land area which, at 1.45 million square kilometres, is over 1.5 per cent of the world's land mass. Under 2.5 per cent is cultivated and the area utilized for agriculture and forests equals less than 6 per cent. Huge oil revenues give the country a high income per capita rate, but the traditional agricultural sector is still dominant in terms of the numbers employed within it.

The tenure of agricultural land in the Kingdom is unlike that of other Middle Eastern countries. There is no concentration of ownership by a few rich individuals and the cultivated land is remarkably evenly distributed. Owner-occupied agricultural holdings make up the bulk of the cultivated areas. By the mid-1970s, 600,000 hectares were under cultivation.

During the Second Plan period (1975-80), the agricultural sector only grew some five per cent per annum – a fifth of the rate of the total Saudi non-oil economy's growth. Farmers were attracted to the new wealth of the cities, creating labour shortages in traditional agricultural areas like date production.

Machines were hard to introduce because most farms are small – 6.7 hectares average in 1976 – and generally not sufficiently cooperative. A few remote areas suffered from lack of infrastructure. These problems were to be tackeld with more cooperatives and more rural roads.

Traditional flood irrigation is wasteful of precious water and increases the poisonous salinity of otherwise fertile soils – with sufficient water and the Saudi sun they can be up to five times as productive as Europe. Subsidies and investment assistance did not always produce significant improvements, especially with livestock and crops competing with subsidized imports. Fishing resources too were barely exploited along the 1,000 mile Red Sea and 350 mile Gulf coastlines. The annual catch by some 4,400 fishermen on 1,400-odd small boats was estimated at 16,000 tonnes during the late 1970s. The UN's Food and Agriculture Organization, however, estimated the potential annual catch to be as high as 3-500,000 tonnes.

Insufficient emphasis was placed on the vital agricultural sector during the first two plans, government officials concluded. Significant progress, however, had been made and the Third Plan sought to advance the improving welfare of the Kingdom's rural people, promoted the optimal use of land and water resources, and provided strong incentives to achieve agricultural self-sufficiency. Protection of the environment was safeguarded through reafforestation, stringent zoning of specially protected areas like Abu Hada and parts of Asir, and the creation of national parks. The Fourth Plan has seen the confirmation of these successes. The Government's goals in the 1980s have been to achieve self-sufficiency in basic foodstuffs, to ensure a constant supply of clean water, to balance rural development and employment with that in the cities and industries, and to encourage the growth of the private sector in farming and food-processing.

The consequence has been one of the Kingdom's greatest success stories, with all four goals already realised. Extraordinarily, given its environment, Saudi Arabia is today the most efficient agricultural producer in the Middle East and its largest wheat producer, even exporting wheat, dairy produce, poultry, eggs, fish, fruit and vegetables to no less than 45 countries. Wheat is exported to, among others, the USSR. Agricultural

Irrigation
Fresh water
remains the scarcest
essential. Careful
use of its
underground and
rain water for
irrigation has given
Saudi Arabia its
agricultural
successes. Dams like
those at Abha
(*above*) and Haradh
(*left*) provide water
for modern pivot-
centred irrigation
(*right*).

products make up 30 per cent of non-oil exports. Between 1980 and 1986 agricultural growth averaged 26 per cent per annum. From a land area under cultivation of 150,000 hectares in 1975, 3 million hectares were being cultivated by 1989. Wheat production has increased from 3000 tonnes in 1975 to 3.6 million tonnes today. By 1989, agriculture was contributing around 13 per cent to the country's Gross Domestic product.

How has this astonishing progress been achieved? The Government has mounted a concerted effort through direct funding of infrastructure projects – rural roads, water resources, training centres – combined with interest-free loans through the Saudi Arabian Agricultural Bank. Subsidies have been provided for up to half the cost of machinery,

animal feed, seeds and fertilisers. Wheat has been bought at favourable subvention prices by the Grain Silos and Flour Mills Organization, which has also been responsible for storing and processing it. The government is now targetting barley production in the hope that 1990's 11 per cent increase in wheat output can be transferred to barley. A programme of free land distribution to farmers and agricultural companies was adopted; agricultural support industries in both public and private sectors are also being encouraged.

The effects of all this on individual agricultural and food-producing sectors have been dramatic. By 1985 the Kingdom had become self-sufficient in egg production, and nearly so in poultry. Today, producing 2.5 billion eggs per

Seventy-five per cent of the Kingdom's wheat is exported to over forty countries.

annum and 266,000 tonnes of broiler meat, it can afford to export both.

New wealth and a growing population led to a growing demand for meat which, in the early days, could only be met by imports. Today the production of red meat is catching up with demand. Dairy products are up from 1,800 tonnes in 1975 to almost 500,000 tonnes today, meeting local demand and enabling exports to be made. By 1985 more than 40 large dairy plants were in operation; the dairy at al-Kharj, with 18,000 head of cattle, was the largest in the Middle East. Most dairies drew on foreign expertise and improved their stock with Frisian cattle to increase

milk yields from 14 to 24 litres per day.

At sea, the Saudi Fish Joint Stock Company, founded in 1980, has successfully established a fisheries industry. Investment in modern equipment has brought a huge increase in catches. In 1990 more than 50,000 tonnes of fish were caught and a total of 10,700 men were engaged in fishing activities. Shellfish are also an important element in the industry, with surplus shrimp production being exported to various countries notably the United States and Japan. Once more, the involvement of the private sector is encouraged. The Marine Resources Research Centre in Jiddah carries out research on the Kingdom's fish resources, and has evaluated the possibilities of intensive fish farming, whose prospects appear to be excellent.

As the Saudi diet has become more varied, so the agricultural industry has endeavoured to diversify to satisfy local demand. A wide variety of vegetables and fruits are grown by market gardeners for export and for the urban markets, which the new roads have made more accessible. The Government has improved the supply of high quality seeds. The tomato and watermelon crops produce large tonnages as do onions, grapes and citrus fruits, all are exported.

The Kingdom also contains one tenth of the world's mature, productive date palms. Although dates are no longer a staple in the Saudi diet, they form an important supplementary part of it. Better storage and packaging has meant that dates too are now exported.

None of this would have been possible

without the farmers' skills, and in this agriculture has been no different from other sectors of the Saudi economy: farmers have received training at the three government agricultural colleges, two training institutes and seven agricultural training centres.

Government-backed research into pest control, efficient irrigation and salinity control have all helped to improve yields. At Jizan, in the Kingdom's verdant south-western corner unique for its considerable rainfall, the Al Hakmah research station has been working in dam-water irrigated fields more reminiscent of Europe than Arabia to produce such tropical fruits as pineapples, bananas, mangoes and guavas. Its influence encouraged farmers to improve their already efficient drip-feed irrigation

Healthy flocks of sheep for breeding purposes have been reared under scientific care at Haradh (above).

systems. The Eastern Province's al-Hasa demonstration farm seeks to improve yields from crop-land that was once barren wasteland and rice is now being grown. Work continues at eleven other research centres and experimental farms.

The provision of adequate water supplies underpins the agricultural effort. For much of the 1980s it was thought that agricultural development would outrun water availability. However, with a slowdown during the period of the Fourth Plan in the development of new agricultural land and concentration on maximising the efficiency of existing farms, the Government's programme of building dams and desalination plants, and improved exploitation of groundwater resources, is proving sufficient to meet demand.

Studies by the Ministry of Agriculture and Water have revealed that Saudi Arabia's underground water resources are much greater than was at first believed in the mid-1970s. With caution, they should be sufficient for perhaps the next two centuries. It has been found that the eastern, northern and central areas of the Kingdom are composed of sedimentary rocks containing water-bearing formations which vary in quality and quantity. Such deposits cover the eastern two-thirds of the country. Their aquifers contain considerable amounts of water, some more than thirty thousand years old. Artesian water, once tapped, reaches the surface under its own pressure, as in al-Hasa Oasis, often at a high temperature. Such groundwater is a diminishing resource, and great efforts have been made to replace its use with collecting surface water by means of dams and by desalination.

Saudi Arabia is the largest country in the world without rivers – though its underground resources are said to equal the annual flow of the Nile for six hundred years. The average annual rainfall does not exceed 100mm, although the south-western parts of the country catch the monsoon and the annual rainfall in some areas might reach 500mm. In general, rainfall is sporadic and variable. There can be periods of drought of up to seven years, great humidity, high evaporation, strong wind effects and rapid run-off of floods.

The accumulation of salts in the soil is one of the permanent problems facing irrigated agriculture. All surface water contains some soluble salts in negligible amounts, but after several years of irrigation a harmful accumulation appears. In Saudi Arabia, salinity can be a severe problem, and careful drainage is therefore necessary.

Irrigation agriculture has been and will continue to be by far the largest user of water. Ultimately water availability will limit the amount of land which can be turned over to farming. It is estimated, however, that there is enough water, in rainfall and below ground, for the area of cultivated land to be almost doubled in the short term.

The main means of reducing dependence on groundwater are by dams and desalination of sea water. 200 dams are already built, of which the largest, across the Wadi Jizan in the Coastal Tihamah of the south-west, provides irrigation for 6000 hectares. Work is in progress on an even larger dam in the Bishah area of south-western Najd, which will be the second biggest in the Middle East. The 1,507 metre long dam will constitute the largest artificial lake in Saudi Arabia with a storage capacity of 350 million cubic metres. There are 23 dams in the Bahah region of the Hijaz alone. The greatest of the irrigation and drainage schemes – to rid the soil of its salinity – is in al-Hasa Oasis.

The final protection against lack of water is the sea, and the Government has undertaken an extensive desalination programme. Although costs were high in the initial stages, new technology has brought it down to a level comparable with the extraction of groundwater per cubic metre. Total capacity of the Kingdom's desalination plants now exceeds 500 million gallons per day. Most desalinated water is used for domestic distribution, so freeing groundwater resources for agricultural applications. The programme includes the world's largest water pipeline from Jubayl to Riyadh, which can be used to supply rural areas. The world's most advanced desalination plant, near Yanbu, uses solar energy.

The achievement of an adequate water supply for its agriculture, industry and homes is one of the Kingdom's chief successes. The story of its agriculture is just one illustration of how high initial state inputs have served to stimulate latent private enterprise into action. Government support for agriculture will always be necessary, particularly for its infrastructure, but direct support for farmers is already decreasing – as witness the recent drop in subsidies to wheat farmers. The Government will remain committed to the process of agricultural development.

Statistical sources: Ministry of Agriculture & Water and Ministry of Planning.

Fruit, poultry and honey

Figs (*top left*), grapes (*middle left*) and pimentoes (*bottom left*) speak of diversity of fruit production. Contrary to popular belief, much of the soil of Saudi Arabia is cultivable. Only the sand desert will grow nothing. The great expanses of powdery loess "desert" would bloom if water could reach it. Where this has been possible, vivid patches of green enliven the dun of the landscape. Meanwhile, more specialist areas of food production are being exploited. Saudi Arabia is already a major exporter of fruit to neighbouring countries, and egg farms are run on scientific methods (*right, top and middle*), providing a protein diet for people who, in earlier generations, had depended largely on dates, rice and sorghum. Bee culture (*bottom right*) has recently been added to the country's indigenous industries.

Other successful crops of fruit include water-melon, squash and tomatoes. The development of cash crops has been greatly stimulated by the expansion not only of the water supply (usually from underground), but also of the road system. Many small trucking enterprises have sprung up, linking producers with their markets in other parts of the country.

Local production of such foods is swiftly changing dietary habits. Dates are seldom, today, a staple; although they remain an important supplementary food. At the same time, the reclamation of the desert and the marking out of new smallholdings act as a spur to settlement.

Communications

THE ROMANTIC VIEW that travel and communications in Saudi Arabia still utilize camel caravans and dhows has long been belied by the modern reality. For more than a generation Saudis have enjoyed a sophisticated communications infrastructure from a superb inter-city road system to a satellite telecommunications system. The Ministry of Communications and the Ministry of Post, Telegraph and Telephone (PTT) have become established as two of the most important Ministries in the Kingdom. Their significance has been reflected in each Development Plan since the "Physical infrastructure development" section of the First Plan mapped out their empires in 1975. International and inter-regional transportation networks were developed to handle increased passenger and goods traffic; telecommunications and postal services were upgraded to relay more information; and old road, rail, air and seaport facilities expanded to meet rising traffic volumes, and more new ones were built. The realization of these ambitious plans has necessitated complex planning, energetic recruiting of manpower, enormous budgetary allocations and farsighted commitment from the Government.

As the map on page 150 shows, there is now an integrated road network in the Kingdom which only gained paved roads in the mid-1950s. This first limited system was transformed in the 1970s, when the overall length of paved road in the Kingdom tripled and the rural network grew fivefold. The Kingdom was linked with its neighbours, Jordan, Yemen, Kuwait, Qatar and the UAE. Rural roads were expanded to facilitate agricultural, mineral and industrial development. By 1989 more than SR100 billion had been spent on creating the road network, which comprises over 33,000 kms of asphalted and 64,000 kms of rural roads linking over 700 villages. The express road system extends to almost 4,000 kms, with major highways connecting Riyadh with Dammam, al-Qasim and Makkah, and Makkah with Jiddah and al-Madinah. The King Fahd Causeway connecting Dhahran with Bahrain, completed in 1986, is a major feat of civil engineering. Twenty-five kilometres long, it is used by 1.6 million vehicles per year. A programme of road-

safety research tested road construction, materials and maintenance to ensure all the Kingdom's roads can meet the heavy demands of its vehicular traffic. (*See also* Construction.)

As the demand increased for imported capital and consumer goods to support the development of the economy, the major ports of Jiddah and Dammam, as well as the ports of Yanbu, Jubayl and Jizan, expanded at a remarkable rate. More berths were constructed, and the amount of cargo handled per berth increased. Specialized industrial facilities were set up at Jizan, Yanbu and Jubayl, and minor ports were improved for small boats and fishermen. Improved training of personnel to operate the Kingdom's eight ports was set in hand, as were improved technical and maintenance facilities.

Great distances and difficult terrain has made aviation a vital element in the transport network. Saudia, the national airline, has become the largest in the Middle East, serving 23 domestic and 50 international airports regularly. Four more domestic airports are planned. Saudia has the largest air training centres in the Middle East. Its fleet comprises 91 aircraft, including Tri-Stars, Boeing 747s, European Airbuses, other wide bodied jets and several light aircraft. In 1985 Saudia carried over 13 million passengers. Although this figure fell to 9.8 million in 1986-7, the number is expected to rise again, eventually reaching 15 million. At up to 165,000 tonnes per year, air freight is an important source of revenue.

The airline and the Presidency of Civil Aviation sought to "Saudize" their operations as quickly as possible. With the exception of one tragic incident at Riyadh airport in 1980, they have maintained an excellent safety record.

In 1981, Jiddah's King Abdul Aziz International Airport opened: larger than Kennedy, Newark and O'Hare combined, it handles the annual influx of up to 1.5 million pilgrims bound for Makkah. Riyadh airport was superseded by the King Khalid complex in 1983. By the year 2000, it is planned to house the Kingdom's new aerospace technologies as well as handle 15 million passengers and 145,000 tonnes of cargo.

The Kingdom's newest airport is the

The airports of Jiddah (above) and Riyadh (right) are triumphs of Islamic architectonics in the tradition first set by Dhahran's airport (top).

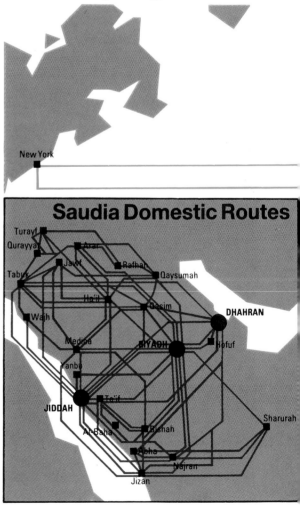

Saudia Domestic Routes

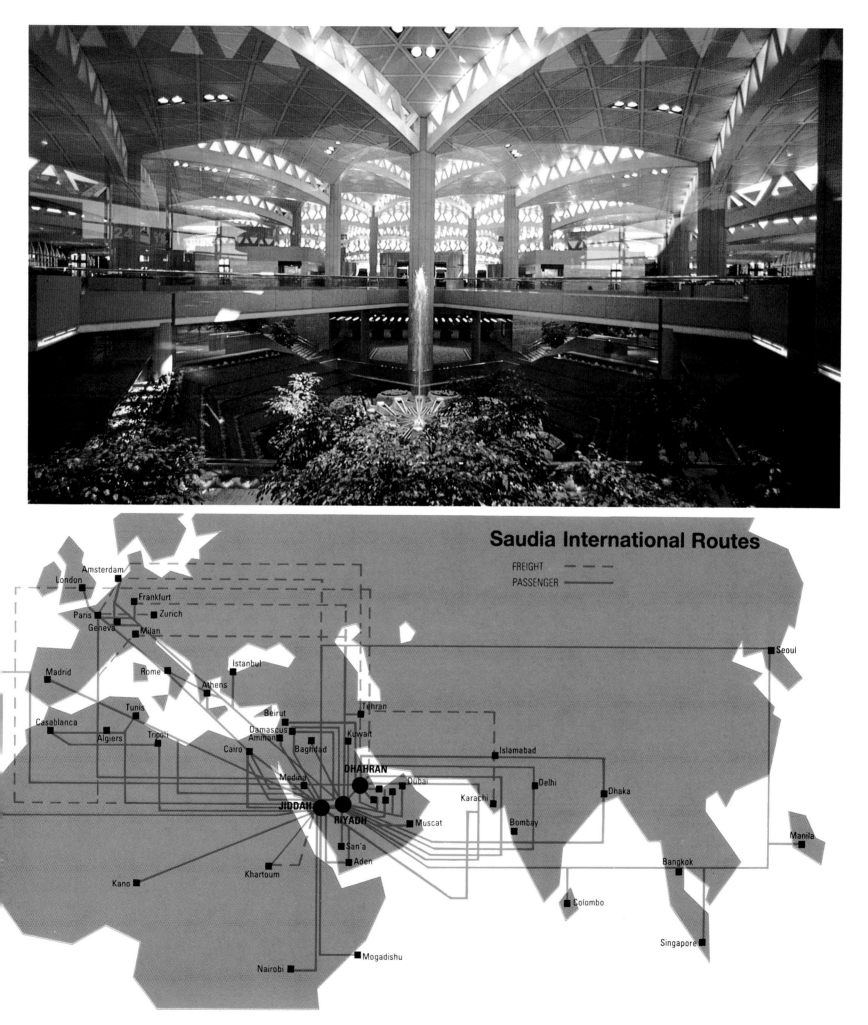

Saudia International Routes

FREIGHT — — —
PASSENGER ————

Amsterdam
London
Frankfurt
Paris Zurich
Geneva Milan
Madrid Rome Istanbul
Athens
Tunis Beirut Tehran
Casablanca Damascus
Algiers Tripoli Amman Kuwait
Cairo Baghdad Islamabad
Medina DHAHRAN Delhi Dhaka
Dubai
JIDDAH Karachi
RIYADH Bombay
Muscat
San'a
Aden
Khartoum Colombo
Kano Singapore
Nairobi Mogadishu
Seoul
Manila
Bangkok

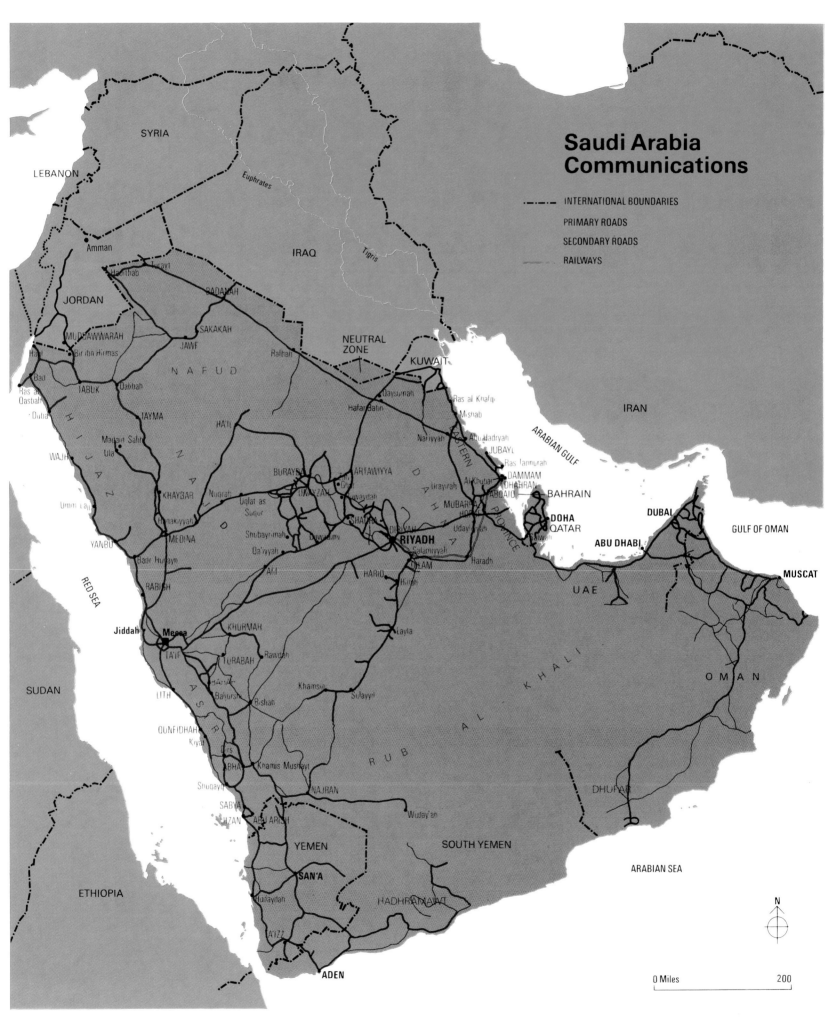

Saudi Arabia Communications

‒··‒··‒	INTERNATIONAL BOUNDARIES
	PRIMARY ROADS
	SECONDARY ROADS
	RAILWAYS

SYRIA

LEBANON

Euphrates

Amman

IRAQ

Tigris

JORDAN

Turayf

Habithab

BADANAH

SAKAKAH

JAWF

Rafhah

NEUTRAL ZONE

KUWAIT

MUDAWWARAH

Bir Ibn Hirmas

NAFUD

Daysumah

Ras al Khafji

IRAN

Had

Ras al Qasbah

JABUK

Qabbah

Hafar Batin

Mishab

Duba

TAYMA

HA'IL

Nariyah

EASTERN

Abu Hadryah

ARABIAN GULF

Madain Salih

Nuqrah

Umm Lajj

Ula

JUBAYL

Ras Tannurah

BURAYDA

ARTAWIYYA

Urayrah

DAMMAM

DHAHRAN

WAJH

KHAYBAR

UNAYZAH

Buraydah

Al Khubar

BAHRAIN

Uglat as Suqur

Huwayyat

ABQAIQ

DAHNA

MUBARR

DOHA

DUBAI

Hanakiyyah

Shubayrimah

SHAQRA

DIRIYAH

Uday ayirah

HOF

QATAR

GULF OF OMAN

MEDINA

Da'iyyah

RIYADH

Salamiyyah

Salwah

ABU DHABI

YANBU

Badr Hunayn

AFI

Duwadmi

DLAM

Harad

MUSCAT

RABIGH

RED SEA

HARIQ

Hilah

Haradh

UAE

Jiddah

Mecca

KHURMAH

Layla

OMAN

TA'IF

TURABAH

Rawdah

RUB AL KHALI

Khamsin

Sulayyil

ITH

BAHA

Bahursh

Bishah

QUNFIDHAH

Kiyat

Dirs

ABHA

Khamis Mushayt

Shuqayd

NAJRAN

Wuday'an

DHUFAR

SABYA

ABU ARISH

JIZAN

YEMEN

SOUTH YEMEN

ARABIAN SEA

SAN'A

SUDAN

ETHIOPIA

Hudaydah

HADHRAMAWT

A'IZZ

ADEN

N

0 Miles	200

King Fahd International Airport, between Dhahran and Jubayl in the Eastern Province. Occupying a 760 square kilometre site, the installations cover 43 square kilometres. The first phase was scheduled to open in the early 1990s.

The General Railway Organization runs and operates a dual line from Dammam to Riyadh as well as a short line to Dammam port. While passenger traffic doubled, freight haulage increased eighteenfold in the twelve years up to 1983, a rise which reflects the increasing importance of Riyadh's "dry port" for customs and warehousing, which was initially established in the late 1970s to ease pressure on congested Dammam. Further increases would follow the halving of travel time between the two cities a decade later. Further expansion, new stock and improved operational efficiency were also being planned. Rail lines from Riyadh to Jiddah with a spur to al-Madinah and rapid transit to Makkah were being considered with a possible reopening of the historic Hijaz pilgrim line; in the meantime, it was decided to develop existing road systems between the Holy Cities and their port and to provide pilgrims to the Holy Places with the specially coordinated services of the Saudi Public Transport Company.

Wireless telegraph stations were established in Makkah, Taif, Jiddah and Riyadh long ago, in the reign of King Abdul Aziz. Telephone systems followed and, in 1956, modern radio stations were set up. The Ministry of Communications (PTT) embarked upon large scale projects, both to develop the services, and to modernize the entire telecommunications system.

Today Saudi Arabia is the fifth largest user of telecommunications facilities in the world, and a major international telecommunications centre. In 1985, it joined the other Arab League nations in launching Arabsat, the Arab world's first communications satellite; its two primary tracking and control stations are at Riyadh, with four further earth stations at King Fahd Telecommunications City near Jiddah and another at

The twisting highway up to Abha is a monument to modern road-building.

Taif. Arabsat now has two satellites in orbit, with a third one planned. It reaches 7.5 million TV sets in the Kingdom, and offers a teletext service. It provides a state-of-the-art international telephone network which, by 1990, will be able to be utilised by the land-based network of 1.7 million telephone lines in operation in the Kingdom.

Postal services have made considerable progress. A 24-hour service for inland mail has been widely established. There is a post-code system and automatic sorting machines have replaced antiquated sorting facilities. Postal services are now available in 4,000 cities, villages and hamlets throughout the Kingdom. The aim is to establish a service of speed and unquestionable reliability to match the rest of Saudi Arabia's ultra-modern communications system.

Statistical source: Ministry of Communications.

151

Ports

The development of a building materials industry in Saudi Arabia caused a decline in the total volume of imports through the major ports in the mid-1980s. Over fifty per cent of the Kingdom's sea-traffic docks are at Jiddah (*opposite and below*) where 13.8 million freight tonnes were unloaded in 1986-7. Once acute congestion at this gateway to the Kingdom obliged ships to wait many weeks to unload. But Jiddah has expanded enormously since then, and especially since the early decades of the century when its principal traffic was shiploads of pilgrims bound for Makkah; the port now boasts 50 of the most modern of the Kingdom's 138 piers.

Further north on the Red Sea coast, Yanbu (*above left*) has been designated to become the country's second port, above all to relieve Jiddah and to provide Saudi Arabia with a terminal expressly designed to handle its growing volume of petrochemical exports (*above right*). Dammam is the largest port in the Gulf, and with Jubayl (*below right*) was built to handle the heavily increased oil traffic of the 1970s; now, as then, the main load of shipped oil takes place by the pipeline off Ras Tannurah. At the same time facilities for small boats and fishermen have not been neglected.

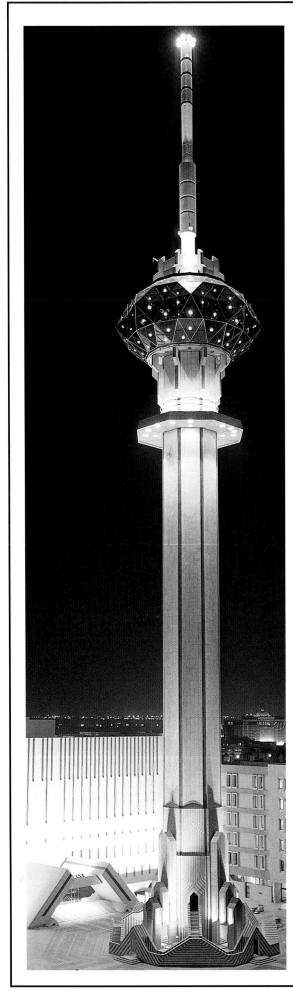

Television

It was the late King Faisal who recognized the potential in television for disseminating information to the Saudi people and bringing them a vivid sense of the unity and achievement of their nation. Now a series of transmission stations and mobile television centres brings informative programming to ninety per cent of the population. There are two television channels, one broadcasting in Arabic, the other in English and French. The Television Complex at Riyadh ranks as one of the world's most up-to-the-minute telecommunications facilities. Linked to the Arabsat satellite in 1985, the Centre's Islamic and news broadcasts can reach most of the Arab League's 21 member countries. The addition of a third satellite to the network is planned before the end of the decade.

Manufacturing

Until recently Saudi wealth had been built on revenues from the sale of a non-renewable asset; hence the growing preoccupation and determination to diversify by building up the non-oil sector of the economy. Capital intensive manufacturing became a priority of the Fourth Plan, and will remain so in the Fifth Plan, with the emphasis on manpower training and stimulation of the private sector.

In Yanbu light manufacturing industries include this plastic bag factory.

Fibreglass lamp posts are exported throughout the Gulf.

INDUSTRY – ESPECIALLY HYDRO-carbon-based – has already become a major source of Saudi Arabia's income, as it diversifies away from its heavy dependence on the export of crude oil.

Several government agencies are at work behind the Kingdom's industrial effort. But it is firm policy that Saudi manufacturing should be profitable in its own right and that private investment and Saudi industrialists and personnel play a central role in the continuing success of the hydrocarbon and heavy industries founded by the Government.

The Fourth Plan established the Saudi Venture Capital Group (SVCG) to promote private-sector participation in industry, and its membership comprises many of the Kingdom's leading companies and business people. Since the mid-1970s the Government's semi-autonomous Saudi Industrial Development Fund (SIDF) has provided viable industrial ventures with cheap finance – up to half the start-up cost to Saudi industrialists, or Saudi-foreign joint ventures with licences from the Ministry of Industry and Electricity. With SIDF, the Ministry monitors industry closely, and licences are curtailed if particular sectors have achieved sufficient or surplus capacity. It has also developed the industrial estates in most cities and towns which have long supplied manufacturers with cheap land and low-priced essential services.

By the end of 1988 the Government had provided more than $51.2 billion to the private sector through specialised domestic credit funds such as the SIDF, which offer interest-free loans for industrial, agricultural and real estate de-velopment, and investment agencies like the National Industrialization Company (NIC). Industrial estates have been created in Riyadh, Jiddah, Dammam, al-Qasim, Hofuf, and Makkah, and six more are planned at al-Madinah, Hail, Jawf, Tabuk, Ar'ar and in Asir. But the biggest concentrations of bulk industrial production are of course at the new industrial cities of Yanbu and Jubayl.

Manufacturing variety is enormous. SIDF's loan policy has shifted from construction materials ventures in the 1970s and early 1980s to encouraging diversification. Apart from down-line petrochemicals products at Yanbu and Jubayl, the Kingdom now produces and in many cases exports iron and steel, processed foodstuffs, fruit juices, cable, piping, glass products, aluminium products, solar cells, air conditioners, various electrical goods, cement and construction materials of all kinds, wood products, leather goods, plastics, paints, medicines and bottled water. By 1988 the Kingdom could boast over 2,000 factories with a combined investment of SR95 billion and a combined workforce of 140,000.

The average value of SIDF loans has risen continuously – a sign that new ventures are increasingly capital-intensive, and that they are investing heavily in the ever-improving technology available. Such a trend also highlights the problems for new projects caused by the shortage of a readily available and qualified labour force. Saudi manufacturing in general continues to be constrained by the smallish size of the Saudi market, making overseas markets essential to its growth. Protectionist tariffs imposed on

Saudi Iron and Steel Company (Hadeed) (Above). Also in Jubayl, the Saudi Shoe Company (Below).

its petrochemical products abroad are now being overcome by means of free trade within the GCC states and with the EEC. Economic cooperation among the GCC states will now increase, coordinated by the Doha-based Gulf Organization for Industrial Consulting which studies and recommends proposals for factories to supply all the Gulf states.

The economic heart of Jubayl is planned to accommodate 20 large capital and energy intensive industries. Except for HADEED – the iron and steel mill – all these industries will use hydrocarbon

resources as feedstock. SABIC completed installation of a basic steel industry when production started at HADEED in 1983. The plant built in co-operation with Korf Stahl of West Germany includes an 850,000 tonnes per year direct reduction process, fuelled by Saudi Aramco's master gas gathering system. Annual capacity from the attached steel rolling mill has doubled since 1983, to 1.6 million mt/y in 1991. Expansion will increase capacity to 2 million mt/y by 1993.

Many industrialists wanted tariff barriers to protect them against cheap im-

ports, but Government policy on viable manufacturing seeks instead to lessen foreign protectionism: the recent free trade agreement with the EEC is a milestone along this route. The Government will continue to encourage foreign participation in manufacturing by licensing joint ventures and allowing them to benefit from the SIDF's soft loans and generous tax holidays for the foreign partner's profits. As manufacturing has been a relatively new Saudi endeavour, there is a shortage of management and technical expertise but this will be over-

The solemn purpose of the country has been to provide an infrastructure that will outlast its age of plenty. Industries firmly based on local resources include an aluminium plant at Al Khobar (above), while a Saudi Mercedes factory (top) shows another aspect of the manufacturing sector. Massive development has changed the face of Jiddah, (left), though quieter, more ancient skills such as wood carving (right) remain in vogue, and highly sought after.

come by the Fifth Plan's priority of training manpower and attracting technology transfer by stimulating foreign participation. Today there are nearly 600 industrial joint ventures: the United States leading (200), followed by Britain (125), Germany (87) and Japan (43).

The first development plans envisaged a worldscale heavy and hydrocarbons industry in the Kingdom, using the plentiful raw materials and energy, particularly natural gas which was in those days being wastefully flared off. By the end of the Fourth Plan, the new industrial

cities of Jubayl and Yanbu were in the last stages of construction. Many of their industries, primed by SABIC as joint ventures with foreign partners are producing and exporting to Europe, the U.S. and Japan. There are over a dozen of these major ventures. Their products include a wide variety of petrochemicals and by-products, plastics, fertilisers and minerals. In 1986 SABIC plants produced 2.76 million tonnes, in 1987 production leapt to 9.7 million tonnes, and in 1988 it fell back slightly to 7 million tonnes.

SABIC is now being increasingly offered to the private sector, and some of its industries are notably successful. In 1991 SABIC shareholders received a total dividend of SR1 billion, about a third of the previous year's profits. It exports its products to 2000 customers in 65 countries.

The SABIC joint venture to produce methyl tertiary butyl ether (MTBE), an octane enhancing fuel additive, has found ready markets in Europe, Japan and the U.S. Methanol is currently in strong worldwide demand, and methanol

plants such as IBN SINA and AL-RAZI are having their capacity increased. The Saudi Petrochemical Company (SADAF) has an annual capacity of 760,000 tonnes of ethylene, 560,000 tonnes of ethylene dichloride, 300,000 tonnes of crude industrial ethanol, and 360,000 tonnes of styrene. The Arabian Petrochemical Company (PETROKEMYA) produces 560,000 tonnes of ethylene, 100,000 tonnes of polystyrene and 50,000 tonnes of butane-1. The Jubayl Petrochemicals Company (KEMYA), a joint SABIC/Exxon project, has an annual capacity of 390,000 tonnes of low-density and high-density polyethylene, which is used for malleable plastics such as films, moulded products and synthetic fibres.

The Yanbu Petrochemicals Company (YANPET), a joint venture with Mobil, has annual production figures of 560,000 tonnes of ethylene, 430,000 tonnes of polyethylene and 250,000 tonnes of ethylene glycol. SABIC's enterprises extend to iron, steel and aluminium, though it is conscious that its production in these sectors should not harm that of other GCC states, such as that of Bahrain's ALBA – one of three Bahrain-based enterprises in which SABIC also has an interest.

A healthy fertiliser industry has also been established. In 1988 the Saudi Arabian Fertiliser Company (SAFCO) had an annual capacity of 330,000 tonnes of urea, and the Jubayl Fertiliser Company (SAMAD), a Saudi-Taiwan joint venture, produces 600,000 tonnes of urea annually.

By 1990 the Kingdom's petroleum refining activities were contributing over 8 per cent to the GNP, and petrochemical exports were soaring. The downstream petrochemical plants not only allow the Kingdom to add value to its crude oil production, but also create the opportunities to train a skilled Saudi workforce for the future. It is envisaged that the Kingdom's very competitive low-priced production will ensure it a continuing share of the world's petrochemical markets of two to eight per cent for different products.

A stripper column (above left) *engineered and fabricated in Jubayl prior to shipment to Shedgum. A trainee on Saudi Aramco's Technical Development Programme* (above top) *tests a water sample in the laboratory. Lube oil is processed in the Saudi Arabian Lube Oil Additive Company (SALACO) in Yanbu. Valve repair at the Dresser-Al-Rushaid Manufacturing Company in Jubayl.*

Mining

MIDWAY TO SUDAN from Jiddah, the Atlantis II hot brine deep, one of many along the Red Sea rift, could prove an exciting source of mineral wealth as the world's first ocean-bed mine.

Thick mud on the seabed 2,000 metres down was found to contain seventeen metallic elements when brought up from the 29 million-year-old rift in the earth's mantle. They include gold, silver, mercury, iron, copper and zinc. The Saudi-Sudanese Commission for the Development of Red Sea Resources considered a mine feasible.

Its work, contracted largely to international specialists, was generating new patents and techniques at the forefront of world research on ocean floor mining, which in most of the ocean's rifts is complicated by legal problems of ownership. Atlantis II, deep in the Red Sea's relatively young and narrow rift – still widening at an estimated 2.5 centimetres a year – is wholly within the two countries' territorial waters. By the late 1980s the Commission expected to establish a pilot plant at Yanbu to process the mineral bearing muds piped by a marine rig from the seabed to shore.

The first mine in the Kingdom's modern mining era started commercial production in 1988. Appropriately it was at Mahd al-Dhahab ("Cradle of Gold"), the Arabian Shield's most historic of mines. The mine produces gold, silver, copper and zinc, using advanced technology.

Originally a joint venture with the London-based Consolidated Gold Fields group, the Government's Petromin assumed complete control of the project in 1982. Raw material deposits are estimated at 1.2 million tonnes.

While the Mahd al-Dahab project is the most advanced, other joint ventures with international mining companies are investigating the several promising deposits which have been discovered largely by the government's sustained and intense geological effort to chart its mineral resources and lay the foundations for a mining industry.

The US-based Arabian Shield Development Company, in a joint venture with the National Mining Company of Saudi Arabia, is working towards production at Masane, where gold, silver, copper and zinc deposits have been iden-

Ancient mine-workings had always hinted that Saudi Arabia would prove rich in much more than oil.

tified, and is investigating a large nickel-iron deposit at Wadi Qatan.

British Steel continues to investigate iron ore deposits at Wadi Sawawin in the north-west on behalf of the Government to assess the commercial viability of supplying the direct reduction steel mill at Jubayl with Saudi Arabian ore when continuing world overproduction has depressed the cost of importing. Minerals policy is to relate closely to industrial needs while mapping resources and investigating the most promising of over 700 mineral occurrences. The exploitation of bauxite at Zabirah may provide the basis for an integrated Gulf aluminium industry. Phosphates near Sirhan and Turayf may promote a phosphoric acid and fertiliser industry. Other deposits reveal uranium at Qurayyat, and copper and zinc at Jabal Sayid and near the ancient Nuqrah mine in northern Najd. Smaller deposits of gold and tin-tungsten encourage wider exploration across the Kingdom: mines at al-Hajjar in the Asir, Shibratah and at al-Amar hold out the promise of gold in commercial quantities.

It is expected that some of this prospecting will lead to small-scale mining to aid the social development of some rural communities.

Quarrying at Mahd al-Dhahab, the Arabian Shield's most historic mine.

Construction

NEW CONSTRUCTION, OFTEN on a massive scale, has taken place in Saudi Arabia, drawing contractors from around the world and creating a new domestic industry. In terms of amenities and standards the Kingdom has been transformed into a modern society as the work has taken place.

By the mid-1980s, the furious pace of building slowed somewhat as the main elements of the essential national infrastructure were substantially completed and attention turned increasingly to operation and maintenance. But despite this relative decline in activity, the

The complex of Conference Palace and mosque (Qasr Al-Mu'tamarat) has given Riyadh one of its most beautiful architectural sites. "Grand Festivals Palace" (left) remarkably reproduces a traditional palace.

Construction

Saudi Arabia's massive building programme inspired the international community of architects and designers to stretch their skills and imaginations. Architects from all over the world have seen the successful construction of such major projects as the Al Hada Sheraton in Taif *(bottom)*. More recently, indigenous designers have made their mark inspiring originality in domestic architecture as in these houses at Jiddah *(top)*, and Al Khobar *(middle)*.

The top of the water tower in Riyadh (top right) affords a splendid panorama of the city and its environs. The striking sports city in Dammam (above), completed in 1979, contains three swimming pools and a multi-purpose gymnasium. A new hotel (left) encloses an elegant stairway. It is the cleanliness of the atmosphere and the strong light that have stimulated architects and designers into attempting forceful new ideas – both in details and on the grand scale – in new townships and universities.

Dammam and Riyadh have been provided with municipal housing on a scale matching Jiddah's (above and right); housing projects, like the one in Taif (below), continue today on a smaller scale.

urban and rural landscape continues to change; the country remains the main focus for construction and allied industries in the Middle East, and projects of immense scale are still under way.

The transformation over the past decades has been enormous. New ports at Jubayl and Yanbu and massive expansions at Jiddah and Jizan paved the way for soaring imports and construction. Even Riyadh received a "dry port", to store cargo brought from Dammam.

New roads have extended the cities which spread for miles beyond their traditional limits – and large numbers of

The tall blocks of downtown Jiddah (left) *dwarf the older parts of the city; its commercial importance makes it a developer's dream.*

International Airport in the Eastern Province – another mega-project on a 760 square kilometre site – was due to become operational in the early 1990s.

New housing included the mammoth rush housing schemes of the three cities as well as thousands of elegant new villas and homes built with the help of cheap government loans. Cityscapes were transformed with new building, whether the dozens of grand new ministries or government buildings in Riyadh or the tall office-blocks of downtown Jiddah. In the towns and villages of the country, new buildings went up, matched, less visibly, by sewage systems, electricity and water – all extended in the cities. A modern telecommunications network efficiently connected the Kingdom nationwide. Thousands of new hospital beds, among the most sophisticated in the world, marked the Government and the private sector's determination to serve Saudi citizens. Schools similarly blossomed to cater for Saudi youth, as well as sports facilities, for example the new King Fahd Sports Stadium in Riyadh – the largest free-span structure in the world – which opened in March 1989. Grand modern hotels, perhaps even too many, were built in the cities and towns, whose industrial estates saw the rise of modern, capital-intensive Saudi manufacturing. Above all, work continues in Jubayl on the Gulf and Yanbu on the Red Sea to extend the new cities built to cater for the Kingdom's increasingly important petrochemical, refining, steel and heavy industries.

It is firm government policy that local contractors should be preferred where possible, but Saudi Arabia's larger projects turned it into an international construction forum drawing keen competition from America, Europe and the Far East for the work. South Korean contractors particularly prevailed for basic building work as they and other Asians, like the Filipinos, undercut Western builders but maintained equally high standards. But American, British, French, German, Italian, Greek, and especially Saudi firms won considerable work. Design – much of it unique in imagination and scope – similarly brought all nationalities, though Saudis themselves took an increasing role.

cars have arrived to use them. Dozens of flyovers in Jiddah and Riyadh sought to ease the flow of traffic, several running for miles above the urban streets. Many of the Kingdom's new generation of roads are outstanding construction feats, like the twisting drive to Taif's escarpment, or down from Abha towards Jizan. These massive schemes, laying thousands of miles of roadway where none existed before, are crowned by the Bahrain causeway, the twenty-five kilometre double-lane highway linking Bahrain and the mainland which opened to traffic in 1986.

In Riyadh, other construction projects abound. The campus of King Saud University, opened in 1984, has achieved worldwide renown. An entire suburb – the Diplomatic Quarter, or 'DQ' – has been built to house the embassies and diplomats relocated from Jiddah. The Qasr al-Hukm project to transform the entire city centre is currently taking shape. And the international airport, operational since 1983, is the largest and most advanced in the world. Jiddah's own international airport, with its award-winning Hajj Terminal, a vast, stunning white fibre-glass "tent", opened in 1981. The first phase of the King Fahd

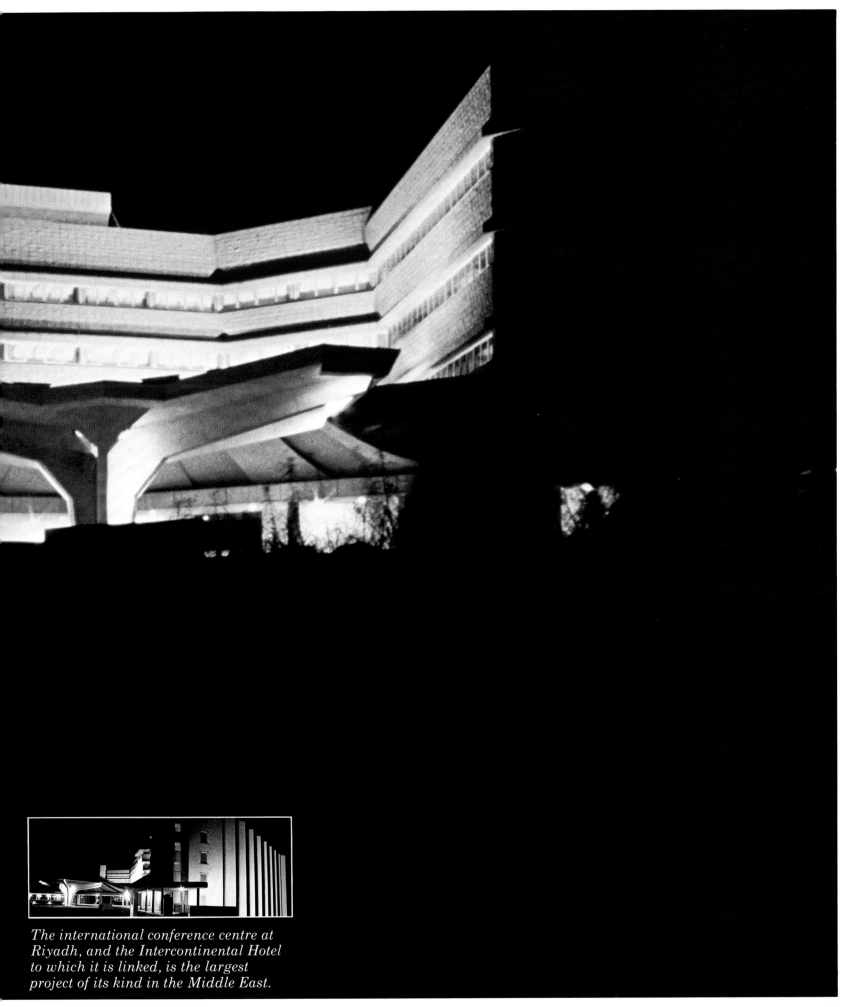

The international conference centre at Riyadh, and the Intercontinental Hotel to which it is linked, is the largest project of its kind in the Middle East.

Petroleum-
Discovery &
Development

THE founder of the modern Saudi State, King Abdul Aziz ibn Abd al-Rahman Al Saud, opened the door to the development of Saudi Arabia's vast hydrocarbon resources in 1933 when he granted a concession to the Standard Oil Company of California (Socal) to explore for oil in the Kingdom. Socal formed an operating company (California Arabian Standard Oil Company), of which Texaco bought a half share in 1937.

The story of the discovery of oil in Arabia is remarkable. Socal was one of the largest oil producers in the United States, but by 1930 its exploration in eighteen foreign countries had produced nothing substantial. Meanwhile, an enterprising New Zealander, Major Frank Holmes, went to Bahrain in the early 1920s to assist in developing water resources, although his principal interest was in the possibility of oil. In 1922 he crossed over to the Arabian mainland and negotiated with Abdul Aziz Al Saud for a concession covering more than 30,000 square miles in the eastern Hasa Province. It was granted in 1923, and, in 1925, Holmes succeeded in obtaining an oil concession for Bahrain.

These concessions were taken in the name of the Eastern and General Syndicate, a British group with which Holmes was associated and which, although not made up of oil operators, hoped to interest British companies who were. In this effort it was unsuccessful. The concession in Hasa was allowed to lapse for want of £1,000 to keep it in operation. Gulf Oil Corporation took up the option in Bahrain, but because of their oil interests in Iraq, assigned it to Socal in 1928.

With Socal established in Bahrain, it was only a matter of time before American geologists were on their way to Jiddah, to the King of Saudi Arabia. By the end of 1933, eight American oilmen were working in the Dammam area. It was Well No 7 that turned the company's fortunes in 1938. Drilled to 4,727 feet, it encountered large quantities of oil in what is now called the Arab Zone.

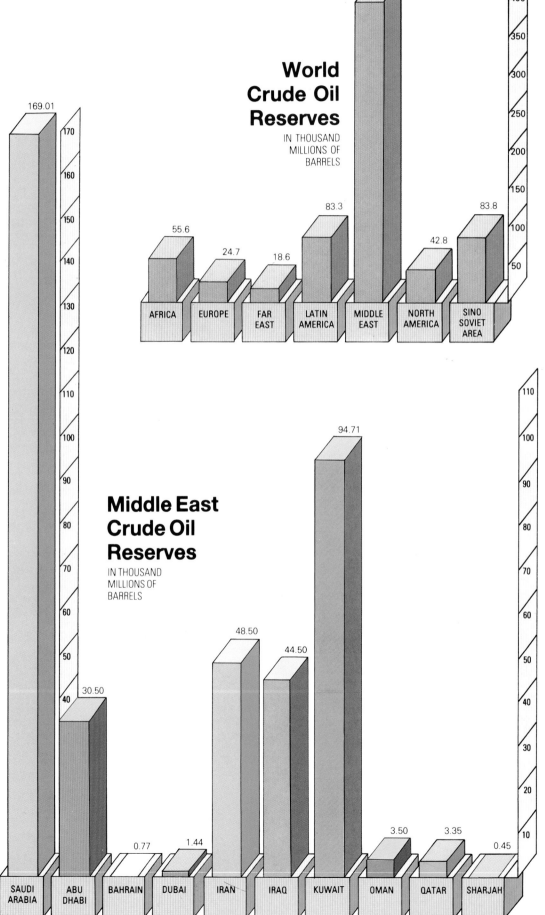

World Crude Oil Reserves
IN THOUSAND MILLIONS OF BARRELS

AFRICA 55.6 · EUROPE 24.7 · FAR EAST 18.6 · LATIN AMERICA 83.3 · MIDDLE EAST 398.4 · NORTH AMERICA 42.8 · SINO SOVIET AREA 83.8

Middle East Crude Oil Reserves
IN THOUSAND MILLIONS OF BARRELS

SAUDI ARABIA 169.01 · ABU DHABI 30.50 · BAHRAIN 0.77 · DUBAI 1.44 · IRAN 48.50 · IRAQ 44.50 · KUWAIT 94.71 · OMAN 3.50 · QATAR 3.35 · SHARJAH 0.45

World Crude Oil Production

INCLUDING NATURAL GAS LIQUIDS IN THOUSAND BARRELS DAILY

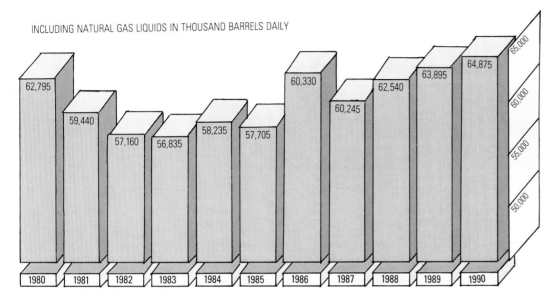

Year	Production
1980	62,795
1981	59,440
1982	57,160
1983	56,835
1984	58,235
1985	57,705
1986	60,330
1987	60,245
1988	62,540
1989	63,895
1990	64,875

Middle East Crude Oil Production

INCLUDING NATURAL GAS LIQUIDS IN THOUSAND BARRELS DAILY

*Aramco Estimate

	1980	1981	1982	1983	1984	1985	1986	1987	1988	1989	1990
UAE	1705	1505	1250	1180	1220	1350	1555	1695	1775	2035	2300
IRAN	1480	1325	2410	2465	2195	2215	1905	2310	2265	2845	3125
IRAQ	2645	895	1010	1105	1225	1440	1745	2090	2600	2825	2005
KUWAIT	1430	965	705	900	985	920	1250	1075	1340	1640	1065
OMAN	285	325	325	390	420	505	560	580	595	590	660
QATAR	460	425	340	310	425	340	355	340	360	410	455
OTHERS	215	215	220	225	220	220	240	285	495	570	630

Saudi Arabia Crude Oil Production

INCLUDING NATURAL GAS LIQUIDS IN THOUSAND BARRELS DAILY

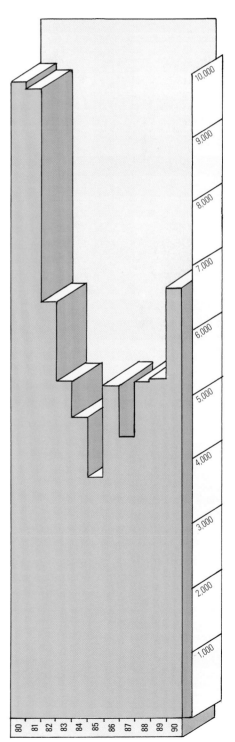

**Probability of
Oil Occurrence**

FAVOURABLE

POSSIBLE

The first tanker was loaded in 1939.

In 1944 the Company's name was changed to Arabian American Oil Company (Aramco). Mobil (formerly Socony-Vacuum Oil Company) and Exxon (formerly Standard Oil Company of New Jersey) obtained shares in 1948, and ownership of Aramco was divided on the basis of thirty per cent each for Socal, Texaco and Exxon, with ten per cent for Mobil.

The discovery and development of Saudi Arabia's oil fields began slowly, affected by transportation difficulties and material shortages resulting from the Second World War. Activity resumed in a limited way in the autumn of 1943 when plans were announced for a 50,000 barrels a day refinery at Ras Tannurah. With the ending of hostilities, Aramco's crude oil production jumped from an average 20,000 barrels a day before 1944 to 500,000 barrels daily by the end of 1949. By 1974 Aramco was producing 8.2 million barrels a day and the capacity of its refinery at Ras Tannurah neared half a million barrels a day.

Aramco then accounted for ninety-five per cent of Saudi Arabia's production, but it was not the only oil company oper-

ating in the Kingdom. The Getty Oil Company was assigned a concession in Saudi Arabia's undivided share of the Neutral Zone in 1949 and, in cooperation with Aminoil (the American company carrying Kuwait's fifty per cent interest in the Neutral Zone), discovered oil in 1953 in what is now called the Wafrah field. The Japanese-owned Arabian Oil Company was assigned a concession by both Saudi Arabia and Kuwait to explore the offshore area of the Neutral Zone in 1958, and two years later discovered oil in the Khafji field.

Through these years the Government's participation in the nation's vital oil sector began to increase; for it was well appreciated that the petroleum resources, no matter how large, were not infinite. In the late 1950s two Saudi officials joined Aramco's Board of Directors, and they were later increased to three.

In 1962 the Saudi Arabian Government established the General Petroleum and Mineral Organization (Petromin) to develop the Kingdom's oil and mineral resources and to establish related industries. Petromin is an autonomous government agency working in conjunction with the Ministry of Petroleum and

Mineral Resources. It entered into a joint venture with the Italian state oil company AGIP, and with Philips Saudi Arabia to explore for oil in the Rub al-Khali and Hasa areas. Under an agreement with Tenneco (the American oil exploration company from Tennessee) it began detailed exploration for oil offshore along the Red Sea coast.

In addition, Petromin established other joint ventures like Argas (Arabian Geophysical and Surveying Company) which has carried out aeromagnetic, geodetic and seismic surveys for local and foreign oil companies. The Arabian Drilling Company has performed drilling and well work-overs on the same basis. In 1967 Petromin Marketing assumed control of Aramco's kingdom-wide marketing network for the distribution and sale of refined products, and thereafter further expanded and modernized its service. The Petromin Tankers and Mineral Shipping Company (Petroship) also purchased a number of oil tankers to haul crude oil from Ras Tannurah to the refinery at Jiddah, then one of a growing number under Petromin's wing (*see* Refining).

Thus, for the first time were the multi-

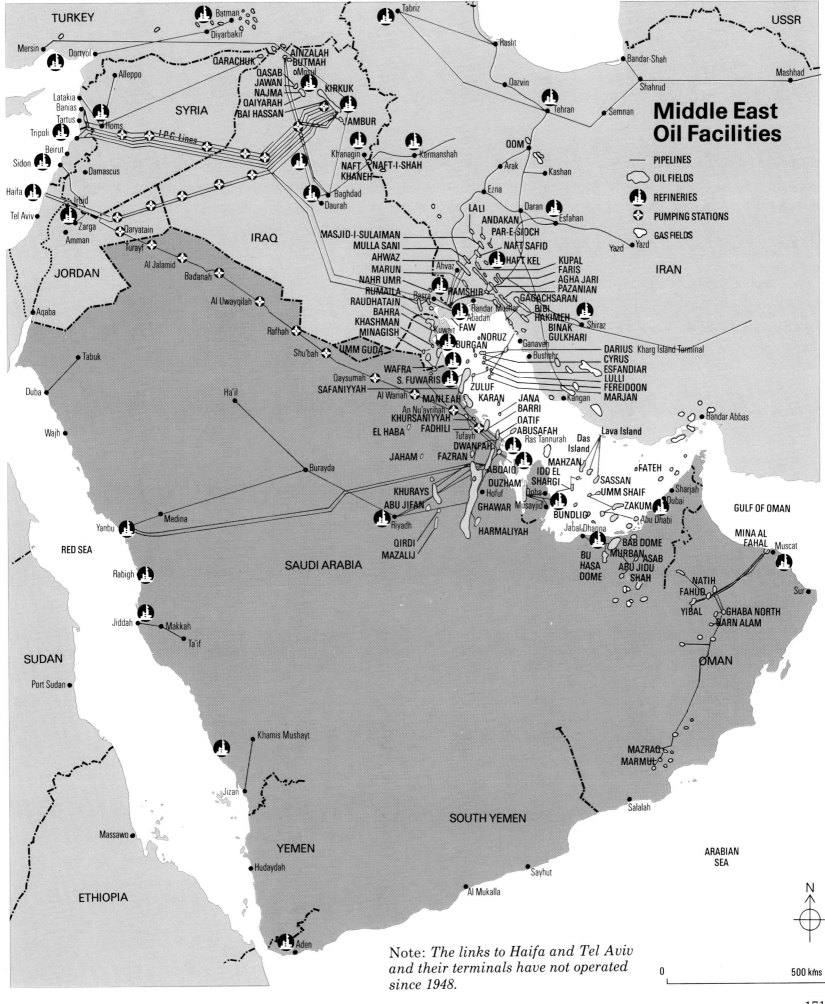

Middle East Oil Facilities

— PIPELINES

◯ OIL FIELDS

⬤ REFINERIES

✛ PUMPING STATIONS

▢ GAS FIELDS

Note: *The links to Haifa and Tel Aviv and their terminals have not operated since 1948.*

0 ———— 500 kms

national oil companies bypassed which, until then, had traditionally handled all international oil flows. Since that time the east-west crude oil and NGL overland pipelines supplying the port and petrochemical plants at Yanbu have superseded the domestic tanker route.

In 1968 the Kingdom's interest in Aramco turned to participation and partial ownership as well as management. In 1972, the Saudi Government acquired a twenty-five per cent interest in Aramco's crude oil concessions rights. On 5 June 1974 this share was increased to sixty per cent. Negotiations were then initiated to bring the Government's participation up to one hundred per cent while still preserving the role of the American companies in providing expertise. The financial takeover was completed in 1980, by which time Saudi oil officials had long been responsible for all aspects of the Kingdom's oil policy. Agreements were reached specifying access to the Kingdom's crude oil for the multinational Aramco partners who continued to supply expertise while Saudi Arabians prepared to take their place. Today the company is known as Saudi Aramco, and is wholly Saudi owned, with all of its management positions, 77 per cent of its supervisory posts and almost half of its professional posts held by Saudis. 1520 Saudis were recruited during 1987-88 alone. As well as its domestic production activities, the company is now participating in overseas refining, distribution and marketing of petroleum products: the joint venture formed with Texaco in 1988 covering the eastern side of the U.S. is a noteworthy development along this route.

When Saudi Arabia and other members of the Organisation of Petroleum Exporting Countries combined to take the power of oil pricing decisions away from the multinational oil companies in the early 1970s, much changed in the Kingdom's oil scene. As OPEC's largest producer it remained a moderating force while oil prices multiplied many times through the years when OPEC prices rose, spurred by the international markets' forces pushing them up many times above the artificially low levels that had been set by the multinationals. Saudi Arabia, when necessary, maintained high output levels to prevent disarray in the Western economies and sought to introduce stabilising pricing formulas for gradual, predictable changes in price. It continued to provide a stabilising force

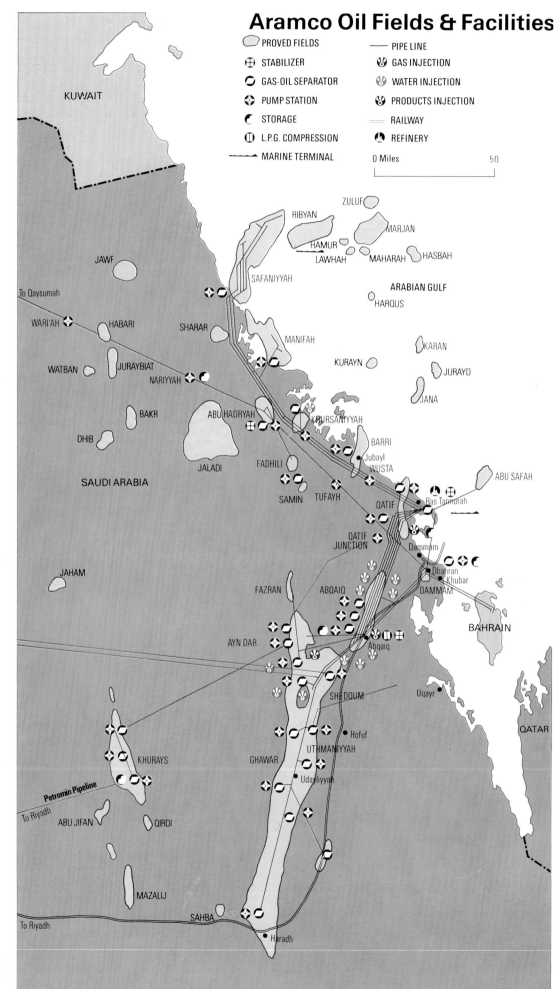

Aramco Oil Fields & Facilities

PROVED FIELDS — PIPE LINE
STABILIZER — GAS INJECTION
GAS-OIL SEPARATOR — WATER INJECTION
PUMP STATION — PRODUCTS INJECTION
STORAGE — RAILWAY
L.P.G. COMPRESSION — REFINERY
MARINE TERMINAL   0 Miles   50

through the early 1980s, when falling world demand threatened real market prices, by pressing for a unified pricing policy and adherence to production quotas among OPEC members. Until 1985, the Kingdom voluntarily acted as OPEC's "swing producer", where it would cut its own quota by up to fifty per cent to maintain the overall rate of OPEC production within the limits set. During these years Saudi exports fell by more than sixty per cent. Since 1986, however, Saudi Arabia has been forced to follow the practices adopted by other OPEC members and has allowed production to rise to accord more fully with its targeted quota. It is stated Saudi policy not to abandon the course it has pursued since 1976 to avoid rapid fluctuations in the price of oil.

In the early 1980s Petromin began to establish direct crude oil export contracts with usually government-backed consumers and also established "incentive" oil contracts which were awarded to those multinational companies investing in the Kingdom's new downstream hydrocarbons industry (*see* Industry). Such direct deals grew to account for two million barrels of oil per day (mbd). However, in the mid-1980s this system gave way to Saudi Arabia's pioneering "netback" arrangement whereby price was to be significantly discounted in advance of sales, in return for guaranteed market access. This ingenious system provided the oil market with a reasonably stable, but responsive framework for pricing. Netback deals have since become standard practice for most OPEC members. Petromin also stabilised the Kingdom's refining at the optimum demanded by domestic consumption and export (*see* Refining). In 1989 Petromin streamlined its subsidiaries which were previously responsible for the refining, supply, distribution and marketing of petroleum products at home and internationally into one major downstream oil company, SAMAREC – The Saudi Arabian Marketing and Refining Company. SAMAREC operations include three refineries for domestic consumption with a total production capacity of 420,000 b/d and three more export refineries with a production capacity of 870,000 b/d.

At the start of 1989, Saudi Arabia's oil reserves were estimated at 252 billion barrels – over one-third of the world's total known reserves. This figure could rise to 315 billion barrels with further ex-

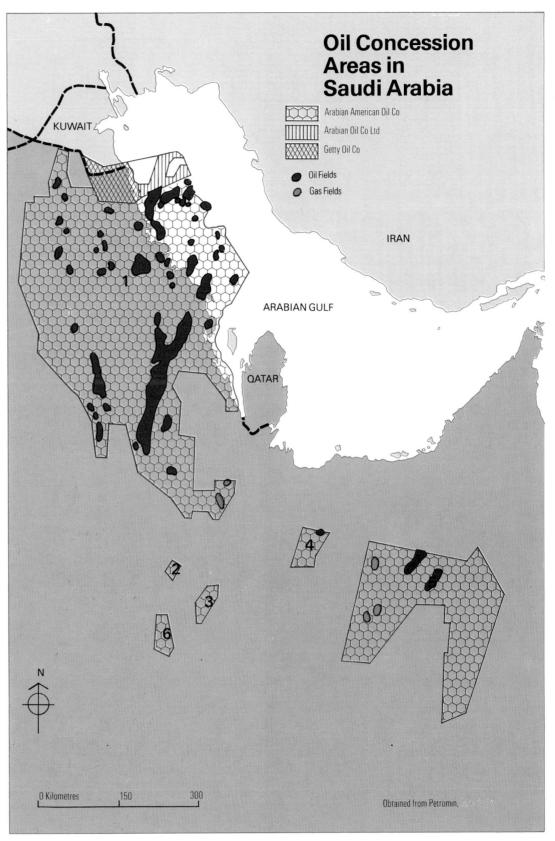

Oil Concession Areas in Saudi Arabia

- Arabian American Oil Co
- Arabian Oil Co Ltd
- Getty Oil Co
- Oil Fields
- Gas Fields

KUWAIT

IRAN

ARABIAN GULF

QATAR

N

0 Kilometres   150   300

Obtained from Petromin.

ploration and improved extraction techniques. Production fluctuated during the 1980s: hit by the world recession and the consequent tightened OPEC quotas, it dropped in 1985 to just over a third of the 1980 peak of 10 mbd. However, production had climbed back to about 5.5 mbd in mid 1990, shortly before the invasion of Kuwait by Iraq. Within three months of

the invasion, Saudi Arabia had responded by increasing production to 8.5 mbd. This figure has climbed steadily and looks set to remain stable at about 10 mbd.

Exploration

Exploration for oil and gas proceeded through the 1970s and early 1980s to establish as precisely as possible the extent of the country's phenomenal reserves. Every year more oil was discovered than was pumped. Saudi Arabia's known reserves, almost double any other country's, amount to over one-third of the world's total. The presence of oil is first calculated from the occurrence of trough-like geological formations; but to strike an oil seam usually involves a lengthy phase of trial and error. By 1985, fifty-nine commercial fields had been discovered, seventeen of them offshore, three partially so, and the rest onshore. The Ghawar field is the world's largest field onshore, and Safaniya the largest offshore. Saudi Arabia divides production from the rich fields in the Neutral Zone which it shares with Kuwait. Fourteen new oilfields have been discovered in recent years.

Heavy drilling materials are dragged across the desert by specially designed vehicles (left and above), *while camps are supplied by helicopters* (above, right). *Rock depths are calculated either by drilling, or seismically by blast* (right). *A gusher may produce black oil, or* (far right), *gas.*

Extraction

Oil from an underground reservoir rises to the surface as a result of an injection of gas. The oil mixed with gas then proceeds to the Gas-Oil Separation Plant (GOSP). The gas is then re-cycled back into the gas injection plant, below ground, to force more oil upwards. The unstabilized oil then proceeds to the crude oil stabilizer, and, as a stabilized oil, it is pumped either aboard tankers, or in pipelines across the desert. Alternatively, stabilized oil may go to the refinery – in Saudi Aramco's case to the refinery at Ras Tannurah. The great size of Saudi Arabia's oil resources, the ruggedly hostile nature of the terrain, the distances over which the oil must be transported before it can be loaded on to tankers, and the vast infrastructure of men and organization required to get the oil out, called for the most modern petroleum technology, much of which has been developed in Saudi Arabia. Saudi Aramco has been a leading innovator in improving water and gas injection techniques to maintain oil-field pressure, so that production levels can be sustained. It also helped to develop the low-pressure, off-the-road sand tyre now commonly used in desert exploration.

Refining

The heart of the oil refinery at Ras Tannurah (*left*), is the bubble car or fractionating column of the crude distillation unit. Into the bottom of the car is fed the heated crude oil, which is flashed into vapours. Crude oil is a mixture of different types of hydrocarbons, all having different boiling points. The vapours of the heavier hydrocarbons condense at a higher temperature near the bottom of the fractionating column. Those of the lighter hydrocarbons, such as kerosene and gasoline, bubble up through a series of trays until they condense at the relatively low temperature at the top. Thus, a process of distillation separates the crude oil into various "fractions". Each fraction in turn must be refined before it is ready for the market. Fuel oil accounts for about half the production of the Ras Tannurah refinery, which refines more than 500,000 barrels of crude oil daily.

It was the first and for many years the only refinery, later joined by smaller export ones operated by Getty Oil and the Arabian Oil Company. Refineries for domestic use were built by Petromin in Jiddah and Riyadh. Jiddah refinery's capacity was then increased to 120,000 barrels per day, Riyadh's expanded to 120,000 barrels per day, and a refinery with a capacity of 170,000 barrels per day built in Yanbu.

Petromin joined with foreign companies to build new export refineries, each with a capacity of 250,000 barrels per day: in Jubayl with Shell, and in Yanbu with Mobil. Both are now in operation and produce benzene, kerosene, naphtha, gas, oil, and liquid petroleum

gas (LPG) among others. A larger export refinery at Rabigh, a Petromin-Petrola joint venture, with a capacity of 325,000 barrels a day came on line in early 1990. The refineries proposed for Qasim and Shuqaiq, however, were placed under a moratorium in 1985, until such time as world demand warranted an increase in the Kingdom's 2 million barrels a day refining capacity.

Increased efficiency in production was stressed to maximise the Kingdom's value-added earnings on its oil. This policy was extended to the lubricating oil plants whose overall capacity had also been expanded. Jiddah's lube oil blending plant was to become more efficient in producing both Petromin's oils, and those from other suppliers using new special additives.

Pipelines

Conceived in the mid-1970s, the 750-mile Petroline pipeline began pumping oil and gas across Arabia in the early 1980s. It is a strategically vital alternative to the exposed tanker route through the Straits of Hormuz and saves 3,550 miles of sailing round the peninsula for supplies to the growing petrochemicals industry at Yanbu. The initial flow of 1.85 million barrels per day on the six day journey would increase to 2.4 million barrels a day when a parallel pipeline came into operation in 1987. Capacity now stands at 3.2 million bpd but is planned to rise to 5 million bpd by 1991. A 500,000 barrel a day spur connected Zubayr in Iraq with the Kingdom's ports in 1985 and expanded to handle a capacity of 1.6 million barrels a day. The Iraqi Pipeline Trans Saudi Arabia (IPSA) was, however, suspended in August 1990 as a result of the invasion of Kuwait. The 48-inch and 56-inch steel lines share eleven pump stations from Abqaiq and Ayn Dar to Yanbu, each with uniquely strategic turbines that can be powered on natural gas, NGL, diesel fuel or even crude oil straight out of the buried line. Petromin, the state agency for petroleum and minerals handed the pipe-line over to Saudi Aramco, who also built the NGL line which carries petrochemical feedstocks to the plants at Jubayl. At Yanbu two very large crude Carrier oil tankers can be simultaneously loaded in thirty-six hours; eleven tanks store one million barrels of crude each. The entire system is operated from a computerized control room in Yanbu where refineries and petrochemical plants process much of the flow. To accommodate an increase in crude oil production, in 1990 Saudi Aramco began a programme to bring back into service 660 km of mothballed pipelines, most are now operating again.

Gas

A process control system console at Saudi Aramco's Abqaiq plant (top).

A team prepares pollution control equipment in the Arabian Gulf (middle).

Earth scientists interpret a seismic cross-section (above). *Marjan GOSP-1 (gas-oil separator plant),* (right).

Saudi Arabia has long realized that no matter how large, its hydrocarbon resources are not infinite and in consequence the Kingdom's industrialization effort has sought to maximuse the benefits of technology with the best possible exploitation of its mineral wealth (*see* Development). The once wasteful flaring of the gas produced in association with crude oil was replaced by a massive, master gas-gathering system for the oilfields of the Eastern Province. The system (*see* map on page 172) provides a source of methane and ethane gas invaluable to the large-scale chemical plants of Jubayl and Yanbu.

Gas production from the northern offshore fields of Safaniyeh, Marjan and Zuluf has been postponed. However, the master gas system developed by Petromin, and designed, constructed, and since operated by Saudi Aramco, now allows Saudi Arabia to utilize almost all of the gas associated with the onshore production of oil.

With an average gas-oil ratio of 500 standard cubic feet per barrel of oil produced, output levels have fluctuated in the mid-1980s from less than 3 billion cubic feet per day to more than 3.5 billion. Total gas reserves in 1989 were estimated at more than 177 trillion cubic feet. Some of this gas is used for reinjection into the oilfields to maintain the pressure necessary for extracting oil. An ever-increasing amount is used to desalinate large quantities of sea water in the country's major desalination plants at Jiddah, Al Khobar, Yanbu and Jubayl. Several thousand megawatts of electric power are also generated from gas for direct consumption in the Kingdom's industrial complexes; for example, the Saudi Cement Company plant at Hofuf has for many years been using gas for thermal heating. At capacity, the country's gas processing plants can yield up to 4,000 tonnes a day of sulphur, most of which is manufactured into sulphuric acid and exported. At Abqaiq, gas is separated into methane. This is used as feedstock for the Saudi Arabian Fertiliser Company's production of urea and also provides the basic feedstock for use in the petrochemical industries, and especially in the methanol plants at Damman and Jubayl. Methanol is also

transformed into natural gas liquids for further processing into Liquified Petroleum Gas (LPG) at Saudi Aramco's Ras Tannurah refinery and into profitable down-line export products such as methyl tertiary butyl ether (MTBE), an octane enhancer for unleaded petrol. This in turn is linked by pipeline to an LPG facility at Qatif where the LPG products are stored for export, or for kingdomwide distribution by truck. Up to two billion cubic metres of fuel gas is manufactured each year from methane. A direct pipeline connects the gas processing plant at Shedgum with Yanbu. Beyond this, three further plants trans-form the remaining natural gas liquids into up to 37 million cubic metres a year of ethane and 375,000 barrels per day of LPG. The ethane provides feedstock and fuel requirements for SABIC's ethylene petrochemical complexes. Much of the LPG is sold abroad, most of it to Japan. The Kingdom's exports of LPG and other gas-based petro-chemical products began to rise to significant levels through the 1980s when Saudi Arabia was poised to become one of the world's major natural gas liquid producers with an eventual world market share envisaged at seven per cent.

Statistical sources: Petromin and Saudi Aramco

PRINCIPAL PETROLEUM PRODUCTS

IN THOUSAND BARRELS
Source: Ministry of Petroleum & Mineral Resources

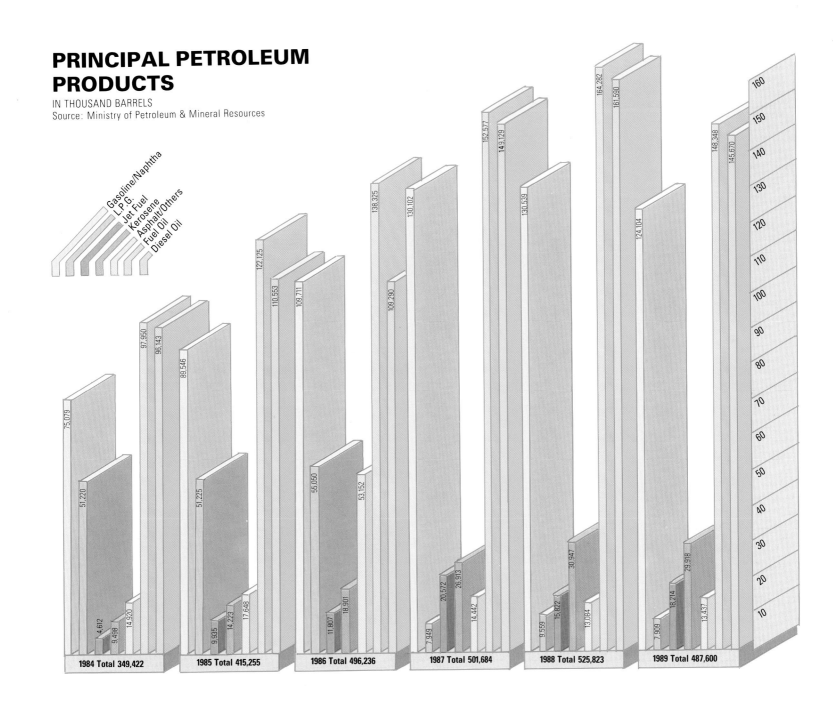

1984 Total 349,422
1985 Total 415,255
1986 Total 496,236
1987 Total 501,684
1988 Total 525,823
1989 Total 487,600

9 Youth

The young of today grew up in a country which their grandfathers, at the same age, would hardly have recognized. This has been the continuing challenge: to provide the young with the opportunities to fulfil themselves and their country's needs, yet shielding them from disorientation through the onslaught of the meretricious from the outside world, and preserving in them the inheritance of wisdom.

At Dhahran's King Fahd University of Petroleum and Minerals, devoted to the study of oil technology, young Saudi students take advantage of the best resources that the world can offer in that field upon which Saudi Arabia's economy chiefly rests. Founded in 1963, it now has over 14,000 students, with a graduate output in 1987 of 3,994. It provides qualified engineers and managers in oil technology for the country.

Policy for Youth

THE youth of Saudi Arabia is growing up in a period of dramatic expansion. They are living at the centre of this drama: it is widely recognized that their innate abilities and talents should be as fully developed as possible. Luqman's proverb "A father's blows upon his son's back are like manure upon a field" could not be more outdated. Education is seen as the true means to build the personality of society's individual members, in order to enable them to continue developing their society. Education is free, but is regarded as imposing a debt on the student which he should repay by his service to the state.

In a Kingdom with a high level of illiteracy in the early 1960s a policy decision had to be made between opting for quality or opting for quantity of education. The urgent need for education led to the rapid expansion of primary and intermediary schooling. This emphasis resulted in a relatively small proportion of students passing on to secondary education. In the early and mid-1970s substantially fewer pupils who qualified for secondary education entered it. Many in fact joined the armed services, vocational schools or religious institutions where their education continued.

At the secondary stage the policy prevails of not allowing pupils to specialize too rigorously, but pupils can choose between the literary and scientific streams after the first year of the secondary stage.

Although many modern textbooks and syllabuses were initially imported from abroad, the aim of the Government has been to keep the study of Islamic beliefs as a basis of the educational system, so that new generations should not only achieve intellectual and practical skills, but should acquire them in the context of an awareness of their duties towards God and man.

Education is seen as a process which develops, controls and guides the life of a community towards its ideal, and awakens individual students to an awareness of their responsibilities towards their country. Different pupils with different aptitudes now have open

to them a wide range of establishments in which they can gain practical and theoretical learning: at the secondary level they can opt for the industrial education programme in technical schools, or the Higher Technical Institute and the Intermediate Technical College, offering

specializations to over 4,000 students in electricity, radio, television, automobile and civil engineering.

Commercial and administrative education has attracted far more pupils than was originally envisaged. Teacher training is being expanded at secondary level institutes, in particular through the establishment of a junior college system for teacher training.

Young people are being encouraged to participate actively not only in intellectual pursuits but also in community activities, such as those attached to Community Development Centres.

School health services were massively expanded and have successfully promoted the benefits of preventive medicine; and sports facilities have multiplied as well. In 1974 the General Presidency for Youth Welfare was formed to formulate policies for future youth welfare. A programme with eight general objectives has been followed since, and the stress has been to ensure that services are comprehensive, integrated and justly distributed, and that all are in harmony with both the Islamic

code for rearing youth and modern knowledge of handling young people. A balanced education is looked for, such as will organize creative capabilities so that they both make an effective contribution to the nation's development, and support the family strucutre, by which great store is set in the Kingdom.

At the same time it is hoped to encourage young people to invest their free time in sporting and recreational activities that both enhance the enjoyment of living and improve physical fitness, so that the nation may raise the standard of excellence achieved in sports at the international level.

The General Presidency supports a hundred and fifty athletic clubs and sporting societies nationwide and provides fourteen clubs and four sports centres in the main cities; sports include football, volleyball, basketball, cycling, table-tennis, swimming, weaponry, karate, judo and athletics (*see* Sport). The General Presidency's literary clubs are increasingly successful, as are its fourteen youth hostels, and Riyadh's science centre.

As part of the Fourth Five Year Plan beginning in 1985, nearly 20 per cent of the Kingdom's resources was allocated for education. The education system is bound to cause some individual problems; yet the frustration of youth which has been a feature of Western societies, and which at times has erupted in anti-social ways, is considered unlikely to appear in the Kingdom since its roots lie in a lack of opportunities.

Saudi Arabia is committed to the provision of superb facilities; few countries have experienced such a proliferation of opportunities for young people, whether male or female, to fulfil themselves as individuals, and as members of a nation.

A policy for youth, in a country where family ties are so strong, must take account of parental attitudes. It is seen as important that parents are themselves involved in the education and wider social activities of the young, and that a living relationship exists between home and school. The "generation gap" so evident outside the Kingdom, and which one would expect to be caused by so rapid a growth of change, may well thus be avoided.

Both the young and the old are enjoined to bear in mind the Prophet's recommendation for the adult to forgive the young and for the young to respect the adult.

Schools

- ☐ FOR BOYS
- ☐ FOR GIRLS

	82/83	83/84	84/85	85/86	86/87
For Boys	5,960	6,198	6,202	6,366	6,790
For Girls	3,683	4,115	4,310	4,347	4,744
TOTAL	9,643	10,313	10,512	10,713	11,534

Students

- ☐ BOYS
- ☐ GIRLS

	82/83	83/84	84/85	85/86	86/87
Boys	899,664	971,412	1,035,051	1,099,652	1,171,671
Girls	641,959	685,178	775,120	856,414	933,230
TOTAL	1,541,623	1,656,590	1,810,171	1,956,066	2,104,901

Teachers

- ☐ MALE
- ☐ FEMALE

	82/83	83/84	84/85	85/86	86/87
Male	60,971	65,493	67,434	68,804	75,066
Female	40,630	45,563	47,142	51,665	56,606
TOTAL	101,601	111,056	114,576	120,469	131,672

Higher Education

- ☐ MALE STUDENTS
- ☐ FEMALE STUDENTS
- ☐ TEACHERS

	82/83	83/84	84/85	85/86	86/87
Male Students	54,112	57,421	62,202	64,304	66,700
Female Students	28,501	34,557	40,507	43,150	47,816
Teachers	8,316	8,561	9,724	9,273	9,950
TOTAL	82,613	91,978	102,709	107,454	114,516

Kindergartens in Saudi Arabia are well equipped with playgrounds in which the children play (far left) and learn group games (below). Young children are alert and enthusiastic (left and opposite bottom) and enjoy even the most demanding of their classroom activities (opposite right).

Infant Education

THE PROVISION OF infant education is a growth area within the Saudi schooling system; but is unusual in that the majority of creches, kindergartens and schools are private, rather than provided and maintained by the established departments in the Ministry of Education. However, several Government and religious organizations, including the Ministry of Defence and the Religious Colleges and Institutes Administration, as well as many of the universities and colleges provide facilities for infant education.

Curricula for the various institutions at this level of the education system are laid down in guidelines set by the General Presidency for Girls' Education. The General Presidency also monitors the standards of the facilities, and the quality of the learning programmes offered by the individual kindergartens and schools. UNESCO (the United Nations Education, Scientific and Cultural Organization) has worked in cooperation with the General Presidency for Girls' Education to provide a range of integrated teaching materials in conjunction with a general curriculum designed to prepare children to meet the needs of the Saudi primary education system.

A typical kindergarten provides a two year programme for children aged between four and six. Many kindergartens and creches also offer a supplementary introductory year suited to the needs of three year old children. At this first stage of their education, boys and girls usually find themselves in mixed groups and classes. By 1984 there were a total of forty six thousand five hundred boys and girls enrolled in the Kingdom's many kindergartens. Three hundred and seventy five institutions employing over one thousand eight hundred teachers were provided under Government auspices. Forty-six of these kindergartens accepted boys only, while the rest were mixed.

In the latter 1980s the General Presidency for Girls' Education is to consider proposals to introduce model infant schools to run training classes in kindergarten courses at some of the girls' colleges for education.

Boys' Schooling

BEFORE THE ESTABLISHMENT of a Department of Education in 1924 the only schools were a few private institutions in the Hijaz concentrating on Qur'anic instruction and rudimentary reading and writing. In its first years the Department was hampered by lack of money. At the same time there were many who feared that a modern educational system would damage the fabric of a profoundly religious society. Expansion was confined to the few large towns and it was only in 1954, when the Department became a Ministry supported by increased funds and headed by HRH Prince Fahd ibn Abdul Aziz, as he was then, that school education began to spread throughout the Kingdom.

The Ministry of Education is not the sole agency concerned with boys' educa-

tion. The Ministry of Defence and the Religious Colleges and Institutes Administration each account for some 1.5 per cent of the total enrolment, while private schools take care of further 4.5 per cent. Education closely follows the pattern of other Arab countries: kindergarten (*rawdah*), primary (*ibtida'i*), intermediate (*mutawassit*) and secondary (*thanawi*). The primary stage lasts for six years at the end of which pupils take the Primary Certificate before entering the intermediate stage. Three years and another exam (the *kafa'ah*), are followed by another three years and the Saudi Baccalaureat (the *tawjihiyyah*) which is the key to the tertiary stage. After one year at secondary school there is a choice of streams, scientific (*ilmi*) or literary (*adabi*). Progression is strictly determined by the end of year exams in May-June, with re-sits in September-October.

At the post-intermediate level there are schools for those not wishing to go on to secondary school: among these are the vocational schools which are a vital source of Saudi technicians. Graduates from the vocational secondary schools

can follow two years higher training at either the Royal Technical Institute in Riyadh, the Model Agricultural Institute in Buraydah, or one of the country's two higher institutes for finance and commerce. The Ministry of Educations' vocational schools should not be confused with the many vocational training centres which take students of low educational level for training as craftsmen and artisans. These are run by the General Organisation for Technical Education and Vocational Training, which works with the Ministry of Labour & Social Affairs.

As Saudi Arabia lacked a university of its own until 1957, many of the brightest students had to go to other Arab countries for their higher education. Because of this, school curricula were largely imported or adapted from those used in other Arab countries. But as most of those countries had changed or renewed their own curricula by the late 1960s and early 1970s to keep abreast of more modern teaching techniques, Saudi Arabia was left with materials that were sadly outdated, and which

Scouting activities at Al Taghr school in Jiddah are taken with obvious enthusiasm (left). Library study provides opportunity for students to further their reading – and a chance to compare notes (right), while open air classes, like the one in the Eastern Province (below), remain popular with pupils.

often reinforced traditional methods of rote learning. The Ministry of Education faced a choice of either continuing to adapt foreign materials to the unique cultural, religious and social background of Saudi Arabia or of producing a curriculum and set of materials specifically designed for the Saudi situation. The Ministry opted for the latter, and most courses had been radically altered by the early 1980s (*See* Higher Education).

Curriculum design and the production of associated teaching materials are carried out under the auspices of the Ministry's curriculum, research and materials department by experts drawn from many quarters. The contribution of Saudi experts to this process has increased over the years as qualified specialists have completed their university studies and entered the specialist departments.

This was not always so. In the early 1970s less than half the teachers in the Kingdom were Saudi, and only one in five of those Saudi teachers taught outside the primary schools. From 1975-80 the number of Saudi teachers increased one and a half times, but at the same time the schools system expanded so rapidly that large numbers of expatriates, particularly at the intermediate and secondary school levels and in mathematics, the sciences and English (the only foreign language taught in government schools) were needed for years to come. Most of these teachers were Arabs with Egyptians, Jordanians and Palestinians predominating.

In these years the Ministry had to rely on the universities – and in particular the colleges of education in Riyadh and Makkah – to provide teachers for the intermediate and secondary schools; but at first the graduates who intended to follow a career in school teaching were all too few. To increase the number of intermediate and secondary teachers that were needed, the Ministry pursued several schemes designed to supplement the output of graduates. One of the most successful of these was the pioneering two-year programme at the Science and Mathematics Centre in Riyadh which provided a model for other centres.

The steady progress in education can be measured by the growth of educational institutions and the increase in pupil/student enrolment and expanding teaching staff. These increases resulted in better classrooms and an improved teacher/student ratio over the decade from the mid 1970s. With enrolment up

Schools in Saudi Arabia's cities are provided with superb buildings and fine facilities (above). *An innovative new school complex in Riyadh* (below) *provides the best of modern educational provisions for its 2,200 pupils and students at the primary, intermediary and secondary levels; schoolboys observe the pull of surface tension* (right).

to nearly 3 million students at all levels of education by 1991. The most dramatic successes have been in higher education, over 19 per cent of female students leaving high school (in 1990/91) entered university, compared with 7.1 per cent of their male counterparts.

For administrative purposes the country is divided into 40 educational zones. These can vary vastly in size and importance – where the Riyadh zone had more than 6,000 teachers in 1975, the rural Aflaj had a mere 200 – but each is a self-sufficient entity with its own health unit, educational aids unit and so forth. The headmaster of each school reports to the zone director who, in turn, is answerable to the Assistant Deputy Minister; the latter reports to the Deputy Minister for Educational and Administrative Affairs who, under the Minister, is the *de facto* chief executive for most matters concerning boys' schooling. Within the Ministry there are departments for primary, intermediate, secondary and technical education; each is headed by a director-general. Attached to each department are a number of subject-specialized inspectors-general who ensure that the centralized curriculum laid down by the Ministry is properly adhered to in the schools. The inspectors-general are assisted by cadres of inspectors based in the larger towns.

The administration of school education has been decentralized with more authority being invested in the three main zone offices – with the Central in Riyadh, the Eastern in Dammam and the Western in Jiddah. The need for on-the-job training and re-training of large numbers of lower grade officials continues to ensure the quality of the system. The Institutes of Public Administration at Riyadh, Dammam, Jiddah and the Ministry of Education have designed courses and in-service training programmes to meet these needs.

The Saudi tradition of right of access to officials at any level by members of the public militates against these devolutionary procedures in education. But this time-consuming contact with members of the public is both an essential part of Saudi democratic practice, and a practical way for senior education officials to monitor the public mood and needs of the people.

Former centralization is most apparent in the financial and supply systems. The zone director has compara-tively little say in financial matters, controls only a very small budget for local expenditure, and is entirely dependent on the central authority for the supply of all equipment. The phase of rapid expansion when new schools were being completed at the rate of three a day strained this system which has worked well since expansion moderated.

The educational planner in Saudi Arabia has faced many challenges, but perhaps the most daunting remains that of finding a way to disseminate modern educational materials, methods and experience without disturbing the country's social and religious heritage.

Girls' Schooling

SINCE THE ESTABLISHMENT of the first school for girls in Saudi Arabia in 1956, female education has become one of the Kingdom's fastest growing areas of social development. By 1987, some three decades since the foundation of the pioneering Dar al-Hanan Institute for orphans, there were around 945,000 girls in full-time education at the kindergarten, primary and secondary levels. Many of these girls will go on to pursue careers that had been closed to women only a generation previously.

Before 1960 girls' education was generally limited in scope and haphazard in organization, available only in the larger cities such as Jiddah, Makkah, al-Madinah and Riyadh. As it was not socially acceptable for a girl to go out of the house on her own she would receive lessons from a private tutor or in a small group known as a *Kutab*.

Sufficiently wealthy families would employ for their daughters private teachers who lived with the family and in many cases acted not only as tutor and advisor, but also as nurse and companion to the children. Sometimes the tutor would be asked also to instruct the mother of the family in reading and writing.

The *Kutab* was the first method of group teaching for girls. A small number could attend classes given by a woman who had been fortunate enough herself to receive tuition from her father or a private tutor. This early form of education was religious rather than technical, but it was usual for pupils to learn to solve simple mathematical problems as well as read and memorize parts of the Qur'an.

In the late 1950s more organized teaching groups started to appear and private schools spread to other cities. The girls who learned at these schools or privately in their homes took the same exams and received the same certificate as boys, but mixed education has not been adopted in Saudi Arabia.

All subjects at the intermediate level demand a high level of concentration.

The history of the Dar al-Hanan Educational Institute for Girls gives an interesting example of the expansion of education in its early stages. Dar al-Hanan was founded in 1956 as a small home and school for orphans by H.M. Queen Iffat Al Faisal, widow of the late King Faisal. It was intended to be a home for needy girls, giving them an opportunity to learn and to acquire a better standard of living later on. In 1957 the Queen, realizing the pressing need for a girls' school, opened some classes at the upper nursery and primary education level, and thus the small institution started its work.

In 1959-60 the first group of girls studying at the school were able to present their primary school certificates. As the Saudi Government approved girls' education in the same year and opened some of the first state primary schools, the need then arose for intermediate (junior high) schools. In 1960 classes for teaching students at intermediate level were opened. In 1963 the first group of girls graduated from the intermediate school (the equivalent of the 9th grade in the American system). This brought Dar al-Hanan to its most challenging step – adding a secondary school (high school) for a small group of girls who wanted to further their studies. Despite the lack of qualified female teachers and equipment and a shortage of space, secondary stage classes were opened with eighteen girls in the first year (10th grade) and nine girls in the second year (11th grade). The nine senior girls had already studied in other Arab cities such as Cairo, Beirut, or Damascus, or at home, and were now able to devote their attention to the sciences.

Intermediate education was taken over by the Government for the first year and the school followed the programme of the Ministry of Education with the help of a very small staff, most of whom were not adequately qualified. At the end of the school year 1964-65 the first group of secondary school pupils graduated from Dar al-Hanan, seven in sciences and one in arts subjects. They were the first group of girls to graduate from any regular school in the Kingdom. At that point the need for a better building was urgent and work started on the new school which now exists. By 1966, the year in which the school moved to its new location, the intake of students had risen to 620, rising further to 1,050 in 1973.

In 1969-70 the General Presidency for

Girls' Education opened a Teachers' Training College in Riyadh, relying on graduates from Dar al-Hanan and the Riyadh Secondary School for the recruitment of their students. By that time a fully developed administrative staff had been established and girls were able to follow a well planned educational programme at all levels.

Dar al-Hanan will continue to forge ahead, opening up new lines of study and developing modern teaching techniques. Some of these will endure for years to come, as in the learning of languages, for example, where many schools now use audiovisual language laboratory methods as standard pedagogical tools in the teaching of English and French. Those girls who fail to further their education at the university level, but who would like to work after completing their secondary education, may enrol in one- or two-year courses in accountancy, arts and crafts, child psychology, administration or secretarial studies. Exchange schemes with comparable schools and colleges abroad have also been made available.

Dar al-Hanan, though a typical Saudi Arabian girls' school in many ways, also exists to fill certain specialized functions. It provides a boarding school for girls whose parents do not live in Jiddah and offers facilities for the daughters of those employed in the Foreign Service who may already have started their education abroad and need reintegration back into the Saudi education system. The institution has established itself as the foremost educational centre and laboratory for women's education in the Kingdom, with well-equipped laboratories, audiovisual facilities, and other modern aids. Its reputation as an innovator in the academic world attracts women lecturers from a wide range of scholastic and academic backgrounds.

In 1960 the Government invested responsibility for girls' education in an august

In the sharp and sunny winter air of the desert, the girls of a school at Hofuf, in the Kingdom's Eastern Province, take a break from their lessons (left). The curriculum at the intermediate level invariably includes the study of the English language (above).

Following the precepts of the ancient Greeks, physical education plays an important part in a girl's education (opposite page). *Modern language-teaching devices* (left and below) *are inevitably bringing an unprecedented cultural diversity within the reach of the next generation of Saudi womanhood.*

The Prophet Muhammad is reported to have said, "To seek knowledge is obligatory on every Muslim, male or female." Complete education is today available to girls in every part of the Kingdom, and many go on to tertiary studies.

group of educational experts and religious leaders who, with the concurrence of religious authorities, approved an education suitable for girls, and formed what is now known as the General Presidency for Girls' Education. This is an agency of Ministerial authority with a full vote in the Council of Ministers, and independent from the Ministry of Education. The General Presidency for Girls' Education administers the Kingdom's system of formal education for girls and is responsible for the 109 colleges and institutes of education which together offer 10,500 places to women for teacher training.

Education for women is now available in every village, town and city. By 1987 the Government school system had been provided with over three thousand elementary schools, and almost 1200 intermediate and secondary schools situated throughout the Kingdom. The total enrolment in girls' schools topped 930,000 by 1987. Provisions set out in the Fourth Plan were to increase this figure substantially.

In the elementary sector, nearly half the Saudi girls between the ages of six and twelve had school places in 1976, and the elementary school enrolment had doubled by 1985. At the same time the provision of new schools and an increase in the number of instructors reduced overcrowding in the existing schools. This emphasis on improving all school welfare facilities continues to be stressed.

Intermediate education for girls had been brought to most of the Kingdom's small communities and rural areas by 1980. In the five years to 1985, over twenty per cent of elementary school leavers were accepted into the intermediate system. The average number of students per class at this level had already fallen below twenty five in 1980, and has continued to be reduced since. (*See* Boys' Schooling.)

Half of those pupils who complete the intermediary stage progress to secondary education. The average number of students per class at this level fell below twenty-three in 1980, and has been

further reduced since.

One of the main difficulties experienced in the rapid expansion of education has been the recruitment of enough people with sufficient academic qualifications and training to become teachers. In the initial years when the present education system was being established, a considerable number of non-Saudi teaching staff had to be employed; during the next decade the increasing number of local staff entering the system led to the steady reduction of foreign personnel. The expansion of education under the Fourth Plan has shown that career opportunities for Saudi teachers continue to be great. By 1987 Saudi teaching staff represented 64 per cent of the total. The secondary level teacher training institute programme has been upgraded to three years, and financial incentives to facilitate student enrolment in teacher training have been increased.

In keeping with the swift emergence of the Kingdom as a developed nation, and with a changing attitude towards the role of women in society, the school curriculum for girls has expanded to embrace sciences and languages as well as Islamic studies. Although some careers are still considered as unsuitable for Saudi women, there are a wide variety of occupations taken up by Western women for which technical and vocational training can be received. Enrolment in the four technical training centres in Riyadh,

Jiddah, Makkah and Hasa doubled from five hundred and fifty students to one thousand two hundred between 1975 and 1980. In the same period new departments were created to provide skills and training along the lines introduced at Dar al-Hanan.

As an alternative to vocational training, girls have the opportunity of continuing their academic studies at university. With the exception of Engineering, all the facilities at Riyadh's King Saud University accept women; the provision of a new campus for up to 10,000 female students is underway. The capital also offers a teacher training college and a School of Medicine. A paramedical institute opened in Rass in 1987 to meet the Central Province's need for medical training. King Abdul Aziz University in Jiddah offers arts and science courses; its facilities based in Makkah offer degrees in social sciences and the Shari'ah (Islamic Law).

Social services required by school education continue to expand. Medical laboratories and dental and ophthalmic clinics have been established in school health units in the major population centres.

To attract staff, housing is provided for the personnel serving in these units. Accommodation is also provided for postings at intermediate and secondary schools and for students at institutes that serve rural areas. Most school bus fleets have been enlarged and updated to increase the efficiency of transport in all the educational districts.

With a sizeable proportion of older women still unable to read or write, an extensive adult literacy campaign is being conducted. Special adult literacy programmes are conducted in schools across the country. Female enrolment in such programmes reached three hundred and eighty three thousand between 1979 and 1980, by which time nearly ninety

thousand women had been taught to read and write. The current syllabus has been modified to emphasize its relevance to women's needs and, in cooperation with the Ministry of Information programme material to reinforce and supplement classroom work is broadcast on radio and television. Short-term training courses for literacy teachers and supervisors have also been organized to augment the successes that have been achieved by the current literacy programme.

These different branches of female education together make up a vigorous programme of learning for the young Saudi woman. The Kingdom now provides universal access to state education at the primary level, and as this spreads through to the higher levels of the education system, future generations will enjoy social, academic and professional opportunities which could not have been envisaged a few decades ago.

Statistical sources: Ministry of Education

Higher Education

THE PROVISION OF higher education in Saudi Arabia has followed the clear guidelines set out in *The Educational Policy of the Kingdom of Saudi Arabia* which, in 1970, laid out a statement on the nature of educational policy. It gave as the basis of educational policy to meet "the duty of acquainting the individual with his God and religion and adjusting his conduct in accordance with the teaching of religion, the fulfilment of the need of society and in achievement of the nation's objectives."

Higher education is thus not beset by the confusion of intent that is encountered so widely in Western European countries concerning the ends of educa-

tion, nor, so far, by problems of student politics. Indeed politics at university are not permitted; the authorities' attitude is that, all education being free, the student owes it to the State, in return, not to attack the State.

Thus by Western standards higher education in Saudi Arabia is determinedly paternalistic at all levels. The political and religious authorities keep a careful watch on the universities and the administrators keep a careful watch on the students. Thus "Any regular student whose attendance at the lectures, exercises and practical work in each of the prescribed courses is less than seventy-five per cent may be prevented by the

faculty board from presenting himself for the final examination. In this case the student is considered as having failed in all subjects." (*General Rules for Students* from the King Saud University Calendar).

In a country where primary education began only in the late 1930s, and where a serious secondary educational programme was only conceived in 1953, it is natural that Higher Education was at first given a lower priority than general education. But once the programme of general education had been established in the early 1970s, King Faisal himself directed that special attention should be given to the post-school level.

199

Technical Education

THE IDEALS SET by King Faisal have been endorsed and continued by his successors. In the late 1970s when the overall education budget was growing at an unprecedented rate, the provision for higher education as a whole accounted for a higher proportion of the education budget than before – a trend which has continued ever since. In 1955 the education budget totalled 15 million riyals: by 1980 it had reached 15 billion riyals, while between 1985 and 1990 spending on higher education alone would account for over 40 billion riyals, 80 per cent of which was allocated to the universities with the remainder set aside for the various institutes offering technical education.

In the academic year 1991 there were 120,000 students enrolled in higher education as a whole, and some 16,000 students graduated that year, 12,000 of them from vocational and technical schools. Today, the Saudi universities and technical institutes prefer to stress the quality achieved by their education

Chemistry teaching at a secondary school in Al-Muharraz (below).

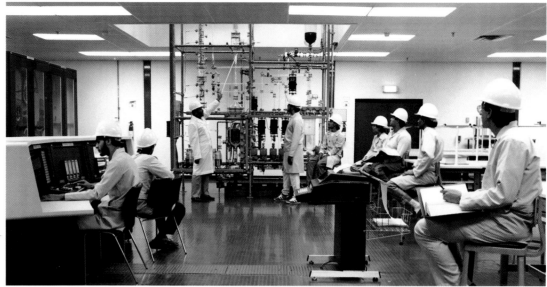

and training.

The goals for development laid down in the Fourth Five Year Plan once more placed the "safeguarding of Islamic values" above "developing human resources", emphasizing the very close links between religion and education. At the same time, Saudi attention is now focussing increasingly on the need to gear education to the demands of the economy. The overall goal in this area is to achieve the Government's long-held policy to "Saudize" the Kingdom's workforce. While previous Five Year Plans have concentrated on increasing the number of places available for students, the Fourth Plan sought to develop more intensively those educational sectors from which graduates are most urgently required – namely the technical and professional – rather than producing more university arts graduates equipped with skills in which the Kingdom is already rich.

Technical training plays a major part in the structure of further education in the Kingdom. There are, for example, the technical school at Hofuf, and the vocational Higher Technical Institute in Riyadh, known as the Royal Technical Institute. Integrated within this technical system are the specialized training schools for those who have completed their primary or intermediary education. As a ground work for this, manual work is taught for two periods each week throughout the Kingdom's education system. Many of the intermediate schools are also equipped with first-class workshops which provide students with technical expertise.

At the Royal Technical Institute (Riyadh) and Hofuf Technical Training

Process control simulator for the petrochemical industry at Yanbu's Industrial College (top).

School particular emphasis is put on electro and automotive mechanics, machine tooling and metal working. The Hofuf school was launched in 1966 with an initial enrolment of seventeen students. By 1980, the student body already numbered over 1,000. Other vocational schools were established in Jiddah and al-Madinah. Plans have been set in motion for the establishment of vocational schools in Abha, Taif, and Unayzah. At the same time the two new technical institutes at Jiddah and Dammam are planned to have a maximum capacity of 1,220 students.

King Faisal himself, at the time, gave his personal endorsement to this area of endeavour. "This country" he declared, "in this particular stage of its development, is in greater need of adopting the vocational trend, because the implementation and carrying out of projects require manpower, and that manpower should be drawn from the country's own sons."

Outstandingly, the largest educational institute is the Royal Institute of Riyadh whose long frontage of arches and massive pink domes are features of the Riyadh landscape. It was built at a cost of 25 million riyals and at once became the best equipped technical institute in the Middle East. It provided elementary courses for skilled workers, which could then be followed by advanced courses, either for engineering or for teachers in technical schools. Already by 1970, over 4,000 students were receiving training in one branch or

In-house language training courses in business English (left). *Diplomas in such fields as electronic engineering provide highly qualified technicians for the Kingdom's industrial base* (bottom).

another of technical education. By the end of the decade, Saudi Arabia had already laid the foundations of its own class of skilled artisans and engineers. A new technical institute in Riyadh is to provide 600 students with training in electronics, engineering and other technological skills required by the country's growing industries.

A leader in this field has been the King Fahd University of Petroleum and Minerals (KFUPM) which is situated at Dhahran in the Eastern Province. It was founded as a college in 1963 with under 100 students; by 1974 it had increased its intake to 1,500 students, and in 1975 was raised to university status. Its intake then was rapidly increasing. The University is an autonomous institution, with the Minister of Higher Education as Chairman of its board. Degrees at Bachelor and Masters level are offered in Engineering (Civil, Mechanical, Electrical, Chemical, Petroleum, Architectural and Systems) in the Sciences (Mathematical, Geological, Physics and Chemistry) and in Industrial Management. Ph.D.s are offered in civil, chemical, electrical, mechanical and petroleum engineering, and in chemistry.

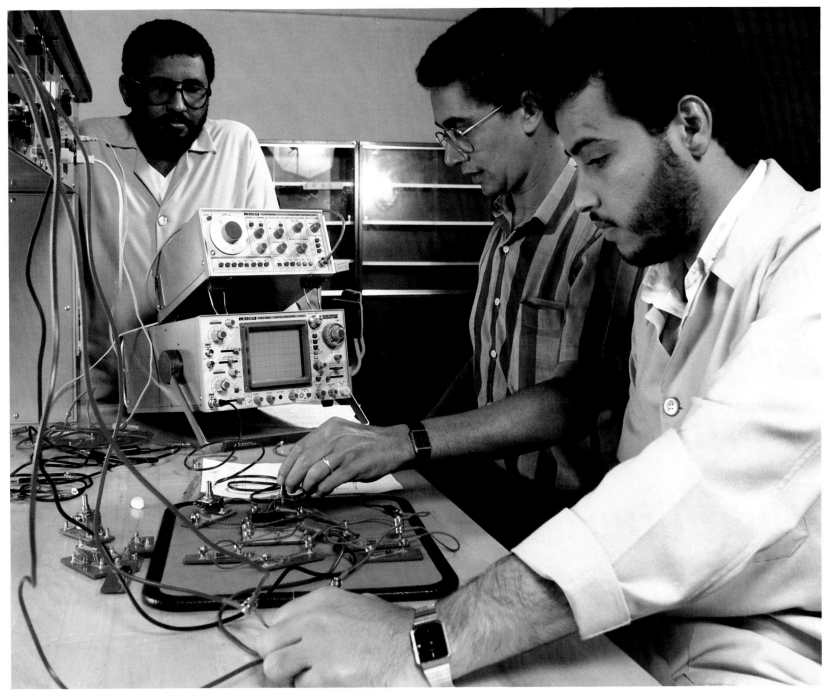

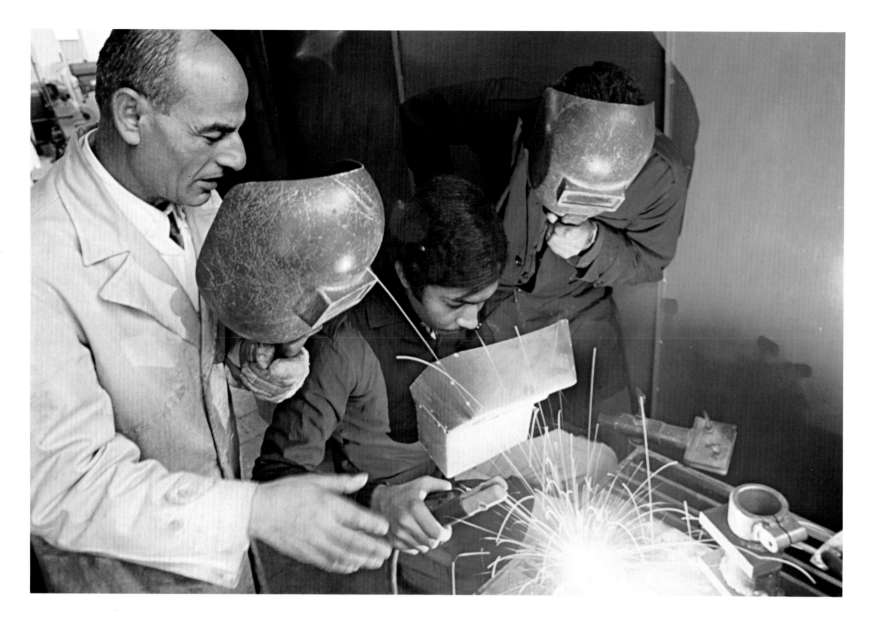

While "in principle Arabic is the language of Education in all its items and stages", here all teaching is in English.

By 1987 student enrolment had reached over 14,000, with almost 4000 graduating that year. Saudis account for 45 per cent of the teaching staff. Though facilities continue to improve, cuts in teaching staff have been forecast to streamline KFUPM to match the general downturn in activity in the oil industry through the mid-1980s, and thus prevent an over-supply of personnel.

The continued development of the University into a Technical University of excellent international standard preparing students with the high degree of expertise necessary to fulfil the professional and managerial needs of the petroleum and minerals industry will nonetheless remain its top priority. A graduate school, Research Institute, and College of Industrial Management have increased the quality of the KFUPM programme

which remains a magnet for students from abroad seeking high training in petroleum technology and the allied fields of the petrochemical industry. KFUPM has students from 51 countries around the world.

The Kingdom's vocational training institutes for women concentrate mainly on the fields of education and the provision of health care. In 1970 the Girls' College of Education in Riyadh opened with a four-year undergraduate curriculum.

The Riyadh College programme initially included seven major fields of study; these were then increased to ten by promoting the minor divisions in history, mathematics and biology to major subjects. In 1976 a further two-year Master's Degree programme was introduced. At the same time a model school was launched to provide students with opportunities for practical application of teaching methods and educational aids.

The much smaller, select College of

All skills connected with mechanics and metalwork are vital to the Kingdom's industrial future. Brazing and welding skills (above) *are taught alongside precision lathework* (far right). *Students are taught automobile engineering and the principles of car mechanics at the Royal Technical Institute* (right).

Arts was added to Riyadh's growing number of institutes of higher education in 1978/9.

Although not anticipated in the First Development plan, a second College of Education was opened in Jiddah in 1974. The Jiddah College was to expand along the same lines as the College in Riyadh, with a structure of ten departments catering for 2,895 students taught by a staff of 289.

The Government's previous development plans have been concerned "to provide female students with a sound education that will fully prepare them for

participation in the social, economic and cultural growth of the Kingdom". The Fourth Plan, however, is concerned "to form productive citizen-workers" and stresses the coordinated development of education to meet the long-term needs for technically skilled manpower and university research. The plan calls for increasingly rigorous entrance requirements; subsidies are to be awarded by merit to studies meeting development needs, or to students in financial need. In 1986 the Kingdom signed a protocol extending for a further five years its technical cooperation accord with West Germany.

Those citizens who have found themselves too old to take full advantage of the explosion of educational facilities in the Kingdom have been provided with the opportunity to fill in the gaps in their education by special classes and courses for adults. The Ministry of Education founded the Department of General Culture to provide programmes of educational training for adults among the communities of Saudi Arabia's vast hinterland. At the same time the Ministry of Information developed special radio and television broadcasts for the wider dissemination of general culture and education. These have successfully augmented the adult literacy programme's efforts in isolated villages and remote areas. Teaching in this field is centred in the regional Community Development Centres which provide art teachers and manual instructors who underpin literacy with practical work. The Ministry of Agriculture has also been involved in practical education through courses in farming based on those offered by its Model Institute at Buraydah.

Statistical sources: Ministry of Education and Ministry of Planning.

Universities

RESPONSIBILITY FOR THE Kingdom's seven universities is vested in the Ministry of Higher Education which was established in 1975. This Ministry is in charge of all policies concerning university education, the disbursement of scholarships awarded to Saudi students for study abroad, and all other aspects of higher education. Within the universities themselves, policy is controlled by the University Boards which are headed by the Minister of Higher Education.

Riyadh's King Saud University was the first of seven universities to be established in the Kingdom of Saudi Arabia. The University was founded in 1957 when its first 9 instructors offered 21 students courses in the Faculty of Arts. By 1964 the number of students had leapt to 1,032. Within a decade this figure had increased to almost 6,000, and the number of lecturers and professors had reached 300. By 1988, the number of

students passed 22,000 to make it the largest centre of education in the Kingdom.

The University's original Faculty of Arts included Departments of Arabic Language, English Language, History and Geography, and, more recently, of Mass Media and Sociology. In the early 1980s a Faculty of Science was opened with Departments of Physics, Mathematics, Chemistry, Botany, Zoology and Geology. The Faculty of Computing and Information Sciences was added in 1985. The University's original Faculties of Pharmacy and Commerce were opened in 1959, followed by a Faculty of Engineering in 1962, a Faculty of Agriculture in 1965 and the Faculty of Medicine in 1969. Later, Faculties of Dentistry and Nursing were added.

In 1967 the University's Faculty of Education was established at a "satellite" campus based in Abha, which has

Students at King Saud University's Diriyyah campus.

since expanded to include the Faculty of Medicine. The education programme here offers a four year course for undergraduates; its Advanced Training Centre has been developed to offer a one-year postgraduate course to train the skills of Saudi graduates who wish to become teachers.

Courses of study for a first degree last three years in all faculties except those of Pharmacy, Medicine and Education whose curricula demand four, and Engineering which asks five. Most faculties treat first year courses as a transitional stage from secondary schooling to university study, and most freshmen are occupied with courses of a general nature.

King Saud University, Riyadh, is particularly advanced in its Faculties of Medicine and of Engineering. In these faculties the original system of lectures given to large numbers of pupils was based on that used in Egypt. This has long since given way to the current system of more individualized instruction which is based on the American-style credit system originally introduced to the Kingdom by the Faculty of Education. The reason for this change lay in the determination of the University that these faculties should maintain their high entrance requirements in standard with the rest, to offer the best education possible. To enter, students must have achieved a grade of at least seventy-five per cent in their baccalaureat examination (*tawjihiyyah*), taken when they are eighteen years old.

By 1984 King Saud University's many Faculties, hitherto scattered across several facilities in Riyadh's various suburbs and lacking a central focus, had been relocated to their present desert site on the edge of the capital at Diriyyah. The campus, which cost 3.5 billion dollars, can accommodate 22,000 resident male students. In 1986 the construction of an independent campus at Riyadh for up to 10,000 female students was an important priority, as was the expansion of the satellite campus facilities at Abha and Qasim. The latter was to provide an extra 10,000 places for students in the faculties of veterinary science, business administration and economics.

Among the facilities on the Diriyyah campus are a library of more than one million books, three auditoria, and 2,000 small laboratories. New faculties, for computer sciences, were among the first established here.

The Kingdom's once outdated teaching materials have been completely replaced by the most up-to-date of techniques which are made available, or have been specifically adapted for Saudi use, by the Research and Materials Department of the Ministry of Education. Thus, for example, there has been a great deal of cooperation between the Faculty of Medicine and various medical universities and research institutions in the United Kingdom which has, on occasion, provided the Faculty with the specialist technical advice and teaching staff necessary to meet its specific needs.

King Saud University aims to stabilize its teacher/student ratio at around one to ten. It has suffered from a shortage of Saudi teachers and administrators (non-

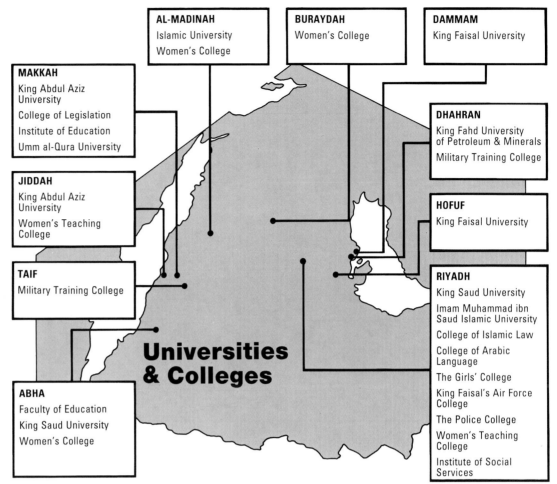

MAKKAH
King Abdul Aziz University
College of Legislation
Institute of Education
Umm al-Qura University

JIDDAH
King Abdul Aziz University
Women's Teaching College

TAIF
Military Training College

ABHA
Faculty of Education
King Saud University
Women's College

AL-MADINAH
Islamic University
Women's College

BURAYDAH
Women's College

DAMMAM
King Faisal University

DHAHRAN
King Fahd University of Petroleum & Minerals
Military Training College

HOFUF
King Faisal University

RIYADH
King Saud University
Imam Muhammad ibn Saud Islamic University
College of Islamic Law
College of Arabic Language
The Girls' College
King Faisal's Air Force College
The Police College
Women's Teaching College
Institute of Social Services

Universities & Colleges

Energy and enthusiasm for education prevails everywhere. Universities are now fully developing their own distinct characteristics and traditions in the pursuit of knowledge.

Saudi staff have accounted for up to seventy per cent of the total); but this situation is expected to improve gradually. With the Kingdom's need for qualified teachers remaining great, 25 per cent of incoming students in the early 1980s entered the Faculty of Education.

King Abdul Aziz University was founded in Jiddah in 1967 when a number of Saudi businessmen, convinced of the need for higher education and the part it would play in building the country, decided to endow a university.

The University developed so rapidly that its founders petitioned the Government to take it over. This took place in 1971, at which time two institutions in Makkah, the College of Education and the College of the Shari'ah (Islamic Law), were incorporated as faculties of the University. Both faculties concentrate on the preparation of qualified

teachers, the latter specializing in the training of judges. Courses last four years and an admission requirement, as at King Saud University, stipulates that "students must undertake to teach, after graduation, for a period equivalent to the time spent at the faculty at government expense".

There are several faculties in Jiddah, of which Economics and Administration (opened in 1968/9), Arts (opened in 1969/70), and Science (opened in 1975) are the oldest. The Institutes of Marine Sciences, and Applied Geology and Mineralogy were opened subsequently. In 1988 there were 2816 graduates, including women.

The University's two campuses lie nearby, one for men, and one for women who were first admitted to the University in 1969. The double campus highlights the problems of higher education for women. Paragraph 153 of the 1970

In 1984 King Saud University's new campus on the edge of the desert at Diriyyah became home for all the University's many faculties which had previously been scattered across Riyadh. The $3.5 billion campus provides 22,000 students with some of the most up-to-date academic, residential and social facilities in the Kingdom. The University's cloisters (left) provide cool shade and tranquility; a refectory in a covered courtyard (right) provides a spacious setting for relaxation between studies.

Coordinated development over the long term was to meet the Kingdom's needs for university-trained manpower and research.

Educational Policy document reads:

"The object of educating a woman is to bring her up in a sound Islamic way so that she can fulfill her role in life as a successful housewife, ideal wife and good mother, and to prepare her for other activities that suit her nature such as teaching, nursing and medicine." And Paragraph 155 states that "co-education is prohibited in all stages of education with the exception of nurseries and kindergartens".

At King Abdul Aziz University the rule until the mid-1970s was that: "Female students can use the Central Library on Thursday evenings under the supervision of female tutors." (*Admission Guidebook*, page 26). Subsequently Aramco helped finance a new library specially for women. "Realizing the special position of women," continues the *Guidebook*, "the University began in 1971-72 to use a closed circuit television system to broadcast a number of lectures, and, when broadcast live, this system enables female students to take part in the question and answer interchange in lectures."

The problem with this television learning is that it is impossible to apply to practical subjects (such as dissection in the Medical College for Women at Riyadh). The alternative is for equal but separate facilities. While expensive, this course has been pursued to provide women with the best education possible. King Abdul Aziz University's female campus was the first in Saudi Arabia to give women facilities that equalled those for men. King Saud University in Riyadh is to follow suit, and so may Dammam's King Faisal University.

Since 1985 King Abdul Aziz University has been one of the first to try to reduce enrolments in those subject areas in which the Kingdom is already well supplied with qualified graduates.

The pure academic in a non-scientific subject in Saudi Arabia is likely to find himself at the country's main, non-secular university – the Islamic University of al-Madinah – which was founded in 1961 and had a student population of 4,000 in 1980. In 1986 the University underwent a major extension programme to increase its existing health, social and administrative facilities which had become stretched as the number of students neared 10,000. The Islamic University serves as a regional centre for Islamic studies, and attracts many students from abroad.

In the early 1980s the Umm al-Qura University opened in Makkah to offer complementary courses of study to those at the Islamic University. The Faculty of Shari'ah (Islamic Law) is the foremost in

Students study the characteristics of high-voltage electricity with a Van de Graf Generator (top left), *and make astronomical calculations at an observatory* (top right). *Study in the library is a feature of University life* (left); *social activities include lively student theatricals* (above).

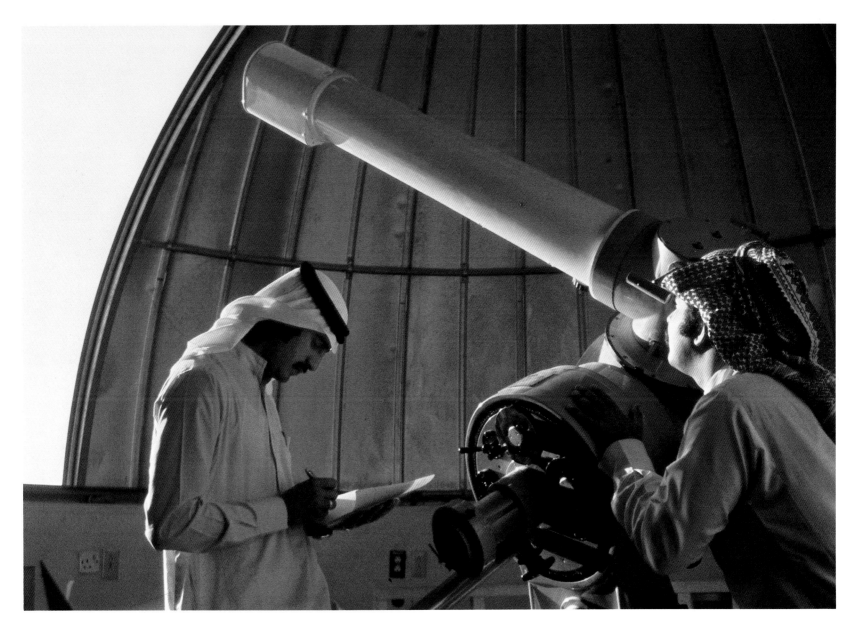

The Kingdom's educational system enters the 1990s with seven major universities, 82 college facilities and 33 vocational training schools. In 1991 there were 120,000 students enrolled in higher education, as student numbers increased, entrance and course requirements were also raised. The government also provides scholarships for Saudi students studying in universities abroad.

wide range of countries indeed. Professors and lecturers at the King Fahd University of Petroleum and Minerals, for example, were drawn from Egypt, Jordan, Iraq, Syria, Canada, Pakistan, Morocco, France, Holland, Great Britain and the United States. While this remarkable eclecticism brings to university life a wide range of influences, and consequent stimulation, one result is that universities themselves are only slowly developing their own distinct characteristics and traditions.

Energy and enthusiasm for education prevail everywhere. And the restlessness and rebelliousness that appear so often elsewhere to be a characteristic of youth have so far been harnessed by the sheer excitement of the acquisition of new and wider skills.

the country, while the University's religious instruction is internationally renowned.

King Faisal University opened the Faculties of Medicine, of Architecture and of Agriculture in 1975-76 with campuses located both at Dammam and Hofuf.

Campus life for students in Saudi Arabia has its own special air of seriousness and commitment to learning. The pace of learning is certainly quickening, yet an atmosphere of conservatism prevails. Increasingly, of course, professors are drawn from Saudi Arabia itself. But the faculties attract staff from a very

Statistical sources: Ministry of Higher Education and Ministry of Planning

The Eastern Province's
King Fahd University of Petroleum and Minerals

Perhaps the most successful architectural achievement of its decade, anywhere in the Middle East, the King Fahd University of Petroleum and Minerals in Dhahran (pictured here) has been a focus of world attention since its launching in 1963. sited on a dominating bluff above Saudi Aramco's headquarters, it

impresses the approaching visitor as a temple of learning. Its Texan architects provided it with a magnificent theatre/conference hall (top) *and mosque; and enriched the natural stone of its water tower* (right) *with subtly tinted floodlighting.*

Sport

THE TRADITIONAL SPORTS of the Arabian peninsula belong, as might be expected, to the desert and to the nomadic people who inhabit the desert. The traditional sporting pursuits have above all been those of hawking or falconry, the hunting of game with saluki hounds, and the racing of camels and fine Arabian horses. These sports are alive, indeed are flourishing, in Saudi Arabia today; but such are the exigencies of an increasingly urbanized life for the majority of the population, and the pressing need to conserve and protect the remaining wildlife of the peninsula, that game sports are now for the few rather than the many. The traditional game of the falconer – the large *hubara* (the bustard), the stone curlew, and the hare – had all diminished as a result of the widespread use of firearms through the decades leading up to the 1970s. In 1977, however, King Khalid banned the use of guns altogether in the interests of conservation, and today hawking and coursing remain as the only forms of hunting that are still permitted (*see* page 44). As for the traditional prey of the hunter's salukis, the gazelle and the oryx are today strictly protected on special reservations and may not be harmed in any way.

Horse racing on the other hand is vigorously promoted and popularly supported. The events at Riyadh's fine race course are always well attended, with

While young soldiers at Khamis Mushayt endure the rigours of army training (top right), *the popularity of such ballsports as basketball* (top left) *continues to grow among the younger generation. The Saudi Olympic team* (below) *has enjoyed success and won honour at the Games. Sailing is an increasingly common sport in Jiddah which enjoys the facilities of an*

impressive yacht club (opposite top); *roller-skating* (opposite bottom) *is a common leisure-time pursuit at the Nassiriyyah Gate in Riyadh.*

the pleasure of the crowd lying in the speed of the horses and the horsemanship of the jockeys. On occasion, camel races, which occur frequently among the desert communities, take their place on the race course, with the camels carrying their owners' colours.

In the last decades group sports and team events of an international variety have become extremely popular among the general population as a whole. Sports of all sorts, including athletics, gymnastics, tracks and field events, have been stimulated by the General Presidency for Youth Welfare, which serves as a fountainhead for many of the sporting enterprises in modern Saudi Arabia, and protectively watches over the standards set by several youth and sporting federations.

The Kingdom's relative isolation from the international community until recent generations has meant that it has

213

been without much experience in international sporting competition. However, this situation has been changing very rapidly ever since Saudi Arabia entered its first team to the Olympic Games in 1976. The demanding standards of world sport have been met with increasing success by the successive athletics teams that the Kingdom has entered for the

Olympics ever since Saudi athletes first made their appearance at the Montreal Games.

The General Presidency for Youth Welfare has set about the construction of major new sports facilities across the Kingdom. The King Fahd International Sports Stadium in Riyadh, inaugurated in March 1988 and built at a cost

The new King Fahd International Stadium at Riyadh has capacity for over 60,000 spectators and facilities for track and field sports including athletics and football (left). *The stadium's stands are sheltered by a series of massive tent-like roofs* (above left). *Football is always a popular crowd-puller* (above).

of one and a half billion riyals, has a capacity of 67,000 spectators. The stadium not only contains running tracks, designed to meet the Olympic standard, set around a football pitch, but also provides a restaurant for 2,000 people, and accommodation for athletes visiting the capital. Sports centres comprising stadia for 10,000 spectators, gymnasia, Olym-

pic-size swimming pools, and track and games fields were to provide Jizan, Bukairiyyah in al-Qasim, and Majma'ah 300 kilometres north of Riyadh, with regional facilities on a par with those in the major cities.

In addition, youth welfare centres, youth hostels, sporting camps and youth club recreation areas have become wide-

215

Horse racing (there is no betting) draws enthusiastic interest in Riyadh – but not at the expense of traditional camel racing, which has recently been brought under racecourse rules for racecourse fixtures; desert rules apply elsewhere.

spread throughout the country. Most major cities and universities now boast advanced sports cities complete with stadia, pools, sports halls, tracks and athletics fields. The specialised Arabian Institute for the Training of Youth and Sports Leaders acts across the country to enrol students of outstanding merit and train them further in their chosen fields of athletic endeavour.

Tremendous enthusiasm for sport prevails among the population, and Saudi Arabian teams have become a familiar sight at the sporting fixtures of the regional international community. At one stage an American sporting organisation was contracted to provide instruction in athletics, swimming, and basketball – as these had become such popular outdoor activities that the demand for coaching outstripped the supply of proficient instructors. Above all, however, it has been the international sport of association football

that has attracted the overwhelming enthusiasm of Saudi youth.

World-renowned football coaches from abroad were given the challenge of bringing Saudi football up to international standards by the late 1970s. A substantial budget was allocated to the project which, by setting up small leagues for all age groups at the district level, had soon established the playing of football on a national basis. The project also promoted training sessions at all levels, and established the necessary administrative staffs, including a national group of some two hundred officials centred upon a national Football Federation, with the result that the Kingdom has produced an effective national team.

Relative lack of experience has not been Saudi Arabia's only handicap where international sporting prowess is concerned. The climate itself makes training difficult: in the heat of the day it is simply not possible to play football,

while the severe aridity makes the maintenance of grassed pitches a constant headache. However, the network of stadia is equipped with flood-lighting for training in the cool of the evening. There is no presumption that success in the challenging world of football, or in the realm of international sport, can be bought. Equipped with the right facilities, young Saudi Arabians have only begun to achieve their successes through the rigours of sustained, hard training and personal discipline.

Football is set to remain at the core of the Kingdom's sporting endeavour, and this enthusiasm for the game has brought its own rewards – memorable moments include the national team's victory in Singapore over the South Korean side. In February 1989 Riyadh hosted the 5th World Cup Youth Tournament, and the Kingdom went on to win the 3rd International Youth Football Championship in June 1989 by defeating Scotland in the final.

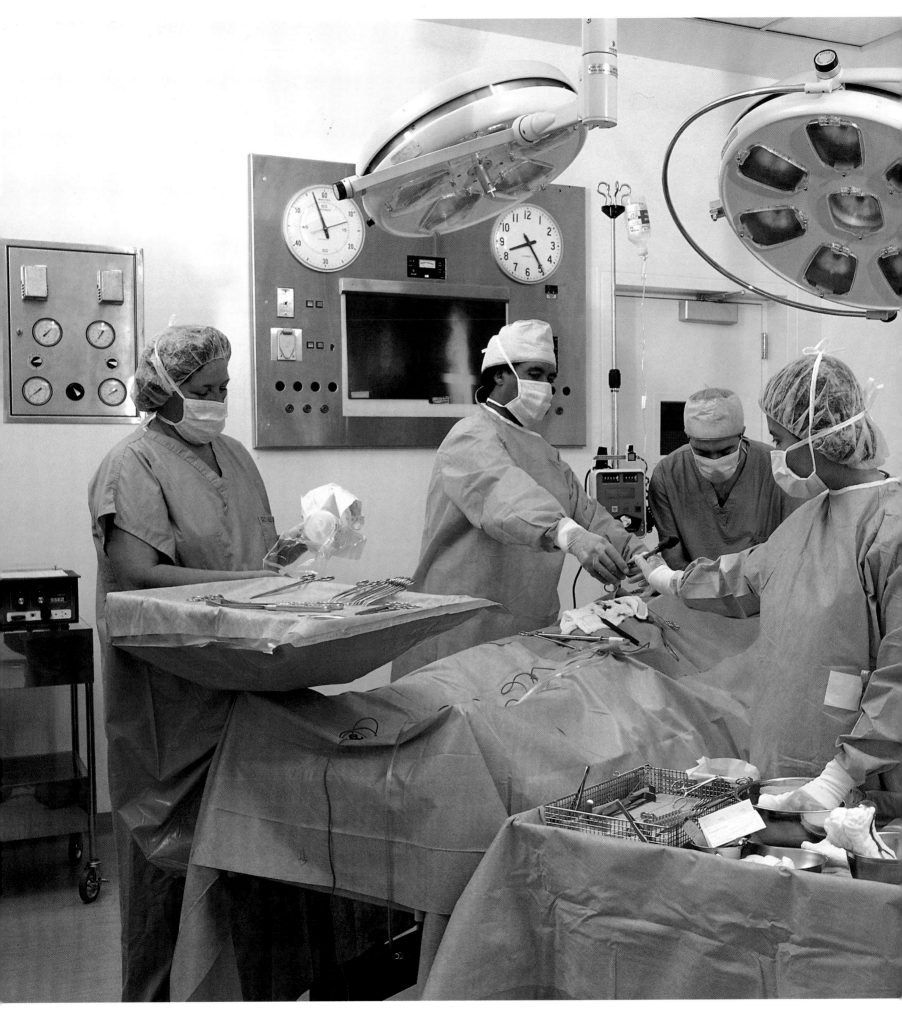

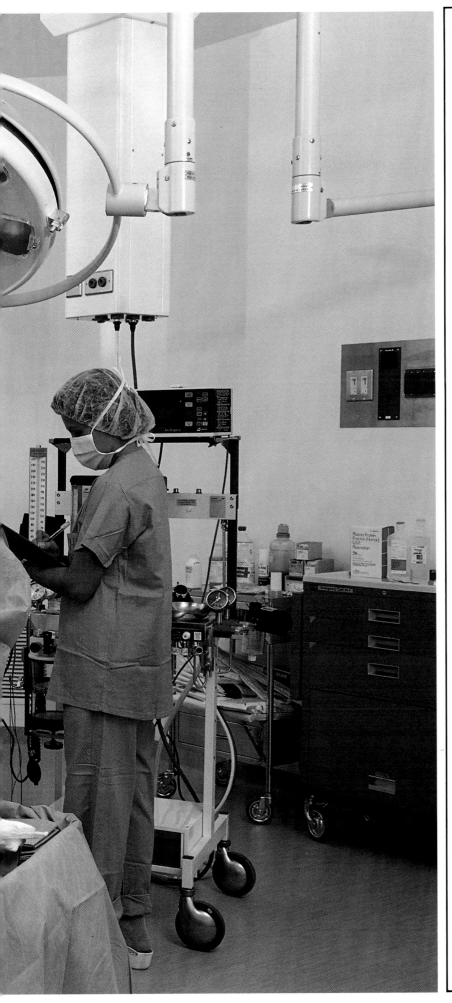

10 Social Development

The Holy Qur'an repeatedly enjoins on man responsibility for his fellows. The Government is the prime dispenser of the nation's wealth. High standards are set in social insurance and welfare for the needy – as high in terms of quality as in thoroughness of coverage.

Medicine, and care of the sick generally, has played a major role in Saudi Arabia's internal allocation of its massive resources. Newly equipped with some of the finest medical technology in the world, it is seeking to establish the human infrastructure of doctors, specialists, nurses and patient aftercare services to make the country self-sufficient in medical terms.

219

Health

ONE of the greatest benefits flowing from Saudi Arabia's new wealth is the enormously improved system of health care which has been made possible. King Faisal decided that the State should provide free medical treatment for all its citizens, and for the pilgrims who visit the holy places of Islam.

By 1980, there were eighty-seven well-equipped modern hospitals with almost 14,000 beds belonging to the Ministry of Health and the private sector alone, including a 1,000-bed TB hospital and a 200-bed hospital for the treatment of leprosy. Over the next nine years the number of hospitals increased to 253 which provide upwards of 40,000 beds. The Ministry of Health was responsible for 86 of these hospitals while, together, the private sector, the Ministry of Defence, the National Guard, the Higher Education Ministry and other governmental agencies supplied the remainder. These various health services maintained 2.4 beds per thousand of the King-

dom's population; a figure that was to improve steadily and reach 3.9 per thousand by the end of the decade.

The Ministry of Health's national network of primary health care centres continued to expand; by 1988 more than 2,150 of these centres were offering local or regional services. A sharp rise in efficiency in the general provision of medical services was recorded between 1983 and 1984 when the average number of sick treated by each doctor rose by nearly a hundred. The ratio of doctors to people improved from the previous record of one in 853 in 1983 to one in 726 in 1984.

The Kingdom's provision of medical facilities and healthcare services for its people continued to improve in the years that followed. Today the World Health Organisation is using Saudi Arabia as a health care model in other developing countries.

As many hospital projects reached the final stages of construction, the emphasis of planning moved away from further construction and concentrated on improving the operational efficiency of current services through effective maintenance and management of existing

facilities.

Throughout its expansion, the Kingdom's network of health services had been continually updated to take advantage of the latest advances in medical technology. A comprehensive national medical record system is being set up, and preventive health measures based on new research into prevailing conditions are proving increasingly effective.

Doctors, nurses and technicians of many nationalities working in the Kingdom today will be supplemented and eventually succeeded by Saudis. The number of physicians working in the Kingdom rose dramatically between 1970 and 1988, from a mere 1,172 to over 19,000. There are new training institutes at al-Madinah and Abha, and training centres at King Faisal University, and also at King Abdul Aziz University in Jiddah where a large, state-of-the-art medical complex was completed in 1986. At the King Saud University campus outside Riyadh, a 760-bed teaching hospital is in operation and plans are going ahead to provide a surgical unit extension to the original facilities there.

A paramedical institute for women at

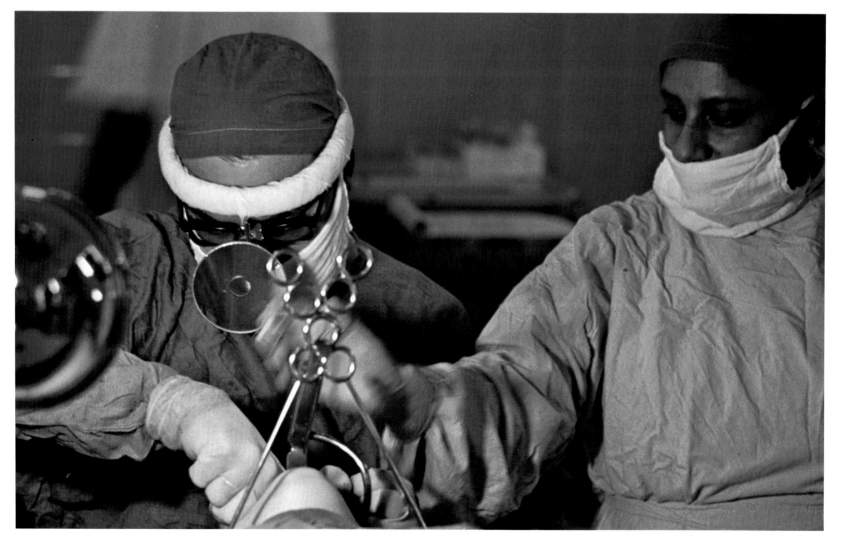

Health Facilities & Personnel

Ministry of Health	1985	1987	1989
HOSPITALS	105	157	254
HOSPITAL BEDS	20,796	25,902	41,123
PRIMARY HEALTH CARE CENTRES	1,306	1,438	3,028
DOCTORS	9,257	11,326	22,136
NURSES & PARAMEDICAL PERSONNEL	30,793	38,779	70,887

Paediatric care is an integral part of medical services; the Saudi birth rate is one of the highest in the world with sixty per cent of the population under 20 years old.

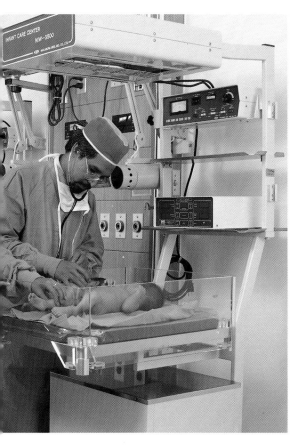

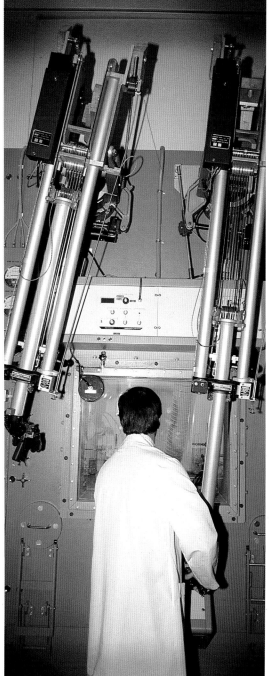

Rass, in al-Qasim adds to the existing medical training facilities at the women's colleges in Riyadh and Jiddah.

In recent years, the Kingdom has made great advances in its programmes of pure medical research, the benefits of which will not be limited to Saudi Arabia alone. New drugs to treat diabetes and trachoma have been developed at King Saud University in Riyadh and are to be marketed world-wide. A preventive treatment for bilharzia has been developed by a Saudi woman doctor. Several Saudi medical institutions are also engaged in a bio-engineering programme with Aerospatiale of France to develop an artificial heart capable of human implant. Saudi medical researchers today win international prizes. The Saudi Pharmaceutical Industries and Medical Appliances Company (SPIMACO) produced the Kingdom's first pharmaceuticals at its plant in al-Qasim in 1988.

Much of the stimulus for Saudi Arabia's impressive medical achievements came from the late King Faisal. A project for which he was particularly enthusiastic, one of the most important hospitals in the country, remains as a memorial to this interest - the King Faisal Medical City on the outskirts of Riyadh. It was the first to provide specialist services for patients who would otherwise have had to travel abroad for treatment.

An elaborate ambulance service was established at King Faisal Hospital for patients in need of intensive care, including air ambulances which land at the hospital's own heliport. Portable cardiac machines and on-board computers in the ambulances and aircraft can relay signals to the main hospital, so that a severely ill patient has, in effect, been admitted to the hospital and is being

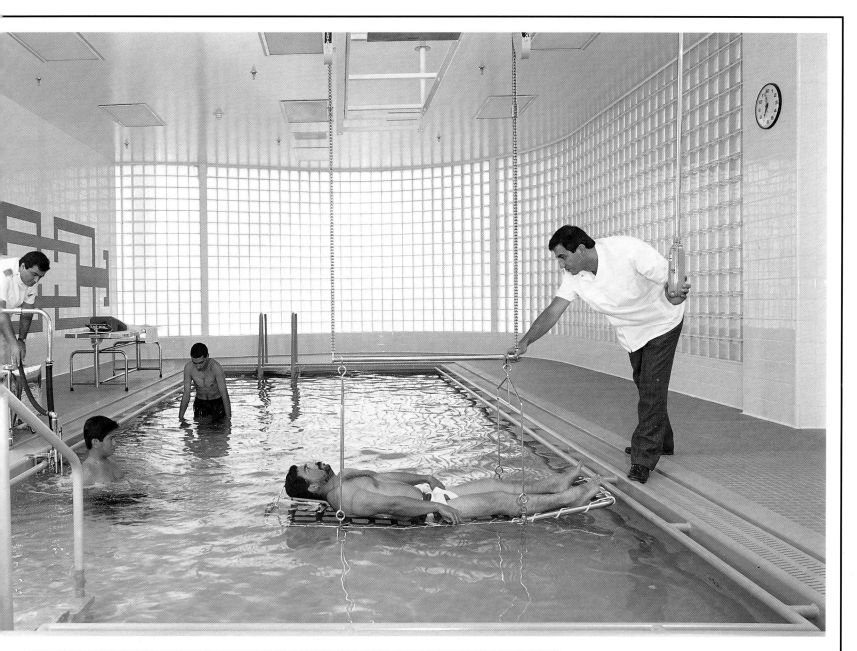

KING FAHD MEDICAL CENTRE

Madinat Yanbu Al-Sinaiyah

Designed to meet the needs of both the industrial city and the region, the Medical Centre provides general medical, occupational and environmental health services. The 342-bed hospital includes specialised departments for ear, nose and throat, renal dialysis, opthalmic surgery and a burns unit.

In addition, there are departments for preventive medicine, environmental and occupational health. Recent statistics illustrate the expansion of the permanent communities with more than 2,300 babies delivered in the industrial cities of Jubayl and Yanbu during 1990. Over the same period more than 12,000 in-patient admissions and 330,000 out-patient visits were made to the hospitals and clinics of the two cities.

King Khalid Eye Specialist Hospital

Since it first opened in 1982, Riyadh's King Khalid Eye Specialist Hospital has established a reputation throughout the region as a leader in its field. The hospital can accommodate two hundred and sixty in-patients and is equipped with twelve operating theatres and two emergency service surgical treatment rooms; two mobile laser coagulators can be used in any one of these facilities.

The eye hospital also offers research, diagnosis and treatment services in its several clinics which include optometry, ultrasonography, radiology, psychophysical and electrophysicology laboratories, as well as a pharmacy and screening centre.

The D.S.F. Hospital in Jiddah provides the city with excellent facilities including maternity, post-natal, paediatric and intensive care units.

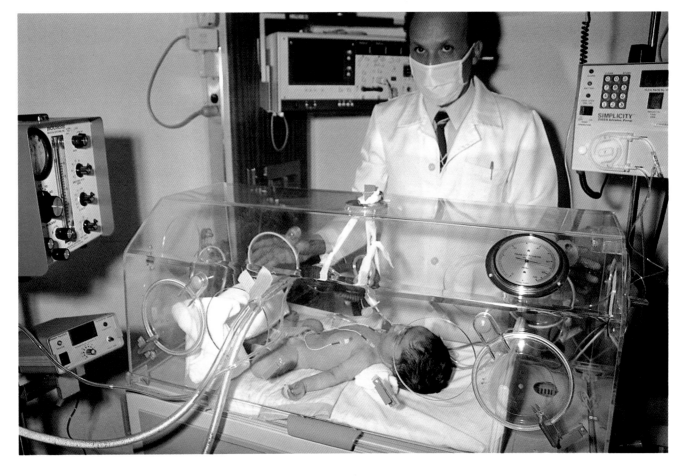

treated before he even arrives.

The Armed Forces Medical Services and some few other hospitals serving in the remoter areas of the Kingdom, also maintain air ambulances and hospital aircraft. The original fleet of mini-hospitals was increased to ten in 1986 when Saudi Arabia took delivery of three L-100-30HS planes.

The Saudi Red Crescent Society, which functions much like the Red Cross in Europe, is an important part of the country's system of medical care. It provides first-aid and emergency services, particularly on the roads and during the period of the *hajj*. From a General Centre in Riyadh, the Society operates 3 branch offices, 8 health centres, 27 first-aid centres which are open twenty-four hours a day, and 120 ambulances. Ambulances in the *hajj* areas are equipped with radios, and a First-Aid Training Institute has been established. The Holy City of Makkah, moreover, has been provided with five hospitals to cater for its own and the pilgrims' needs. There are a further thirteen hospitals in the al-Madinah area.

The annual *hajj* confronts the Kingdom with unique health challenges. Pilgrims from Africa, say, or Asia could so easily enter bringing with them communicable diseases like cholera. Special

medical teams are briefed for such emergencies. Moreover, the main port of entry, Jiddah, is provided with a quarantine centre containing two isolation hospitals in an enormous site comprising a self-contained village of over 150 buildings.

Apart from this special contingency medical centre and fever hospital, Jiddah is provided with five public hospitals to meet the daily health needs of its citizens. In addition to these, there are a maternity and paediatrics hospital, an eye hospital, and a specialist chest hospital. Construction work on the new 440-bed King Abdul Aziz General Hospital was completed in 1988.

The populations of the conurbation in the Eastern Province are served by eleven hospitals. Qasim's total of seven is to increase to eight with the opening of a 200-bed hospital in Rass in 1989. Taif has three large hospitals, while Bahah, Najran and Hail have one each. The populous Asir in the southwest is provided with seven hospitals spread throughout the region; and the Northern Province has four.

The greatest concentration of health facilities is in Riyadh where there are eleven general hospitals. Riyadh has also become Saudi Arabia's capital for most specialized health care. The city

has maternity and paediatric, chest, and fever hospitals. A surgical dental health clinic was opened in 1986. The clinic is attached to the Ministry of Health's central hospital and provides specialist treatment for cases referred from the Kingdom's local dental clinics, and has been equipped to perform jaw and facial surgery. The Armed Forces Hospital's Cardiology Unit has an international reputation.

Saudi Arabia's eye specialists at the King Khalid Hospital have made it a leader in the treatment of trachoma. It has been selected by the World Health Organisation as the centre for combatting blindness in the region. The Kingdom's improved public health conditions are expected to have decreased the incidence of trachomas among the general population. The number of people afflicted with blindness is also thought to have halved over the last two decades. By 1988 King Khalid Eye Hospital had performed 37,000 eye operations and had done much to alleviate the suffering of numerous individuals with trachomas who have been drawn from many countries by the hospital's reputation for treatment.

Statistical sources: Ministry of Health, Ministry of Planning and SAMA

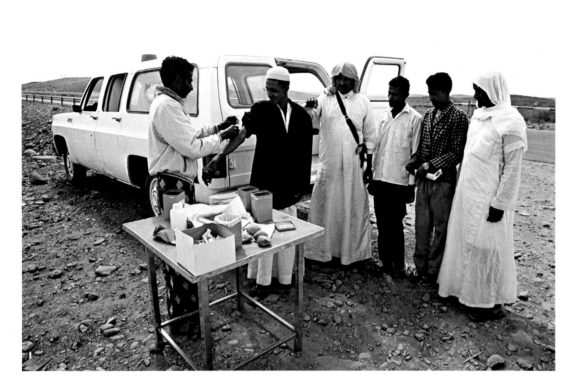

Preventive Medicine

Clinics cut infant mortality.

SAUDI ARABIA is, climatically, a healthy country. The arid atmosphere, the traditional hardihood of a desert people, sensible dietary customs and the rules of hygiene strictly observed by all good Muslims, combine to prevent the spread of sickness.

There is, for example, one of the lowest rates of heart disease *per capita* in the world. This is particularly true among those living the Beduin life.

Communal health hazards do exist, however, especially in certain areas. On the south-western coast bilharzia and malaria still occur; however, malaria had been eradicated from the Northern and Eastern Provinces and its spread checked elsewhere by 1986. The trachoma virus which attacks the eyes, is a common scourge, as in hot dry climates. And epidemics – of cholera, diphtheria and smallpox – are still a constant threat.

There is no settled community in Saudi Arabia beyond the reach of the network of medical care now provided. The urban areas are served by major general and specialist hospitals: elsewhere there are district dispensaries and health centres, and even the smallest and most remote desert community has

access to mobile clinics and dispensaries, the "flying doctor" and other emergency services.

At the same time, there is a continuous programme of vaccination, nutritional instruction, pre-and post-natal care for mothers, x-rays and dental care. Sources of carrier-bred disease, such as malaria and bilharzia, are systematically treated. Among the obstacles to be overcome is the over-readiness of unsophisticated people to accept disease as an inescapable fact of life. But by 1988 it was estimated that the Kingdom's vaccination programme was reaching 90 per cent of infants, 19 per cent up on 1985.

The improved medical care of the last two decades has increased the average life-expectancy by eleven years. Infant mortality, once as high as twenty per cent in some desert communities, has fallen sharply, to 16 per 1,000 in 1988-9 in, for example, Jiddah. The linking up of road systems, especially in the northern and north-west parts of the country, should accelerate the process; so one of Saudi Arabia's chief obstacles to development – the lack of indigenous population – is being diminished in the most desirable way.

Meanwhile, Saudi Aramco and Har-

vard University have, for a long while, been engaged in joint trachoma research. In an effort to develop an effective vaccine, studies have been made of the natural immunity which occurs in some young people as they become adults. Other research units are planned, and there will also be a network of mother and child care clinics.

Health education is itself a form of preventive medicine, and widespread efforts are being made to increase the public's awareness of health problems, their causes and how best to deal with them.

Mental Health

The Qur'an enjoins kindness.

THE mentally defective or retarded constitute a special category of handicapped people, and one for which Islam has traditionally been particularly solicitous.

By and large the Kingdom has escaped the widespread mental health problems that afflict Western countries. This is ascribed to the strength of family ties and the security that the extended family provides: it is rare indeed for an Arabian infant or child to be deprived of the continuity of love and care within the family. The other factor that brings to society balm and balance is the depth and ubiquity of religious conviction. But there are, inevitably, a number of citizens suffering from mental defectiveness or brain damage.

An institute for retarded children was opened in 1968, offering full boarding facilities for fifty boys and fifty girls; and there are other institutes to care for the mentally retarded of all ages. Attached to each insitute are social workers, whose responsibility it is to make a special case-study of every pupil. They visit homes and parents, and try to establish a relationship of trust.

Everything is done, as far as possible, on an individual basis. At the institute for retarded children, the maximum number of students in any house or class is five. A clinic is available for psychotherapy. Monthly meetings are held, to which both parents and pupils come. The discussion may be led by a visiting psychologist or social worker.

Blood tests, quarantine and vaccination programmes all reach remote parts of the country. Below, *the mentally sick – a relative rarity in Saudi Arabia – are cared for in a specially built hospital.*

The Handicapped

THE SAUDI ARABIAN Government, in accordance with the principles of Islam, makes special provision for the care of handicapped people.

In 1959, the Ministry of Education established an evening institute for the blind. Within a year the institute had come into being. Based in an existing school in the suburbs of Riyadh, it provided classes for a hundred students. During the daytime they attended religious institutes; in the evening they came to this new Institute for the Blind, where they learned Braille and received vocational training.

When it was reorganized as a day school in 1960, the Ministry accepted full responsibility for the academic and technical education of the students, whose number had then grown to 110.

Two years later, institutes for the blind were also established in Makkah and Unayzah. Their teaching staff has been trained, and had acquired experience, at the Riyadh Institute. In the same year, 1962, the Ministry created its own Department of Special Education.

During the next few years several similar, or related, establishments were founded – institutes for the blind at Hofuf, al-Madinah and Qatif: two institutes for the deaf and mute at Riyadh (one for men, the other for women); and an institute at Riyadh to train women teachers of the handicapped.

The Department of Special Education provides everything necessary – buildings, audio-equipment, books in Braille and so on. The students are entitled to free transport from their homes to the institute; and they receive a small monthly grant throughout their training.

There are now several centres where teachers can learn how to care for, and work with, handicapped students; and the Department offers fellowships for advanced training abroad.

Over 20 institutes for the handicapped have been built. Workshops, such as those at the Dammam Institute, train pupils in carpentry, tailoring, secretarial skills, painting, agriculture, horticulture, telephone operating and computer programming. Planning policies for these and future institutions have been evolved in the light of experience.

In the institutes for the blind, two courses – one academic, the other voca-

Respect for Qur'anic principles lies behind Saudi Arabia's particular concern for the handicapped, the blind and the crippled. Schools and institutes give education and work to the handicapped; lip-reading for the deaf (right), art therapy for the handicapped (bottom right) and occupational therapy with the use of a prosthesis for an employee at Saudi Aramco (below).

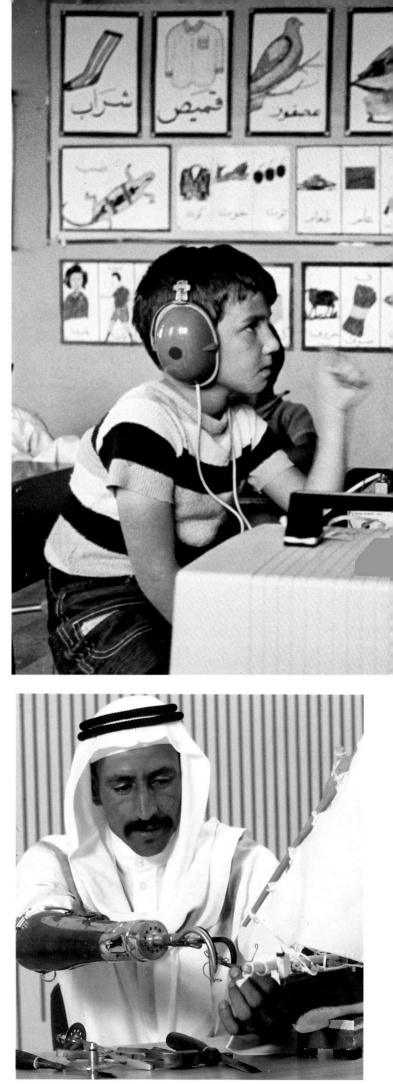

tional – are normally provided. Pupils are admitted to the academic courses from the age of six to the age of eighteen, when they can sit the examination for a Secondary Education Certificate. Teaching methods are not dissimilar from those of ordinary schools, except for the use of Braille.

For pupils between the ages of six and twenty, vocational training courses are available in such subjects as basketwork, weaving and the manufacture of household equipment. These courses usually extend over six years, and culminate in the examination for a certificate in technology. Some general education is included as well and all pupils are trained to read and write Braille. Amply equipped workshops are available. The items which the pupils can make – chairs, beds, baskets, cane tables, brushes, cloth, carpets – are usually of good quality, and sell quite readily on the open market.

The institutes for the deaf and dumb have to cope with even more difficult problems. A preparatory course is provided for young children aged four to six. Deaf and dumb pupils are fed and clothed, as well as receiving their monthly grant and enjoying the medical and welfare services available to all handicapped people. They are taught in classes containing not more than ten, or fewer than five, pupils.

Every institute has social workers and a full-time nurse on the staff. The hope is that all students will acquire a trade, with the encouragement of the Labour Law's stipulations that companies employing more than fifty should give two per cent of their jobs to disabled workers. In 1985 a General Directorate for Women's and Children's Affairs was set up under the terms of the Fourth Plan with specific provision to provide a section devoted to following up the education of the Kingdom's disabled, and thereafter with monitoring their employment.

Saudi Arabia's successive Development Plans have consistently sought to provide and expand the care and facilities necessary to the broader development of each disabled individual's personality. Those children who are in care have long been encouraged to participate in the Kingdom's everyday life through a full range of extracurricular activities; a policy which has seen the flowering of many an active and fully socially-adapted adult.

Social Insurance

NO major developing country has exceeded Saudi Arabia in its concern for its workers and their families.

Social Insurance is a system originally based on Islamic principles through which the State ensures the worker's safety and provides for a secure future in which he and his family can lead a decent stable life. The General Organization for Social Insurance (GOSI) began enforcement of the Social Insurance Law in 1393 AH (1973 CE). This Law lays down several types of protection for workers regardless of nationality or sex – disability, old age and death benefits (Annuities Branch), occupational injuries and occupational diseases (Occupational Hazards Branch), temporary disability due to sickness or maternity, and family grants in cases where the insured has several dependants. Unemployment compensations are made available and there is good protection for the self-employed.

The Annuities Branch includes: old-age annuity, non-occupational disability, payment of lump sums to insured persons who do not qualify for pensions, funeral expenses grant, heirs' annuity, marriage grant to widows, daughters and sisters, and voluntary insurance for old age.

When the insured workers retires at the age of sixty or more, the General Organization for Social Insurance pays him a monthly annuity for the rest of his life. The amount of the annuity depends on the contributory period and the average of his wage during the last twenty-four months of insurance. It is calculated on the basis of two per cent of his average monthly wages during the previous twenty-four months, multiplied by the number of years of his contribution in insurance. Added to the annuity is a dependants' allowance – ten per cent of the annuity for the first dependant, five per cent for the second dependant, and five per cent for the third dependant. Annuities are paid monthly for the rest of his life, and the annuitant's heirs, after his death, are also entitled to monthly payments.

If the insured sustains a non-occupational disability and is crippled before he reaches retirement age, he is entitled to receive from GOSI a disability annuity payable to him monthly for the duration of his life. The amount of this annuity is computed in the same way as the old age annuity, at two per cent of the average monthly wage for the twenty-four months preceding the occurrence of the disability, multiplied by the number of years of his participation in insurance or forty per cent of such an average, whichever is the higher figure. A total disability allowance of fifty per cent of such annuity is added if the disabled person needs the assistance of others in the performance of his everyday activities. Both the annuity and the allowance is paid to the annuitant as long as he is incapacitated. If he is still disabled at the age of sixty, the annuity is then payable for life. After his death, the dependent members of his family are entitled to heirs' annuities.

The insured who has reached the age of sixty and who for at least six months has been without a job subject to insurance, and likewise the insured who is afflicted with a non-occupational disability before he reaches sixty, receives from GOSI a lump sum equivalent to his total contributions (five per cent of his wages) paid throughout the insurance period, plus a grant of five per cent of the total of such contributions, provided that he has completed a minimum of twelve insurance months and does not qualify for an old age disability annuity. If he dies, GOSI pays the lump sum to the widow or to the children, to the father and mother or, in the absence of any other person, to the brothers and sisters.

A grant of SR 400 is paid to the person who undertakes to pay the funeral expenses of an insured worker who dies in service after completing at least six insurance months during the last year before his death. A similar grant is available on the death of an aged or crippled annuitant. Upon the death of an insured person who received a non-occupational disability annuity, his dependants are entitled to the same annuity which used to be paid to their supporter (minus the dependants' allowance or total disability allowance). The heirs are entitled to the annuity if the deceased was not an annuitant, on the basis of the disability annuity to which he would have been entitled had he sustained the disability on the date of his death. If a son or daughter has lost both parents, the annuity is doubled.

The widow is given one half of the husband's annuity, and each of his other dependants receives twenty per cent of such annuity, provided that the total monthly amount payable does not exceed the original annuity; if the annuities exceed one hundred per cent of the deceased worker's entitlement, all the annuities are reduced in proportion. The widow is entitled to the annuity provided that the marriage took place at least six months before the death of the insured if he was in service, or at least twelve months before his death if he was an old age pensioner or crippled annuitant. She continues to receive it until she remarries, in which case she is given a marriage grant. Male orphans under twenty years of age are also eligible for the annuity. The age limit is extended until they are twenty-five, if they are pursuing their studies in an educational or vocational institute. If they are unable to work by reason of a chronic disease or an infirmity, the annuity is paid to them as long as they are thus afflicted. Female orphans are supported until they marry, provided that they were supported by the deceased at the time of his death. Brothers and sisters of the deceased are provided for, subject to the same conditions applicable to orphans. Parents of the deceased who were supported by him at the time of his death, provided that the father is over sixty years of age and unable to work, are also entitled to the annuity. If an old age or disability annuitant's widow, daughter or sister marries, she is given a marriage grant equal to eighteen times the annuity she used to receive, and payment of the annuity ceases at the end of the month during which the marriage takes place. The allocation of this grant terminates any right derived from the insurance.

The Hazards Branch provides for insurance against employment injuries and occupational diseases. The accumulation of benefits in kind and cash is not conditional upon any qualifying period of insurance. The rate of contribution is fixed at two per cent of the wages of the insured and the employer alone is responsible for its repayment.

The Social Insurance scheme operates on a contributory basis, that is, GOSI revenues comprise contributions from both employees and employers, as well as investment revenues and government subsidy.

Statistical sources: Ministry of Labour & Social Affairs and Ministry of Planning.

Social Life

ALL over Saudi Arabia today traditional patterns of life are being affected both in their outward form and more intimately by swiftly rising levels of education, the dramatic impact of increased income, and the consequences of industrialization. Television, sound broadcasting, and the surge towards literacy are swiftly expanding the knowledge both of those living in cities and towns and of the peasantry and villagers. The new metalled roads and the internal airline system and railroad, linking rural areas with towns and cities, and the major centres with the outside world, have brought about an unprecedented flow of new ideas.

Simultaneously, the cities are attracting from the outlying areas, at an accelerating pace, people whose way of life in the desert has scarcely changed for centuries. They are brought into the towns and cities by the promise of work and are at once confronted by the complexities of modern urban life and the racket of a culture where technocracy rules. An industrial revolution which, in Europe, gathered pace over generations, is in Saudi Arabia being compressed into a matter of years. There is an advantage – to which those guiding the country have laid claim – that lessons can be learned from the experiences, both achievements and mistakes, of the already developed nations.

The strains and pressures within Saudi Arabian society today are recognized as inevitable. Yet the intent to preserve what is right and true in traditional values, while accepting the enlightenment of education and the challenge of so-called progress, wins the admiration of all who look at Saudi Arabia today closely.

Al fresco coffee on rug-covered rooftops is characteristic of Najran.

The central point is that Saudi Arabians put first their role as guardians of the holy shrines of Islam and as the inheritors of the homeland of the Prophet. This role in their peninsula is their *raison d'être* as a people. They have standards to maintain on behalf of Islam. They grow up in the knowledge of this unique heritage. Whatever the temptations, they refuse to dispense with it.

The outsider is at once struck by the restraints which Saudi Arabians at all levels willingly accept. A devoutness prevails at all levels of society, even when luxury or great wealth is easily within reach. Sophisticated young men and women who may have completed their education in the West will return to Saudi Arabian society and, with apparent effortlessness, shed those

The central factor in Saudi Arabia's social life is the strength of the family. In a period of swift outward change, widely spread family links produce a complex of allegiances which ensure continuity and high standards of personal conduct.

aspects of indulgence and licence which the West takes for granted. The Qur'anic prohibition against alcohol is taken seriously. Modesty is indeed expected of womenfolk, and the segregation of the sexes in open society – while it is being modified in certain aspects – is widely accepted.

One of the central strengths of the Kingdom is that this subtle balance between traditional values and the modern world is struck by the Royal Family. By its vast network of relationships, it permeates almost all areas of authority in the Kingdom. Yet it has a subtly and determinately liberal attitude which is evident in general attitudes towards women. Up to the early 1960s there was no formal education for girls. Twenty five years later, over 850,000 girls (probably accounting for over three quarters of the girls in the country) were attending school, and the number and proportion are still continuing to grow. The impulse for this remarkable development came directly from the top. By and large, this profound change has been achieved smoothly through the years and without ruction.

Similarly, for example, in the field of broadcasting and television the late King Faisal was alive to the educative potential of the medium. Some of his counsellors were not so persuaded. The King presented a closed circuit demonstration of readings from the Qur'an. The doubters soon became impressed. Today television plays a notable role in the religious life of the nation, indeed a role which reaches beyond that into general education and information, right into the home, where the women and children are to be found.

Traditionally in Saudi Arabia, the women's role centred exclusively on the home. Social contact with men outside the home was forbidden. While in the intimacy of the home a wife would play as full a part as her energy and intelligence and strength of character allowed her, the basic definition of a wife's role could be defined as that of serving her husband by obeying him, and serving her children by caring for them. If such a role has meant restrictions on the lives of women, it has nonetheless brought remarkable strength to the family unit in the country.

For womenfolk would meet womenfolk within the family, and family links have always been broad and often far-flung. Today the restrictions on the life

Commerce (above and opposite) *brings social intercourse. Conversation is lively in a student café* (above left), *the atmosphere relaxed at a Hofuf picnic* (left).

and activity of women is often more apparent than real. The outsider can easily be deceived. In the streets women go veiled; in their homes, as in the schools and universities, they are unveiled. Indeed, they are unveiled when they enter the shops now selling expensive women's fashion in the major cities. The visitor from outside the country will not normally find himself in the company of women when taking a meal at the home of a Saudi friend. But this would not be so if he were a member of the extended family.

There is no woman in Saudi Arabia – of any nationality – to be seen behind the wheel of a car. On the other hand, Saudi

233

Many of Saudi Arabia's best hotels provide conference, business and social facilities as well as accommodation for foreign visitors. The Intercontinental Hotel is linked to the international conference centre in Riyadh (see page 167), *while the prominent Al Hada Sheraton in Taif offers businessmen a wide range of meeting facilities* (see page 167). *The Marriott Hotel in Riyadh is famous for its lobby* (top left) *which is a favourite meeting place for those in the capital. The Oberoi Hotel* (top right) *is one of Dammam's well-known landmarks. The capital's Hyatt Regency* (centre) *is the flagship for the group's provincial hotels in cities like Jizan* (lower centre). *The Meridien Hotel* (bottom) *combines an exciting structure with first rate accommodation.*

women are taking university degrees in their own universities. The problem of listening to lectures given by male professors is overcome by the use of a closed circuit television. At the same time, more and more Saudi women are travelling abroad with their husbands, many of them executives in the modern structure

of Saudi government or in Saudi-based international firms. Saudi women now carry their own passports, their unveiled faces appearing in their passport photographs.

It has been speculated that women may soon play their part in industry and government, and they are readily accepted as doctors, teachers, nurses and social workers. For a great many years they have been employed as radio and television announcers and commentators.

Furthermore cautious moves towards the participation of women – many of them quietly instigated following the accession of the late King Faisal, who was known to respect the relatively progressive views of his wife Iffat – have included education, developing work opportunities and the opening of special bank branches for women under their Qur'anic right to engage in business as many do. There are few Saudi women who would not vigorously defend the virtues of the paramountcy of the woman's classic role as wife and mother, and there are few who wish to rush headlong into the much vaunted but often unhappy emancipation of womanhood in the West. But a wider role in the Kingdom's economic life is emerging for them. The law states the right to work, and in the mid-1980s a senior ministerial council was, with the World Bank, investigating ways to increase women's participation in the workforce. For women represented a major pool of precious Saudi labour which could help displace the large numbers of foreign workers who, it was thought, threatened the delicate balance of traditional Saudi life.

However, despite these singular moves towards the participation of women, the system of marriages being arranged between families is universally honoured as its success has long been proved. Westerners often forget that it is a system that prevailed successfully in the West itself until a few centuries ago.

Traditionally, it is the girl's parents who negotiate her marriage and the dowry which the future husband is expected to provide. Such is the basic system prevailing today. But an element of choice by the young people themselves is creeping in, especially among those girls who are beginning to become wage earners and therefore have more influence in their families. But this is not to imply that marriages take place against parental wishes. And if marriages in Saudi Arabia are seen by both families clearly not to work, the way in which married partners are separated is far less fraught than in, say, Western societies. Because divorce may not be a complicated process, it does not mean that it is excessively frequent. Qur'anic law provides quite clearly for marriages which do not work. Divorces take place privately, without fuss.

Privacy is a virtue of Saudi Arabian life. As elsewhere in the Islamic world, homes are built around an open centre. They do not look outwards. They are self-contained. Their freedoms are internal freedoms. Indeed, the liberality and ease of relationships within a family are well known.

Beyond the towns and cities, among the Beduin – perhaps ten per cent of the population – it is the tribal allegiances that still strongly prevail. The influence of the ancient, disciplined and dignified way of life markedly pervades all levels of Saudi Arabian society. And although the force of tribal loyalties is certainly diminished in town life, the loyalties are not forgotten. Among those from the families who hold the leadership of tribes and who have come to live in cities and to make their fortunes there, there is a widespread tendency to maintain the tribal links. The Beduin "wing" of the family or tribe is visited at festival times throughout the year. Conversely,

Beduin Life

In the desert, the social life of the Beduin – literally "the desert people" – retains much of its time-honoured forms and styles. Life is centred on the family tent. The traditional black tent is woven by the women of goat hair (the most waterproof), sometimes mixed with sheep's wool and camel hair, in strips which are sewn together. Gaily coloured woven internal "walls" divide the men's section from the general living quarters where the women do the cooking and the small children's leather cradles are slung between tent poles. Many of the desert artefacts are of camel leather or goat hide – belts and waterskins, bags (often decorated with beads and shells) and saddles and cradles and, in the past, shields.

The well-ordered tented home is the responsibility of the women while the camels, herds of goats and milking, are the men's responsibility. Pick-up trucks have supplemented, but not supplanted, the camel, just as bore holes and pumps have supplemented wells. The camel is irreplaceable in true desert travel, which the Beduin's search for grazing requires. An Arabian camel can survive in winter, when there is moisture in the pasturage, for about a week without being watered, although in high summer only for two or three days. She-camels are the most useful. They produce milk for up to six months after giving birth, and they possess greater stamina than the male. It is the she-camel that is used for riding by

mankind; the male camel carries the baggage. White camels are widely admired in Arabia, although in the past the darker-hued well-camouflaged camel was sometimes preferred in the chivalrous activity of raiding, in which the tribes were often engaged.

By night, camels are often hobbled to keep them close to the tent, though the family herds (of an average number of forty or fifty beasts) always preserve the homing instinct. The branding mark, or *wasm*, distinguishes tribal or clan ownership.

Desert hospitality is invariably generous and leisurely, and attendance upon the guests involves distinct obligations. The visitor is welcomed by a rug spread on the ground. He will first be offered tea, and in due course the ceremony of coffee will begin. A few coffee beans are roasted on an iron skillet, then placed in a decorated pot to cool. Three times the coffee is brought to the boil, then poured into the characteristic sharp-snouted coffee pot containing ground cardomom seeds, from which it is served in tiny handleless cups. Then, if the visitor is to stay, and is of significance, a young goat or sheep will be slaughtered, and at length served up on a great heap of steaming rice.

The Beduin way of life is hard, uncluttered and unhurried; it brings a closeness to God to those who live it fully.

tribesmen visiting cities or towns unfailingly find hospitality at the homes of relatives or tribal leaders who now reside in the urban communities.

The Western visitor is frequently struck by the way in which drivers or servants may be ushered into the presence of the mighty along with distinguished visitors. The practice is exemplified by the accessibility of the Monarch himself, whom many subjects may visit at appropriate times and, in visiting, bend to kiss his cheek in welcome. Similarly – and in accordance with a Qur'anic principle – does the Saudi leadership eschew expressions of obeisance. All are equal in the sight of God; bowing and scraping do not take place in the Saudi court or society.

In the desert, the life of the women is relatively less sequestered than in the cities. Veiling is largely unnecessary. There are no strangers in the group. Worship takes place within the group. In the Beduin encampment, there is no mosque – always a male preserve – to separate the sexes. Tasks of every kind must be performed jointly.

Despite the onslaught of technology, Saudi Arabians as a whole seem in no doubt as to where their values lie. As the decades have passed they have left the structure of those values largely intact, for as a people, the Saudis have proved themselves unafraid of what technological progress can bring; at the same time they have proved themselves indifferent to the shallow carpings of those ignorant of the meaning of Saudi social traditions.

Population Distribution and Growth

Figures for the early 1990s put the total population at about 12 million, more significantly 60 per cent of the population is under 20 years old. As with other fast developing countries, there has been considerable movement of people from the land to the towns. The population was for a time swollen by large numbers of foreigners, although numbers from Europe and North America have since fallen. The largest contingents have come from such Arab states as Egypt, Jordan, Sudan, Yemen, Palestine, and also from Pakistan. Lebanon and Syria have also provided temporary additions to the population. So too did such non-Muslim countries as South Korea, Taiwan and the Philippines, besides the U.S., Britain and other European nations. Conversely, the large numbers of Saudi Arabians resident abroad have begun to decline as many return from

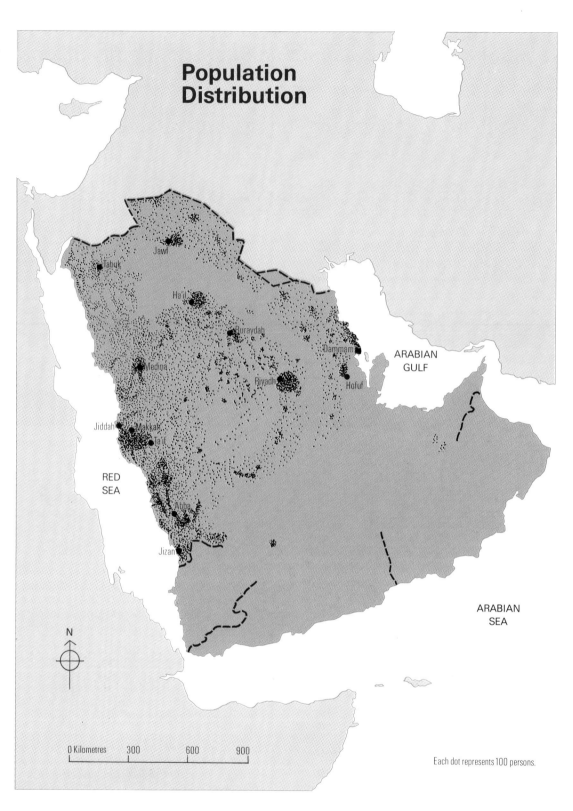

Population Distribution

Each dot represents 100 persons.

periods spent in study or research.

In the report issued in 1976 by the Central Statistics Department of the Ministry of Finance and National Economy, the administrative area with the largest population was that of Makkah, with 1,754,108 people; the Eastern Province had 769,648, Asir 681,648, al-Madinah 519,694, Jizan 403,106, al-Qasim 316,640, Bahah 185,905, Najran 147,970, Northern Frontiers 128,745, Jawf 65,494 and Qurayyat 31,404. These figures were drawn from the national

census of 1974.

By 1986 the administrative area of Riyadh contained the largest population which was rapidly approaching the 2 million mark. Beduin residing in the border areas were numbered at 210,000 and Saudis residing abroad were listed as 73,000.

Statistical sources: Ministry of Labour and Social Affairs and Ministry of Planning.

The Westerner in Saudi Arabia

The Saudis are most decidedly masters of their own house. But in meeting its responsibility as a power in the world of today, and in its commitment to adopt for its people the benefits of modern technology and systems, Saudi Arabia has invited the help of many specialists from abroad. The appropriate relationship is, as Saudi Arabians see it, one of host and guest.

FOR Western readers of this work, who may be visiting Saudi Arabia for the first time, the Publishers deferentially offer the following guidance on certain aspects of form in Arab society.

As providers of **hospitality**, Arabs are well renowned. There is a genuine delight in social interchange, and most Arabs take pride in the range and variety of their friendships.

The most familiar gesture of hospitality in Saudi Arabia, whether it is Arabians entertaining one another or foreign visitors, is the serving of coffee. The coffee is offered in small cups without handles, which are usually only half filled when offered. The coffee itself is strongly flavoured with cardamom, and sometimes with cloves and saffron. It is admirably refreshing in a hot climate. The server of coffee will refill the cup until the guest returns the cup to him giving it a little shake. To accept three such cups of such coffee is normal; more may be considered excessive. Sweet milkless tea often follows.

An invitation to dinner may prove to lead to the offering of a meal in the Western style. Alternatively, it may be a more grand affair in which Arab food is served in large dishes placed on a table-cloth on rugs on the floor, and the guests assemble seated on the floor, as round a table, to eat with the fingers of the right hand. The central dish could be a young camel, or a sheep – either boiled or roasted whole – served on a mound of steaming rice on large copper or brass trays. To eat with the left hand is not regarded as acceptable. Before and after such meals the right hand is washed.

Women do not mix with strangers in Arab society. Dinner engagements and more elaborate feasts are all-male affairs.

Westerners are often surprised at the ease of relationship between various ranks in society. This equality of men in the eyes of God derives from the teachings of the Holy Qur'an. Frequently, drivers or others in relatively humble capacities will accompany those in whose service they are employed into the presence of those of standing and high rank. There is little rigidity in social stratification, so far as it exists at all. The *sayyids* and *sharifs*, or descendants of the Prophet Muhammad, are accorded, however, special esteem.

It is customary to shake hands on meeting and parting. Hearty behaviour seldom impresses, and to give a sense of haste can cause affront. Those seeking to discuss matters with people in high positions may find that when they are admitted there are several others present who have quite different business to discuss, or who are simply paying their respects. Conversations may thus overlap, and frequently be prolonged by interruptions.

It is customary for hosts to accompany visitors to the door of the house or of the office, or to an awaiting car. Such gestures should be reciprocated by Westerners receiving Arab guests; and a Western host should not be misled by the protests that his journey from desk to front door are hardly necessary.

As for **dress**, Saudi Arabians of virtually all ranks hold firmly to their traditional manner of dress in their own land, and may well prefer to keep the head covered indoors. To be less than well turned out is unacceptable.

Most Saudi Arabians rightly consider their own form of dress to be more appropriate to the climate of their country. Men wear the headcloth, *ghutrah,* on the head, held in place by the *taqiyyah* beneath, and the black woven circlet, *'iqal,* above. The *ghutrah* is usually of chequered red and white in the cooler months and of white in the hot months. The main body garment is the long white shirt, *thawb,* above which may be worn the loose and flowing gown, *mishlah,* not infrequently of a brown colour. Women

Hotels like the Intercontinental have luxurious leisure facilities.

wear the *abaya.*

The ubiquity of English among educated classes can easily mislead the visitor into overlooking the pleasure a knowledge of Arabic can bring to the Arabs with whom he may be associated. Even to be able to greet and to reply to a greeting in Arabic is regarded as a mark of some deference towards the society which the visitor is entering. Frequently **Arabic salutations** are extended. Here are a few of them:

Salutation	Response
is-salaam 'alaykum Peace be upon you	*wa-'alaykum is-salaam* And upon you be peace
sabaah il-khayr Good morning	*sabaah in-nuwr* "Morning of light"
masaa' il-khayr Good evening	*masaa' in-nuwr* "Evening of light"
kayf haalak? How are you?	*tayyib, il-hamdu lillaah!* Well, praise be to God!
fiy amaan illaah Good-bye – "in the care of God"	*fiy amaan il-kariym* "in the care of The Generous One"

The usual term for *please* when requesting something or a service is *min fadlak*; and when offering something *tafaddal*. Use of the term *shukran* is perhaps most common for the English *thank-you*, but *mashkuwr* and *ashkurak* are also used.

The Structure of Planning

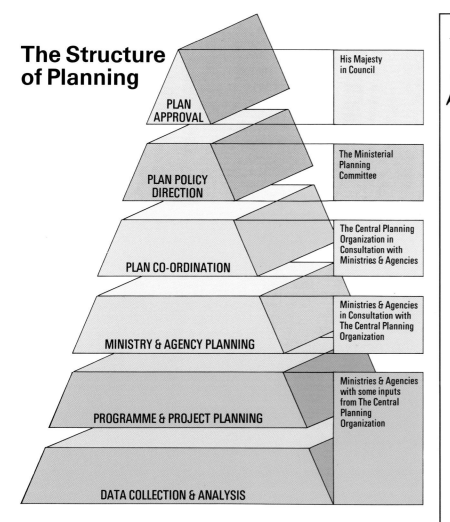

PLAN APPROVAL	His Majesty in Council	
PLAN POLICY DIRECTION	The Ministerial Planning Committee	
PLAN CO-ORDINATION	The Central Planning Organization in Consultation with Ministries & Agencies	
MINISTRY & AGENCY PLANNING	Ministries & Agencies in Consultation with The Central Planning Organization	
PROGRAMME & PROJECT PLANNING	Ministries & Agencies with some inputs from The Central Planning Organization	
DATA COLLECTION & ANALYSIS		

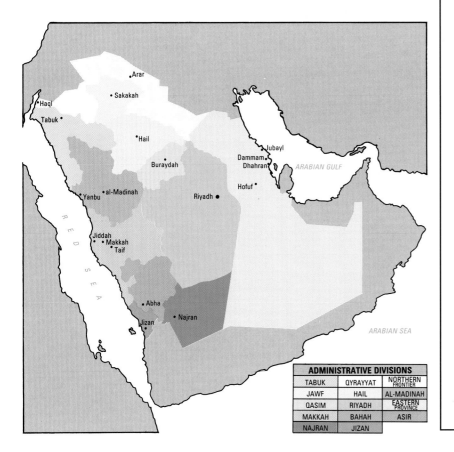

ADMINISTRATIVE DIVISIONS

TABUK	QYRAYYAT	NORTHERN FRONTIER
JAWF	HAIL	AL-MADINAH
QASIM	RIYADH	EASTERN PROVINCE
MAKKAH	BAHAH	ASIR
NAJRAN	JIZAN	

11 The Future

Perhaps the first requirement is to have the resources. The next is to have the vision. But the resources and the vision are not in themselves enough for reality. The planning is the third requirement – coordinated effort linking money, minds and hands, that month by month and year by year allows achievement to catch up with hope.

Power generation and electrical distribution are vital to the Kingdom's urban and rural development programmes. Electricity output has increased to almost 11,000 megawatts.

Planning Ahead

The first requirement: To maintain the values of Islam; the second: Assure the Kingdom's defence.

SAUDI ARABIA IS, in one conspicuous way, remarkable – and it is a way which touches everything in the Kingdom. The country's spectacular annual revenue from oil has provided the financial resources to implement a growth in development more rapid and wide-ranging than has ever been possible for a country of comparable population.

This fortunate circumstance continues to offer the Kingdom the opportunity to improve the prosperity, security, education and general well-being of present and future generations of its people. The Kingdom has long been meeting the challenge to demonstrate that abundant financial resources can be successfully used to produce, in a very short time, a modern nation capable of sustaining a high standard of living for all its people through the development of its material assets, without destroying its traditional values. Strong central planning has been a key to the Kingdom's successes.

The Fifth Five Year Plan of 1990-1995 seeks to consolidate and maintain the rise in living standards of the Saudi people. The period of the Fourth Plan demonstrated that Saudi Arabia is able to exercise flexibility and foresight in the face of uncertain international conditions. During a time of reduced oil production and the difficult years of 1985-87, an adequate public-spending programme was maintained throughout a time of deficit budgeting. The Fifth Plan allows for total Government expenditure over the five years of SR753 billion ($200 billion), of which civil sector spending will total SR498 billion. The remaining SR255 billion has been allocated to defence and security.

The priorities of the development agencies, who will command SR395 billion, remain similar to those of the Fourth Plan: human resources development leads with an allocation of SR140 billion; followed by infrastructure maintenance and expansion with SR116 billion; economic resources SR73 billion; and health and social services with SR66 billion.

The new "programme approach" of the Fourth Plan required all Government agencies to examine and control spending between programmes, since their

The 25km long King Fahd causeway (above) *connects Saudi Arabia and Bahrain. Traffic at Riyadh's King Khalid airport* (below) *is expected to reach 15 million passengers a year by the year 2000.*

proportional balance reflects the Kingdom's overall development priorities. More advanced planning was demanded from the private sector, which was expected to respond constructively to the long-term signals and opportunities provided in the Plan's economic perspective. Indeed, one of the successes of the 5-year period up to 1990 has been the steady growth of the private sector.

The Fifth Plan continues to focus on developing the nation's manpower, essential to a secure future, emphasising compulsory school education, free academic and in particular vocational training, encouraging Saudis to establish themselves in new jobs in modern factories, offices and banks. The era of the Saudi work ethic has arrived.

Two of the chief issues in developing human resources are "Saudization" and the employment of women. The filling of jobs at all levels by trained Saudis is vigorously promoted, and many women are working in health care, social welfare, women's education, and in business – especially businesses catering for other women. With some 3 million students at all levels in 1991 – 45 per cent of them women – there is a pressing need for educated and trained young Saudis to be absorbed usefully into the economy. With education now reaching all parts of the population, the emphasis will be placed increasingly on quality rather than quantity.

To care for the nation's health, a comprehensive system of health care is now in operation. A hierarchy of primary health care centres, rural clinics, general and specialist hospitals provides an unrivalled service which has been augmented by the private sector, stimulated by the Government, and by the hospitals of the armed forces.

The social welfare system provides a safety net for the disadvantaged, by providing income support and loans for housing. There is comprehensive care for the disabled.

With the Kingdom's infrastructure substantially complete by 1985, the industrial emphasis turned from construction to maintenance and production processes. Despite the downturn in oil revenue, all other economic sectors apart from the construction industry have registered satisfactory growth rates. A downward trend from the artificially high levels of wages, prices and rents caused by the phenomenal rate of development during the Second and Third

Plans, took place as predicted. There has been considerable capacity for cost-cutting, and the period of the Fourth Plan saw a large-scale adjustment to the labour force with a substantial cut in the number of foreign workers in the Kingdom.

At the same time, the private sector has played an increasing role in the economy, starting up new businesses, investing in new ventures, and responding to the Government's drive to privatise state industries. As a result, the private sector in 1991 accounted for more than 50 per cent of non-oil GDP. Saudi exports continue to rise, and an increase of 13.5 per cent in exports from the private sector was recorded in 1989. A dramatic improvement in the foreign trade balance occurred at the end of the eighties, although imports from other Arab countries, Asia, Latin America and Western Europe are on the rise.

The country's natural resources – hydrocarbon, mineral and agricultural – are being exploited to the full. Oil exploration continues, with the discovery of a new oil and gas field rich in high quality oil, 120km south of Riyadh. Saudi Aramco's management of reserves concentrates on efficient production and cost awareness. Diversification into the downstream, value-added aspects of oil exploitation – production of petrochemicals, plastics and fertilisers, as well as marketing and distribution of products

The Kingdom's industrial colleges provide a range of technical skills such as draughtsmanship (above). A visitor to the Aramco Exhibit in Dhahran looks at an astrolabe, which simulates the apparent rotation of the stars around the celestial pole (below).

abroad – proceeds apace. SABIC's role in large-scale production of a range of petrochemicals, steel and aluminium will remain pivotal, while its enterprises, many of them joint ventures with foreign partners, are increasingly offered to private investors. SAMAREC, formed as a result of the merging of Petromin's subsidiaries in 1988, is now a major player in domestic refining and in the international marketing of the Kingdom's petroleum products.

The industrial cities of Yanbu and Jubayl, with their infrastructures complete, are ready to take centre-stage in the Kingdom's industrial future.

One of the Kingdom's greatest success stories has been the agricultural sector, and encouragement in this area through subsidiaries and research will continue. Natural resources and their careful exploitation also feature under the Fifth Plan. Approval and funding has been given for the drilling of 450 new wells and 49 new dams. Mineral wealth is also being exploited – with gold, silver, zinc, copper and iron all in production. The Kingdom has developed the world's most advanced solar energy collection system at al-Uyaynah, north-west of Riyadh.

A fractionation plant at Ju'aymah Gas plant in the Eastern Province. The module's de-ethanizer column stands in the foreground.

Transport systems across the Kingdom are constantly being improved. The new King Fahd International Airport in the Eastern Province is now scheduled to open in 1993. And in the field of telecommunications, Saudi Arabia is the world's fifth largest user; the Fifth Plan will fund the addition of half a million telephone lines to the existing network. The Arabsat system is also scheduled for the addition of a third satellite.

The objectives underlying the policies of the Fifth Plan are six-fold:

Increasing government revenue by expanding the non-oil sector.

Encouragement of the contribution of the private sector to the national economy – through facilitating the investment of private capital in new ventures and the privatisation of state owned industries.

The development of human resources to increase opportunities for Saudis.

Replacement of foreign imports with local products by improving the competitiveness of national industries.

Diversification of the economic base with new initiatives to develop high technology, capital-intensive industries.

Greater emphasis on balanced development in the various regions.

The Kingdom's defence and security will continue to be given priority particularly in the light of the recent conflict. The Government of the Kingdom will continue to work for peace in the Middle East as a whole.

It has never been the intention in Saudi Arabia to develop a labour-intensive industrial base, as cheap Saudi labour does not exist. Rather, the aim is to develop capital-intensive, high-technology industries depending on a highly skilled and productive workforce. Saudi Arabia's industrial advantages lie in plentiful supplies of raw materials and energy, together with a highly efficient infrastructure. It is by exploiting these advantages that the Kingdom intends to diversify and develop its industries.

In the 1970s and early 1980s the Saudi economy was driven by Government expenditure. During the Fourth Plan the private sector was encouraged to participate in investment. The Fifth Plan will see a further development of this trend: the private sector is expected to diversify even more vigorously into import substitution. Having tested its products on the domestic and regional market, it will then seek out global markets. To some extent, the process of diversification and

import substitution has already taken effect: import bills in 1989 were SR90 billion, as against SR120 billion in 1984.

The Government has eschewed protectionism, and its industries will therefore be expected to compete on equal terms. However, it also recognises that infant businesses require special nurturing. Some special factors will be a permanent part of the Saudi industrial scene, such as low raw material and energy costs. But to stimulate the private sector, various other start-up incentives are offered. These resemble those offered by other free-trade zones: no currency restrictions, free movement of capital in and out, no personal income taxes and 10 year tax holidays for manufacturing ventures on condition that there is a minimum 25 per cent Saudi participation in the equity. There is no duty on raw material and equipment imports, and soft loans provided by the Saudi Industrial Development Fund are available for up to 50 per cent of the cost of a new project. In addition Yanbu and Jubayl, and industrial parks at Riyadh, Dammam, Makkah, and others under development elsewhere, provide an infrastructure far superior to that which the Kingdom has hitherto been able to offer.

This package of incentives applies equally to foreign participants in joint ventures with Saudi state or private enterprises. The Offset programmes with the U.S. (Peace Shield) and the U.K. (al-Yamamah) are aimed at actively encouraging partnership between foreign and Saudi organisations, on a profit-making basis, to start up high technology businesses in the Kingdom. The foreign partner is seen as offering not only capital but expertise in technology, management and international marketing, which will thus be transferred into the Saudi business scene.

As is now the case with agriculture, where subsidies have declined from their peak in 1982-83 of over $400 million, to less than $260 million today, this package of incentives is supposed to assist at the birth of the new industries, not to maintain them throughout their lives. The ultimate objective is that Saudi goods should become globally competitive in price and quality in their own right. Nevertheless the Kingdom continues to support Saudi industries, most notably in construction, where under the new 'Thirty Per Cent Rule' at least 30 per cent of government contracts must be awarded to Saudi companies.

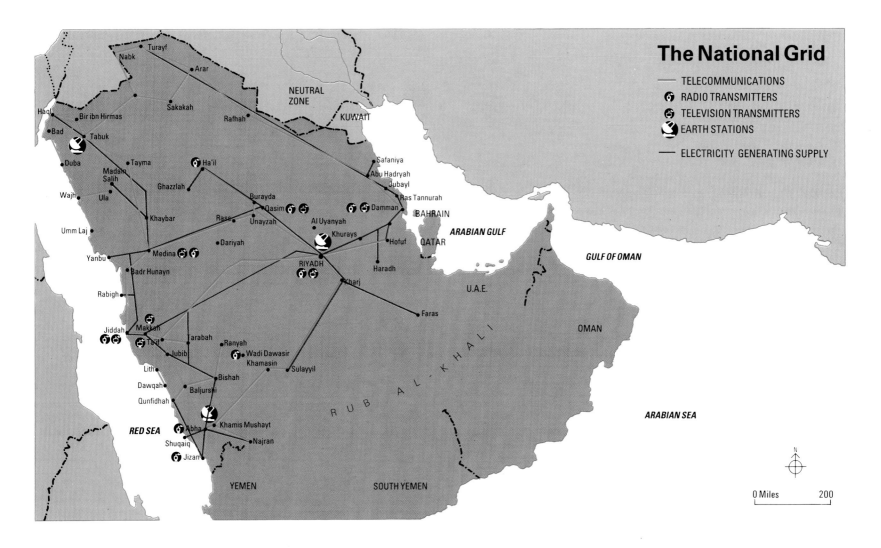

The National Grid

— TELECOMMUNICATIONS
🎧 RADIO TRANSMITTERS
📺 TELEVISION TRANSMITTERS
🛰 EARTH STATIONS
— ELECTRICITY GENERATING SUPPLY

As the Saudi economy and industry enter their mature phase, thoughts are turning to how best to stabilise the effects of development on the environment. Saudi Arabia like other Gulf states has long been noted for its concern for the environment and wildlife, but now this concern is being translated into a nationwide effort to conserve existing resources and, in some places, even to reverse such damage as has been done.

Prince Sultan ibn Salman ibn Abdul Aziz Al-Saud, payload specialist and crew on the space shuttle mission in 1985.

The National Commission for Wildlife Conservation and Development is responsible for eight wildlife sanctuaries throughout the Kingdom, and for breeding programmes of species facing extinction. Bans on grazing and any kind of hunting in some areas, such as the Harrat al-Harrah reserve in the north-west, have illustrated how dramatically the landscape can be transformed in a very short time. National parks, such as that in Asir, play an important part in the drive to increase public awareness of the Kingdom's natural riches. Efforts will be made to halt the decline of the famous juniper forests in the Asir mountains.

The NCWCD is drawing up a strategy for further environmental conservation, which will include the setting up of more sanctuaries, including marine ones, and establishing a national natural history museum in Riyadh.

In what will rapidly become a highly educated society, the application of science and technology will increasingly be seen as the key to successful diversification of the petrochemicals industry, to the provision of jobs, and to safe-guarding the environment. Research, develop-

Saudi science plays an active role in international projects exploring and utilizing space. Saudi involvement in Arabsat has made the Kingdom the regional communications centre (above).

ment and the transfer of technology will intensify during the Fifth Plan period. Saudi researchers, particularly in medicine, have already begun to make an impact on the international scene, and other sectors can be expected to follow suit. Amongst the highlights of Saudi involvement in science and technology, was the participation of Prince Sultan ibn Salman ibn Abdul Aziz as a payload specialist on NASA's space shuttle in 1985. Further Saudi involvement in space projects is expected.

During the period of the Fifth Plan, the world can expect to become increasingly familiar with Saudi Arabia as a developed industrial country, and with its energetic and sophisticated young people making their mark on the international scene in business, sport, research and academic life. The "Made in Saudi Arabia" logo will become an increasingly familiar sight abroad.

243

Jubayl and Yanbu

For centuries Al-Jubayl flourished as a small port on the trade routes between the Arabian Gulf and the Indies. The town, whose name in Arabic means 'small mountain', is believed to have been inhabited by the Phoenecians as early as 3,000 BC. Subsequently it became a centre of the pearl industry and then later, due to changes in the trade routes, fishing became the town's main industry.

Yanbu Al Bahr on the Red Sea coast was, similarly, a small historic port. An ideal stop-over on the caravan route used by merchants trading in myrrh and frankincense. The rise of Islam in the 7th and 8th centuries CE brought an increasing and regular tide of pilgrims coming overland or by sea to the holy cities of Al Madinah and Makkah. These travellers and the commerce that thrived as a result, enabled the town to prosper in the centuries that followed.

The two ancient ports now lend their names to two enormous industrial cities, the pillars of the Kingdom's phenomenal industrial growth over the past decade. They are a testimony to the determination and energy of the Saudi Arabian government in its policy of diversified economic growth.

The idea of developing Jubayl and Yanbu into twin industrial cities was conceived by the late King Faisal. He believed that a well-planned programme of diversified industrialisation would achieve greater prosperity and decrease Saudi Arabia's dependency on the export of crude oil.

Geographical factors, similar to those which had caused the two ports to thrive centuries previously, were the prime reasons for choosing Jubayl and Yanbu. The former's accessibility to the Gulf's deep sea-lanes, and its proximity to energy sources and raw materials for refining and petrochemical production were both major advantages. Whilst Yanbu, to the south of the Suez Canal and the Mediterranean sea lanes, was in a prime position for exporting petrochemical products to western markets.

The royal decree issued in 1975 by the late King Khalid established the Royal Commission for Jubayl and Yanbu,

King Fahd Industrial Port at Jubayl Harbour includes twenty deepwater berths.

granting it full responsibility for the infrastructural development and management. Special powers were vested in the Royal Commission to facilitate their rapid development, which included an independent budget and administrative autonomy.

The work of the Royal Commission for Jubayl and Yanbu has been informed by the objectives of the Five Year Plans – particularly the aims of the 4th and 5th Plans to increase the contribution of the private sector; to develop work opportunities for the growing Saudi population and to substitute local production in place of imports wherever possible. As a result new industrial projects are successfully maturing in both cities.

New industries were selected to make efficient use of Saudi Arabia's petroleum and other feedstocks. Generating both export and domestic products, these industries range from heavy to light and from capital to labour intensive.

They fall into three main categories: primary, secondary and support or light

manufacturing industries. Each area is provided with the infrastructure and services to meet projected industry requirements into the next century.

Most recently, as a result of increased Saudi production during and after the Gulf War, there has been a boom in petrochemicals, now the Kingdom's second industry after oil. Saudi Basic Industries Corporation (SABIC), whose affiliates produce the bulk of Saudi petrochemicals, is one of the world's ten most profitable petrochemicals producers. The availability of raw natural gases and an almost limitless supply of domestic feedstocks give SABIC a strong advantage over competitors in non-oil producing countries. Parallel pipelines carry crude oil and natural gas liquids from the oil fields of the Eastern Province to Yanbu, distributing resources to create a regionally balanced industrial base.

The Royal Commission has also pursued the implementation of intensive manpower training programmes to ensure a qualified Saudi workforce is available to operate the Kingdom's industries. At the end of 1990, Saudi Petrochemical Company (SADAF) was able to announce that, as a result of massive investment, including training in the US, 70 per cent of their employees were Saudi nationals. Priority was given from day one to the planning and construction of comprehensive training institutes at Jubayl and Yanbu. The largest and longest established of these is Jubayl's Industrial College – JIC – formerly known as the Human Resources Development Institute. Founded in 1978 with a few training courses for construction workers, it has now graduated over 3,600 Saudis in over 21 different areas of expertise. Based upon the industrial and business requirements of the industrial city, courses teach everything from process control technology to engineering skills and business administration. JIC accommodates 1,200 full-time and 500 part-time students in its modern campus.

The College continually assesses the manpower requirements of Jubayl's established industries and those starting up. Its courses were designed to respond to these trends to meet specific industry skill requirements. Training periods run for nine to eighteen months depending on the course, with graduates looking to

Yanbu's primary industries including the Saudi Yanbu Petrochemical Company (YANPET) are all served by a superb infrastructure.

Jubayl as their primary source of work.

The Yanbu Industrial College is located on a 62 hectare site on the southern tip of the community area near King Fahd Port and the primary industries area. Complete technical training for up to 1,000 full-time students is provided by the College.

A number of companies operating in Jubayl and Yanbu have signed agreements with foreign companies. Twelve of the primary industries operating today at Jubayl are SABIC affiliates, either wholly owned by SABIC or joint ventures with international companies such as Exxon, Mitsubishi, Lucky-Goldstar, Shell and Neste. One of SABIC's other three manufacturing affiliates is a joint venture with Mobil at Yanbu. Another joint venture between SABIC and private Saudi investors – SAFCO – is due for start-up in 1993 at Jubayl.

Amongst the light industries, Olayan's existing partnership with a Pakistani engineering firm, Descon, is expanding in the Light Industries Park at Jubayl where they produce parts for plant maintenance. Whilst in Yanbu, Best Foods is a joint venture with the American Corn Products Corporation which rapidly took over 20 per cent of the national market in corn oil and was exporting within months. Such agreements are further evidence of a move towards

The administration headquarters, Jubayl, is an inverted pyramid designed to provide maximum shade.

an expansion of the private sector.

Evidence of successful development in the non-oil sector comes from HADEED, the Saudi Iron and Steel Company, a major presence in Jubayl. In the summer of 1991, the first in a series of shipments of iron left Dammam for the Far East. A particular triumph, showing how the Kingdom is now exporting to those countries from whom it imported in the past.

Yet expansion in both Jubayl and Yanbu has been carefully monitored to make sure that the industries of today threaten neither the architectural heritage of the past nor the natural environment of the future.

Both complexes have been carefully sited to preserve the ancient towns from which they take their names. Jubayl Industrial City – Madinat Jubayl Al-Sinaiyah – is located 15km north of the historic al-Jubayl, whilst Madinat Yanbu al-Sinaiyah lies 18km south of the original Yanbu al-Bahr. Preliminary plans for development at Yanbu were redrawn to avoid damage to one of the significant plots of mangroves and there are now three Royal Commission conservation areas in Madinat Yanbu al-Sinaiyah ensuring that the coastal habitat continues to provide a natural refuge for the large numbers of birds visiting the coastline.

In Jubayl the Wildlife Rescue Centre cares for injured birds and turtles. As a result of the Gulf War large numbers of oil-stricken birds were in need of rescue.

Jubayl

Jubayl Industrial City lies at the heart of a superb infrastructure. Locked into the national highway system of four- to six-lane motorways, it is also served by specialised access roads designed for transporting large loads of up to 2,500 tonnes. For travellers leaving the Kingdom, the new King Fahd International Airport is only forty minutes drive away. The city's land communications are supplemented by the recent extension of the railway from Dammam, 100 kilometres to the south.

This vast industrial complex, now covering an area over 1,000 square kilometres, is probably the largest public construction project in modern times. Work started in 1976 and at its peak nearly 52,000 workers were employed, representing 62 nationalities. Much of the site was a low-lying coastal plain with extremely saline water lying just below the surface. As a result, enormous amounts of fill material were needed to ensure that the new city would lie above the marine flood threshold. This was 'borrowed' from inland high points and also from the extensive dredging operations necessary for the construction of Jubayl's King Fahd Industrial Port. By

Saudi Arabia's policy of industrial diversification is represented by more than 100 primary, secondary and support industries operating in Jubayl and Yanbu.

1988, 270 million cubic metres of earth had been moved: enough to construct a belt around the Equator, 6 metres wide by 2.5 metres high.

The city itself is divided up into the community residential district of Haii al-Fanateer to the north, and to the south the industrial area with its primary, secondary and support industries. Between the two is a broad, landscaped buffer zone containing some administra-

The King Fahd Medical Centre in Yanbu includes a 342-bed hospital and specialist departments.

tive and educational facilities.

The main community zone is on the peninsula and coastal land, giving Jubayl a total of 45 kilometres of continuous coastline. By the year 2010 it is planned that Jubayl will be a city of more than 200,000 inhabitants living in eight

districts bordered with green-space corridors: each with a population of about 2,500 and its own mosques, schools, shopping and recreational facilities.

The industrial area is serviced by a seawater cooling system, believed to be the world's largest canal system; it carries 10 million cubic metres of seawater per day to cool the factories and refineries.

The economic heart of Jubayl is the Primary Industries Park which is planned to accommodate 20 large capital and energy intensive industries. With the exception of HADEED – the iron and steel mill – all of these industries use the Kingdom's hydrocarbon resources as feedstocks. Much of this output is for export, although increasing amounts are becoming the feedstock for downstream industries. Principal downstream industries are located in the Secondary Industries Park or within the primary industries area near a parent feedstock supplier.

Planning is the primary instrument of development in the Kingdom.

tries area near a parent feedstock supplier.

The task of the secondary industries is to upgrade primary industry products by further processing thereby yielding petrochemical intermediates, plastic and steel products, and chemical derivatives for agricultural and other uses. The resulting added-value products may be sold or undergo further conversion into more refined products either for domestic or international markets. The Support and Light Manufacturing Industries Park contains smaller enterprises, ranging from heavy commercial enterprises such as industrial laundries to equipment dealerships offering goods and services required by other industries and the Jubayl community.

Primary industries have demonstrated continuous growth over the last decade with 15 plants now operational. These include PETROLUBE producing lube oils, lubricants and greases, and IBN-ZAHR producing MTBE (methyl, tertiary butyl ether). This latter is the major octane additive for unleaded gasoline worldwide. Production of MTBE at the Ibn-Sina and Ibn-Zahr plants will increase to 1.7 million tonnes by 1993. An

The permanent communities of Jubayl and Yanbu continue to attract Saudi professionals and their families from all over the Kingdom.

SR3.76 billion flexible feedstock cracker is being built by Petrokemya (wholly owned by SABIC). Based on liquid gases, it will add 500,000 tonnes of ethylene capacity and introduce propylene, butadiene, and benzene by 1993. Saudi Arabian Fertiliser Company (SAFCO) together with Chiyoda of Japan are building an ammonia-granular urea plant and are set to increase SABIC's output by 500,000 tonnes of ammonia and 600,000 tonnes of granular urea by 1993.

Secondary industries include the Saudi Urethane Chemical Company manufacturing polyether polyols and formaldehyde. Over 70 support and light industries are now operational, including manufacturing facilities such as Saudi Ega which produces PVC conduit. These represent the last step in the value-adding process that begins with one of Jubayl's primary industries.

Yanbu

Madinat Yanbu al-Sinaiyah, Yanbu Industrial City, is 350km north of Jeddah on the Red Sea Coast. Yanbu's development plan which outlined the city as a 24km linear development was announced in 1977, a couple of years behind Jubayl. However, in the first ten years of its development, investment totalling around SR33 billion was poured into the city.

The infrastructure and facilities have been completed and the industrial area is served by a network of corridors which feed into the coastal highway. Among the support facilities is a solar-powered desalination plant providing 56,000 cubic metres of water a day, testimony to the determination to use natural resources to the full. Yanbu as a whole has a seawater intake capacity of 3,000 million cubic metres a day, satisfying the industries' requirements for cooling, desalination and electricity.

The primary industries already in operation include the Saudi-Yanbu Petrochemical Co (YANPET), ARAMCO Natural Gas Liquids (NGL), ARAMCO Crude Oil Terminal, Petroleum-Mobil Yanbu Refinery (PEMREF) and SAMAREC's Yanbu Refinery. The latter, after a series of experiments, has recently begun processing naptha received from the Jeddah refinery at an average of 7,000 barrels per day.

Amongst the secondary industries LUBRIZOL and SALACO both have Lube Oil terminals. Other presences include Arabian Gulf Oil and Arabian Chemical Terminals and National Titanium Dioxide have a new Cristal facility producing titanium dioxide.

As the industrial city establishes itself, there has been an increasing emphasis on private investment and development. As well as the new titanium dioxide facility, private development has included the financing of a residential project by the Al-Shaghdali Establishment.

Other changes signpost the successful implementation of the objectives of the Five Year Plans. The percentage of the permanent Saudi population in the city has increased from 6% in 1981 to almost 53% in 1989, the projected total population is set to rise to 90,000 by 2010. At present, over 30% of the total residents are under 18.

As a reminder for these young citizens of the skills and culture of their ancestors, the museum of Yousif Najjar has been established on a permanent basis with help from the Royal Commission. The collection shows examples of artefacts from the lifestyles of both the bedouin and the villager. These include examples of wood carvings, silverwork and traditional household items. Such objects might seem out of place in a new industrial city, but they are an important symbol of the way in which the values of the community have not been overlooked by the planners of these cities of the future.

Statistical source: Ministry of Planning

Bibliography

This selected bibliography includes books covering a wide range of aspects of Saudi Arabia, but does not attempt to be definitive.

Abdel Wahab. *Education in Saudi Arabia*, Macmillan, London, 1971

Al-Farsy, Dr. Fouad. *Saudi Arabia, a case study in development*, 2nd ed., Routledge, 1986

Ali Abdullah Yusuf. *The Holy Quran*, Lahore, 1938

Aramco *Handbook*, The Arabian American Oil Company (Dhahran), revised edition, 1986

Armstrong, H.C. *Lord of Arabia*, Khayyat, Beirut, 1954

Asad, Muhammad. *The Road to Mecca*, Simon and Schuster, New York, 1954

Assah, Ahmed. *Miracle of the Desert Kingdom*, Johnson, London, 1969

Azzam, Abdel Rahman. *The Eternal Message of Muhammad, Devin-Adair, New York, 1964*

Bremond, E. *Yemen et Saoudia*, Paris, 1937

Brockelmann, Carl. *History of the Islamic Peoples*, Putnam's, New York, 1947

Brown, W.R. *The Horse of the Desert*, Macmillan, New York, 1948

Bullard, Sir Reader. *The Camels Must Go*, Faber and Faber, London, 1961

Burckhardt, J.L. *Travels in Arabia, 1826*

Cheeseman, R.E. *In Unknown Arabia*, Macmillan, London, 1926

Collins, Robert O. (ed.). *An Arabian Diary: Sir Gilbert Clayton*, California, 1969.

Cornwallis, Sir Kinahan, *Asir before World War I*, Oleander Press, New York and Cambridge, 1976

Cragg, Kenneth. *The Call of the Minaret*, Oxford University Press, 1956

De Gaury, Gerald. *Arabia Phoenix*, Harrap, London, 1946

De Gaury, Gerald. *Arabian Journey and Other Desert Travels*, Harrap, London, 1950

De Gaury, Gerald. *Faisal, King of Saudi Arabia*, Arthur Barker, London, 1966

Dickson, H.R.P. *The Arab of the Desert*, Hodder and Stoughton, London, 1957

Dimand, Maurice S. *A Handbook of Muhammadan Art*, The Metropolitan Museum of Art, New York, 1958

Doughty, C.M. *Travels in Arabia Deserta*, Jonathan Cape, London, 1964

Esin, Emel. *Mecca the Blessed, Madinah the Radiant*, Elek, London, 1963

Fisher, Sydney N. *The Middle East, A History*, Knopf, New York, 1969

Fisher, W.B. *The Middle East: A Physical, Social and Regional Geography*, 6th revised edition, Methuen, London, 1971

Gibb, Sir Hamilton A.R. *Mohammedanism*, Oxford University Press, London and New York, 1953

Glubb, Sir John Bagot. *The Life and Times of Muhammad*, Hodder and Stoughton, London, 1963

Graves, P. *Life of Sir Percy Cox*, London, 1941

Guillaume, A. *Islam*, 2nd edition, Penguin Books, Harmondsworth, England, 1956

Hartshorn, J.E. *Oil Companies and Governments*, 2nd revised edition, Faber and Faber, London, 1967

Hitti, P.K. *History of the Arabs*, 7th edition, Macmillan, London, 1961

Hogarth, D.G. *The Penetration of Arabia*, F.A. Stokes, New York, 1904

Hopwood, Derek (ed.). *The Arabian Peninsula*, Allen and Unwin, London, 1972

Howarth, David. *The Desert King*, Collins, London, 1964

Keiser, Hélène. *Arabia*, Silva, Zurich, 1971

Kiernan, R.H. *The Unveiling of Arabia*, Harrap, London, 1937

Lebkicker, Rentz and Steineke. *The Arabia of Ibn Saud*, Russell and Moore, USA, 1952

Le Bon, Gustave. *The World of Islamic Civilization*, Minerva, Geneva, 1974

Lenczowski, George. *Oil and State in the Middle East*, Cornell University Press, New York, 1960

Lenczowski, George. *The Middle East in World Affairs*, Cornell University Press, New York, 1962

Longrigg, S. *Oil in the Middle East*, 3rd edition, Oxford University Press, 1968

Mauger, Thierry and Danielle. *In the Shadow of the Black Tents*, Tihama, Saudi Arabia, 1986

Meinertzhagen, Richard. *The Birds of Arabia*, Oliver and Boyd, Edinburgh, 1954

Meulen, D. van der. *The Wells of Ibn Saud*, John Murray, London, 1957

Monroe, Elizabeth. *Philby of Arabia*, Faber and Faber, London, 1973

Musil, Alois. *The Northern Hejaz*, American Geographical Society, New York, 1926

Musil, Alois. *Arabia Deserta*, American Geographical Society, New York, 1927

Niebuhr, Carsten. *Description de l'Arabie*, Amsterdam, 1774

Palgrave, William Gifford. *Narrative of a year's journey through Central and Eastern Arabia 1862-63*, 2 volumes, new edition, Macmillan, London, 1868

Pelly, Lewis. *Report on a Journey to Riyadh (1865)*, Oleander Press, New York and Cambridge, 1978

Pesce, Angelo. *Colours of the Arab Fatherland*, Riyadh, 1972

Pesce, Angelo. *Jiddah – Portrait of an Arabian City*, Falcon Press, 1974

Philby, H. St. John B. *The Heart of Arabia*, Constable, London, 1922

Philby, H. St. John B. *The Empty Quarter*, Henry Holt, New York, 1933

Philby, H. St. John B. *Arabian Jubilee*, Robert Hale, London, 1952

Philby, H. St. John B. *Saudi Arabia*, Ernest Benn, London, 1955

Philby, H. St. John B. *Arabian Oil Ventures*, Middle East Institute, Washington, 1964

Philips, C.H. (ed.). *Handbook of Oriental History*, Royal Historical Society, London, 1963

Pickthall, M. *The Meaning of the Glorious Qur'an*, new American Library, New York, 1953

Purdy, Anthony (ed.). *The Business Man's Guide to Saudi Arabia*, Arlington Books, London, 1976

Ross, Heather Colyer. *Bedouin Jewellery in Saudi Arabia*, Stacey International, London, 1978

Ryan, Sir A. *The Last of the Dragomans*, London, 1951

Safran, Nadav. *Saudi Arabia: The Ceaseless Quest for Security*, The Belknap Press of Harvard University Press, Cambridge, Mass. and London, 1985

Sanger, Richard. The Arabian Peninsula, Cornell University Press, New York, 1954

Shroeder, Eric. *Muhammad's People: A Tale by Anthology*, Bond Wheelwright, Portland, Maine, 1955

Smith, Wilfred Cantwell. *Islam in Modern History*, Princeton University Press, Princeton, 1957

Thesiger, Wilfred. *Arabian Sands*, Book Club Associates, London, 1959

Thomas, Bertram. *Arabia Felix*, Scribner's, New York, 1932

Thomas, Bertram. *The Arabs*, Butterworth, London, 1937

Tibbetts, G.R. *Arabia in Early Maps*, Oleander Press, New York and Cambridge, 1978

Twitchell, K.S. *Saudi Arabia*, 3rd edition, Princeton University Press, Princeton, 1958

Vidal, F.S. *The Oasis of Al-Hasa*, Arabian American Oil Company, 1955

Vincett, Betty. *The Flowers of Arabia*, 1977

Wahba, Hafiz. *Arabian Days*, Arthur Barker, London, 1964

Wallin, Y.A. *Travels in Arabia (1845 & 1848)*, Oleander Press, New York and Cambridge, 1979

Ward, Philip. *Ha'il: Oasis City of Saudi Arabia*, Oleander Press, New York and Cambridge, 1984

Wellsted, J.R. *Travels in Arabia*, John Murray, London, 1838

Winder, R. Bayly. *Saudi Arabia in the Nineteenth Century*, St. Martin's Press, New York, 1965

Yale, William. *The Near East: A Modern History*, University of Michigan Press, Ann Arbor, Michigan, 1958

Zirikli, Khair al Din. *Arabia under King Abdul Aziz*, 4 volumes (in Arabic), Beirut, 1970

Glossary

abal	scarlet-fruited shrub; eglantine
abaya(h)	woollen outer cloak
adabi	arts stream at secondary school
adat	customs
Ahadith	see Hadith
alim, pl. ulama	Muslim scholar; scholar of Islamic law
arfaj	yellow-flowered shrub
arikah	half-baked dough covered with honey
bayt Allah	house of God
dabb	plant-eating lizard
Dhu 'l-Hijja(h)	the twelfth month in the Islamic calendar (in which the *Hajj* occurs)
Diwan al-Mazalim	Board of Complaints
ghutrah	headcloth worn by Arab men
hadh	prickly saltbush
Hadith, pl. Ahadith	traditions giving the sayings or acts of the Prophet Muhammad
Hajj	pilgrimage to Makkah and other holy places obligatory for every Muslim
hajj, hajji	Muslim who has performed the *Hajj*
hara	quarter of a city
Haram	the Holy *Ka'bah* sanctuary
Haramayn	the two holy cities of Makkah and al-Madinah
harrah	extensive lava fields
Hijra(h)	the migration of the Prophet from Makkah to al-Madinah
hijrah	encampment; agricultural settlement
hubara	MacQueen's bustard
ibtida'i	primary stage of education
Ihram	pilgrim's dress
ijma	consensus of non-specialist opinion on points of Islamic law
Ikhwan	"the Brethren"; specifically a religious movement founded by King Abdul Aziz
ilmi	scientific stream at secondary school
iqal	rope-like circlet holding *ghutrah* in position
jar Allah	God's neighbour
jihad	holy war
Ka'bah	venerated square stone building in Makkah, the house of God
kafa'ah	examination taken at end of intermediate school stage
Kiswah	black cloth covering the *Ka'bah*
kutab (kuttab)	small group of children to whom private tuition is given
majlis	session for meetings and audiences
marsum	royal decree
mashrabiyya	lattice window in the Egyptian style
maslaha	welfare
Mataf	parts of the pilgrimage area around the *Ka'bah*
mihrab	prayer niche in mosque (cf. qibla)
mishlah	loose outer cloak worn by Arab men
muqallid	lawyer who accepts as binding precedent in legal decisions
mutawassit	intermediate stage of education
mutawwif	guide for pilgrims performing the *Hajj*
nizam	regulation
qadi	judge; ruler
qibla	recess in a mosque indicating the direction of the *Ka'bah* in Makkah; prayer niche
Qiran	combined performance of *Hajj* and *Umrah*
rababa(h)	simple violin
rajaz	song with lines of four or six beats
rawda(h)	kindergarten school
rimth	saltbush
sabkhah	salt basins
Sa'y	the running from as-Safa to al-Marwa in the *Hajj*
sayyid	descendants of the Prophet
Shari'ah	Islamic law derived from the Qur'an
sharif	the Prophet's descendants and their families (a wider meaning than *sayyid*)
Sawahil	coasts of East Africa
Sunnah	orthodox interpretation and commentary on the life of the Prophet Muhammad and on the Qur'an
suq	space in town where the market is held
Talbiyah	words of acceptance of the pilgrimage duties chanted by the *hajj* pilgrims
Tamattu	separate performance of *Hajj* and *Umrah*
taqiyyah	cap worn under the ghutrah
Tawaf	circumambulation of the *Ka'bah*
tawjihiyyah	the Saudi baccalaureat, taken at end of secondary education
thanawi	secondary stage of education
thawb	inner gown worn by Arab men
ulama	see alim
Umm Salim	"Salim's mother", hoopoe lark
Umrah	short form of pilgrimage to Makkah only
uruq	crescent sand-dunes
usul al-fiqh	sources of Islamic legislation
wadi	former water course, now dry
Wudu	ablutions before prayers
Wuquf	final prayer of the *Hajj* made standing on Mount Arafat
Zakah	regular giving of fixed alms
ziggurat	(from Assyrian ziqquratu) Sumerian brick tower

Note on transliteration

The system of transliteration employed in this work reflects the influence of two main aims which, to some extent, are in conflict with one another.

First, it was deemed important that the general reader should be spared the complexities of the elaborate system developed for scholarly purposes, and that transliterated forms should be similar to those encountered in the British and American press.

Second, it is clearly desirable that transliterated forms should represent the original as accurately as possible.

Where names have been in use in English and have achieved an accepted and established form, the latter is employed even where this results in some inconsistency with the rest of the system, e.g. Taif rather than Ta'if.

Hamza (glottal stop) and 'ayn, where marked, are shown as ' and are not differentiated.

Arabic and vernacular words have been italicized except where words may be regarded as in common usage among non-Muslim people throughout the world – e.g. *ijma*, and *taqiyyah*; but Qur'an, and sheikh.

Quotations from the Holy Qur'an

Unless otherwise indicated, the quotations from the Holy Qur'an have been taken from the rendering of Mohammed Marmaduke Pickthall. The rendering by Arthur J. Arberry has been preferred where the requirement has been to indicate the tonal flavour of the original Arabic.

In deference to Muslim readers, the usage CE (Christian Era) has often been used in place of AD (Anno Domini), more familiar in Christendom.

Index

Mainly for reasons of regional variations in sound values, no generally accepted transliteration of Arabic nomenclature into Roman lettering has been established, nor indeed of Arabic usages in this volume (see note on transliteration on page 249). The difference in accepted usages in various contexts (e.g. historical, religious, commercial) is sometimes unavoidable.